UNEXPECTED
BRITAIN

About the Authors

Stuart Laycock has a degree in Classics from Cambridge University. He has worked in advertising and marketing and TV, and also did aid work in Bosnia during the war there. He has authored or co-authored a number of books, including *Britannia the Failed State* (nominated for Current Archaeology Book of the Year) and *UnRoman Britain* (described in the *Sunday Times* as 'thrillingly provocative'). His most recent book was the hugely popular *All the Countries We've Ever Invaded*.

Philip Laycock has a degree in History from St Andrews University, where he was also captain of the shinty team. He has been a history teacher in Essex for more than thirty years and is currently Head of Humanities at St Helena School in Colchester. He is also an experienced climber whose achievements include climbing the Matterhorn and Mont Blanc.

UNEXPECTED BRITAIN

A *Journey* THROUGH OUR HIDDEN HISTORY

STUART LAYCOCK & PHILIP LAYCOCK

AMBERLEY

First published 2014
This edition published 2015

Amberley Publishing
The Hill, Stroud
Gloucestershire, GL5 4EP

www.amberley-books.com

British Library Cataloguing in Publication Data.
A catalogue record for this book is available from the British Library.

ISBN 978 1 4456 5116 3 (paperback)
ISBN 978 1 4456 3284 1 (ebook)

Typeset in 10pt on 12pt Sabon.
Typesetting and Origination by Amberley Publishing.
Printed in the UK.

Contents

Tudors and Stuarts

Eighteenth and Nineteenth Century

Twentieth Century

Introduction

Many Britons like to think they have a basic understanding of Britain's amazing history. The Roman invasion, Alfred and the Danes, 1066, Magna Carta, Bannockburn, Agincourt, the Wars of the Roses, Henry and his wives, the Reformation, etc., etc. The trouble is that concentrating on just a few over-familiar landmarks like these can give a distorted picture of this land. What would our history look like if, instead of looking at all the bits everybody knows, we started telling it through some of the bits not everybody knows? We set off to find out.

The result is *Unexpected Britain*, tracing the story of Britain from a time before Rome to a time within the lives of people still living, but going beyond the well known to explore a world of different angles and fascinating little-known facts that bring fresh life to the story of what Britain has been and what Britain is.

Modern life is busy and time for reading can be short; we've therefore divided the book into fifty-two chapters. So if you get the book for Christmas or your birthday, you can, if you like, read one chapter a week; allowing yourself, again if you like, extra time to read around the chapter subject a bit in other books and online, and by next Christmas or your next birthday you'll have had a glimpse of British history from before Roman Britain almost to the present. Of course, if you'd prefer to sit down and read it from beginning to end, in one go, that's fine too!

This isn't supposed to be anything like a comprehensive list of Britain's unexpected historical gems. It would take a book (or indeed a series of books) far, far larger than this modest effort to accomplish anything even a bit like that, particularly as we approach the more recent centuries, of which so much more is known than about earlier times. Nor is this supposed to be any value judgement on Britain's unexpected historical gems. If one that you're aware of isn't in here, that doesn't mean it's not as important, or indeed more important than some that are in here. With so many to choose from, we had to make a selection somehow.

So this is as a bit like an effort by one of those travel writers who goes off the beaten track to give an impressionistic view of one journey through the countryside. It's not going to cover everything you could see there, and it's not going to cover what you could see if you took one of the many other different available routes, but hopefully, nonetheless, it incorporates a genuine and exciting flavour of the region and its unexpected delights.

And obviously some readers will probably already be aware of a few of these stories, but hopefully you won't know a lot about many of them. If you enjoy it, and if you know of other unexpected historical gems that you think we should cover on another historical meander through Britain's history, we'd love to hear from you. Thanks for reading the book.

We'd also like to thank all those who've helped us with the book on the photo front, including Elaine Laycock, Rebecca Laycock, Richard Laycock, Ross Laycock, Harvey Scott and Nicky Somerville-Jones.

1

African Emperors in Britain

The first humans arrived in Britain many hundreds of thousands of years ago. But humans haven't lived in these islands ever since then. Populations came to this country a number of times in prehistory and then disappeared again as the weather changed. And even since Britain was settled for the last time, it has seen a steady stream of new people arriving on these shores.

In 55 BC, someone stepped ashore that we've all heard of: Julius Caesar. He returned again, in 54 BC. In the process of writing his accounts of his 'victory' in Britain, Caesar introduces us to two of the first inhabitants of this island for whom we have names. Cassivellaunus was a tribal leader who had been fighting loads of other British chiefs until Caesar turned up, and Mandubracius was King of the Trinovantes, an enemy of Cassivellaunus, who, also showing scant regard for any idea of British solidarity, promptly teamed up with the Romans to inflict at least a short-term defeat on Cassivellaunus.

What Caesar spends less time dwelling on in his memoirs is that unlike Gaul, where he came, saw, conquered and made sure it stayed conquered, with Britain he came, saw, conquered a bit, came up with a peace deal with his British enemies that he could make sound good in his memoirs and then promptly returned south across the Channel. After his brief second visit, he never landed here again. In fact, it wasn't until AD 43, almost a century after their conquest of Gaul and a long time after most of the rest of their Empire, that the Romans arrived here to stay.

Once ashore in AD 43, again probably with support from some Brits keen to see the existing powers in Britain toppled, the Romans gradually spread their control across the whole of what is now England and Wales. In parts it wasn't a particularly quick process and it was often quite brutal. For instance, it took the Romans a long time to conquer what is now Wales. We've all heard of Boudica, the queen of the Iceni who rebelled with some temporary success against Rome. And then, of course, the Romans under Agricola – a general with a Latin name that curiously means 'farmer' and who anyway was born in the south of France, at Fréjus, now a delightful holiday town on the beautiful Mediterranean coast – steamed on into what is now Scotland. The Caledonians fought a guerrilla war against the Romans, lost a battle when Agricola finally managed to corner them, but then eventually sat and watched as the Romans withdrew, unable or unwilling to put in the necessary effort to take and hold the whole of Scotland. By the end of the first century AD, Rome controlled little north of the Tyne–Solway Firth line and, of course, a permanent stone frontier was built along that border soon after. Yep, it's the world-famous Hadrian's Wall.

A little flurry of activity a decade or two later briefly saw Rome's frontier pushed north to the Antonine Wall that runs through the Scottish lowlands. A large percentage of the wall was made of turf and earth, and it's not anything like as well known as Hadrian's Wall, but there are still some really interesting bits of it left to visit today. Nevertheless, Rome once again found out it couldn't or didn't want to maintain a border in what is now Scotland, and shortly after AD 160 Hadrian's Wall was the frontier again.

All of which rather lengthy introduction brings us to the late second century and the story of African emperors in Britain. It's a story that sheds an interesting light on a number of different aspects of Britain's experience with Rome, including the difference in experience south and north of Hadrian's Wall.

We sometimes think that a multicultural society is something new in Britain, yet cultures and people, sometimes from quite far away, have been mingling on this island for a very long time. The Roman Empire itself had strong regional variations, but on some level was also a multicultural institution. This story concerns four Roman emperors, one of whom was definitely North African, two of whom were half-North African and one of whom is said to have been North African.

It also concerns the fact that we sometimes think that, apart from some occasional vicious palace intrigues, the Romans brought peace to their Empire, Pax Romana. In fact, the Roman Empire throughout its history, and particularly from the late second century onwards, was regularly thrown into chaos by rebellions and vicious civil wars. Britain saw plenty of these rebellions.

It raises once again a point that we've already touched upon. Rome never conquered what is now Scotland, never for any long period of time taking and controlling the territory north of Hadrian's Wall. But it wasn't that they never ventured north of Hadrian's Wall. They did, on a number of occasions spread across much of their time in Britain. Even in the fourth century they ventured north of the wall, but they never stayed there. So Britain would never become a part of the Empire to the extent that Gaul or Italy or Greece was. It had sea borders accessible to those from outside the Empire anyway, to those from across the Irish Sea and from across the North Sea, but it would also always have a land border to be defended as well. Britannia would always be a little spot on the edge of the Empire, separated from the European mainland and the Empire's Mediterranean heartlands by a finger of ocean, the sea that the Romans believed was the edge of the world.

In AD 193, Commodus (yes, the guy in the film *Gladiator*), the last in a line of linked emperors who had succeeded to the throne in a fairly peaceful and orderly fashion, was assassinated. What followed was an unseemly and very violent battle for power, of the sort that was going to become all too common in the next century.

Commodus's immediate successor, Pertinax, was himself

assassinated shortly afterwards, after which the Praetorian Guard put the Empire up for sale. Yep, one Didius Julianus was the lucky high bidder, although lucky isn't really the word since he was soon bumped off as well. The remaining competitors for power were Pescennius Niger, supported by the army in Syria; Clodius Albinus, Governor of Britain and supported by its army; and Septimius Severus, supported by the armies of Illyricum and Pannonia. Septimius Severus was from Leptis Magna (also known as Lepcis Magna) in what is now Libya, while Clodius Albinus is said by the *Historia Augusta* (not always the most reliable of sources, admittedly) to have come from Hadrumetum, which is now Sousse in Tunisia.

Septimius Severus, having seized Rome, was in a fairly strong position, and Clodius Albinus allowed him to finish off Pescennius Niger. This was possibly not the wisest move on Albinus's part because he soon found that he was next in the firing line. However, not wishing to wait around for Septimius Severus to polish him off at his leisure, Clodius Albinus decided to invade Gaul – not by any means the last time a Roman general in Britain would do so, and, of course, very far from the last time a British army would cross the Channel to attack people on the other side. However, it was to be pretty much the last of everything for Clodius himself since he ran into Severus's forces at Lugdunum, now Lyon, in February AD 197; after a lot of death and destruction on both sides, Clodius lost the battle and lost his life as well.

The North African Septimius Severus was now master of the Roman Empire, including Britain, and by AD 208 he'd decided to have another crack at Caledonia. In a somewhat familiar pattern, he thrust northwards towards the old Antonine Wall and then beyond it, reoccupying assorted old Roman forts as he went, while the Caledonians waged a guerrilla war against the advancing Roman legions. There was something of a clash of cultures, too. Severus's wife commented unfavourably on the sexual morals of Caledonian women, to which the wife of Caledonian chief Argentocoxos retorted that, actually,

Caledonian women were better than Roman women because Caledonian women openly did what they wanted with the best of men, while Roman women secretly let the worst of men do what they wanted to them. Great putdown.

It all resulted in a peace treaty with which the Romans could say they'd won, only they hadn't really. Assorted Caledonians rebelled soon after the treaty was signed and then Severus, after muttering genocidal threats and trekking north yet again, suddenly fell ill, retreated to York and died, after allegedly giving his two sons the famous, or indeed infamous, advice to look out for each other, keep the soldiers sweet and scorn everybody else.

Caracalla and Geta, the two sons, promptly abandoned their father's campaign and hotfooted it to the joys of Rome instead, and by the end of AD 211, completely ignoring his father's advice, Caracalla had had Geta bumped off.

We tend to know him as Caracalla because of a type of Gallic coat that he wore and made popular; he was originally named Lucius Septimius Bassianus, and later acquired the names Marcus Aurelius Septimius Bassianus Antoninus. And, again reflecting the multi-ethnic nature of some aspects of the Empire, while his father had been North African, Caracalla and his brother, who became Roman emperors in the north of Britain, were themselves half-North African and half-Syrian, because that's where Severus's wife, Julia Domna, came from.

Caracalla himself was also dead by AD 217, supposedly stabbed during a roadside loo stop at the other end of the Empire, near Carrhae. Ahead lay plenty of rebellions and civil war, both for Britain and the rest of the Roman Empire – which was never permanently going to include Caledonia.

2

The First British Heretic

The Roman occupation of Britain lasted quite a long time and, in the south and east, the locals eventually adopted a lot of Roman culture. We're never going to know to what extent they actually liked Rome, or whether it was just that they liked some of the products of the Empire. Plenty of Britons today, for instance, regard the EU with suspicion but are very happy to buy French wine and German cars. In the north and west, Roman culture wasn't adopted so enthusiastically and extensively.

We know plenty of names of those who lived in Roman Britain, but almost all the names we have come from things like inscriptions found here. Named British individuals of the period hardly ever got mentioned by Roman and Greek authors.

Finally, in the late fourth century AD, as Rome's grip on Britain weakened, one of the first people from the British Isles whose career we know much about, a man who became famous across much of Europe and the Mediterranean, was born. For Pelagius is a man who remains controversial even today, and who has managed to get himself and his theological views reviled by both Catholics and Protestants.

The details of Pelagius' early life are sadly obscure. It is not even entirely clear where in the British Isles he is supposed to have come from. Orosius and Prosper describe him as a Briton, St Augustine calls him Brito and Marius Mercator describes him as '*gente Britannus*' by race, a Briton. It is also worth pointing out here that he seems to have had quite a following in Britain, because in the fifth century a deputation was sent from Britain to the bishops of Gaul to tell them that the teachings of Pelagius had spread like wildfire. St Germanus of Auxerre was, in response, despatched across the Channel to face the British Pelagians (described as rich, well-dressed and surrounded by crowds of fans) in debate. This being (literally) hagiography, Germanus is unsurprisingly described as conclusively winning the debate.

St Jerome (not a fan), however, describes Pelagius as being of Scottish ethnic origin from somewhere 'in the vicinity of Britain' and rather more graphically '*Scottorum pultibus praegravatus*', 'weighed down by Scottish porridge'.

This was a time long before the emergence of Scotland as we know it today; a time when the Romans generally regarded the Scots as a people living in Ireland. They were best known to the Romans as pagan raiders crossing the Irish Sea and attacking anyone they could get their hands on in Britain.

Some have used Jerome's comments to argue that Pelagius was Irish. Many Romans regarded even Britain as (fairly literally) the end of the earth (or at least in that direction), a wild place about which they knew little and wanted to know even less. To such people Ireland would have seemed even more remote, wild and generally sinister. Not all saints have been permanently immune from tetchiness and occasional exaggeration; it may be that Pelagius was indeed a Briton with Irish/Scottish blood in him and a liking for porridge, or it may be that Jerome was attempting to draw attention to what he saw as the (quite literally) outlandish nature of Pelagius and his theology.

Anyway, wherever he came from in the British Isles, the first we really know about him is when he turned up in Rome. Here he acquired a sidekick in Caelestius (though some people would argue that Pelagius became the sidekick), an aristocratic lawyer turned ascetic, and started developing his own ideas on sin and grace. The details of exactly what he believed are slightly hazy since much of the evidence for it comes from people strongly opposed to it. It does not, however, seem that Pelagius was preaching anything that would shock the average Briton on the street today. He was not, for instance, suggesting that it was essential to marry your grandmother, nor that tiger-skin clothes were essential for salvation. However, his views on sin and grace do seem to have stood in particularly sharp contrast to those of a theological superstar of the time, the African St Augustine.

For St Augustine original sin was a central problem for humanity, one that could only be solved by divine grace. For him, flawed humanity corrupted by original sin could only avoid sin and could only do good things through divine grace. By contrast, Pelagius seems to have taken the view of Rufinus the Syrian that the original sin could not be transmitted and that, while divine grace was an essential aid and guiding principle to the Christian, humans had the ability to choose to do good or not do good. To many, particularly non-Christians, such questions may seem an attempt at saying similar things from a different angle, but equally to many believers they can define a crucial difference in how God deals with man and how the universe works.

However, before the Church could deliver a final verdict on Pelagius, the man from the British Isles was off on his travels again. In AD 409, the people of Rome had other things to worry about besides theology – Alaric's army was on the rampage in Italy. Pelagius and Caelestius fled the city for the safety of North Africa. Alaric sacked Rome in AD 410, while far to the north in Britain things were changing too as Britain moved beyond the reach of the ailing empire.

Shortly afterwards, Caelestius faced the Council of Carthage. He was accused of holding six beliefs which the council condemned. These were:

1) Even if Adam had been sinless he would still have died
2) By sinning Adam only harmed himself not the whole of humanity
3) Newborn babies are like Adam before he sinned

4) The whole of humanity is not condemned by Adam's sin nor saved by Christ's resurrection
5) The Law, as well as the Gospel, can lead to heaven
6) Even before Christ some men lived who were without sin

It's impossible to know if this is precisely what Caelestius believed, and it's certainly impossible to know whether it is exactly what Pelagius believed. However, it is possible to see again a battle over the basic idea of whether humanity is innately sinful and can only be good through God or whether humans on their own can do good things. Having been condemned in Carthage, Caelestius left Africa and headed for Asia Minor, where, by contrast, he managed to get himself ordained as a priest.

Pelagius had meanwhile headed for Palestine, where he was strongly opposed by St Jerome but found much less resistance from Bishop John of Jerusalem. A Spanish priest, Orosius, arrived to lend his support to Jerome and Pelagius ended up being accused in front of a diocesan synod in Jerusalem in AD 415. Orosius, however, seems to have managed to score a bit of an own goal, ending up accused of holding the belief that the original sin had so corrupted humanity that even with God's grace it could not avoid sin. Orosius vigorously denied this, but it had taken the focus off Pelagius. In December AD 415, Pelagius persuaded a council in Diospolis that he was not a heretic.

But that was not to be the end of it. In 416 two councils in Africa condemned Pelagius and Caelestius, and in early 417 Pope Innocent I did too. Innocent died soon after and Caelestius persuaded the new pope, Zosimus, to look again at the situation. Things were not moving in the direction Caelestius and Pelagius hoped. On 30 April 418, Emperor Honorius, the emperor who had lost Britain from the empire, decisively rejected the man from the British Isles. He condemned anyone who rejected the idea of the Fall and barred Pelagius and Caelestius from Italy. St Augustine and a Council of Carthage issued a vigorous statement of views on sin and grace the following day, asserting, for instance, that all humans are affected by the original sin and that good works can only come through God's grace. After this, Pope Zosimus excommunicated both Pelagius and Caelestius. Pelagius was forced out of Jerusalem and fled to Egypt. It is not clear what happened to him after that.

The man from the British Isles was gone, and the Church continued to act against his followers. However, the debate between Pelagius and Augustine and the furore that it sparked in significant chunks of Britain and the Empire is still of interest today because of how it helped shape Christian thinking on fundamental questions about the nature of man and the nature of God.

3

Saints, Stones and the Origins of England

In AD 43, Roman power had come to Britain to stay; by AD 410, having completed its stay, it was pretty much gone.

A lot of people tend to think of the period after the end of Roman Britain as a period in which Britain drops off the historical radar almost entirely; a period about which only archaeology can give answers (and even there the evidence is pretty slim). On some levels, this is true. We have little written by contemporaries or near contemporaries about what was happening in the couple of centuries after Britain slipped from Roman control. Yet three saints have left a historical legacy linked to the period that throws a fascinating light on it and played a major role in shaping how the Welsh and English have come to think of themselves. More than this, rather unexpectedly these three saints' stories have also left something of a concrete (well, stone at least) legacy that is still around today.

The first biography of St Germanus (whom we already met briefly in the previous chapter), that composed by Constantius, was probably written about AD 480, about seventy years after the end of Roman Britain and a few decades after the death of the saint. This is the biography of a saint. It is literally hagiography, and contains plenty of stories of miracles. However, at its heart is a story of the saint's visit (or visits) to Britain, the first portrayal in any detail of what was happening in Britain after the end of Roman control.

Constantius indicates that St Germanus himself had been born to high-status parents in Auxerre, south-east of Paris, and then became a barrister in Rome and a military commander. As it turned out, both of these experiences were to be of use later in Britain. Eventually, however, he became bishop of his home town Auxerre.

When a deputation arrived in Gaul from Britain complaining about the spread of Pelagianism there, Germanus and Lupus were dispatched by a synod of bishops to do spiritual battle in Britain. They preached their faith around the country and eventually faced the Pelagians in open debate. According to Constantius, Germanus' arguments destroyed those of the Pelagians. However, the debate with the Pelagians was not the only thing Germanus got up to in Britain.

He was a busy saint. He cured a girl of blindness and he visited the shrine of St Alban, who had been martyred outside Verulamium, on the site of what became, of course, St Albans. Its beautiful abbey still contains a shrine to St Alban. Germanus also miraculously dealt with a fire, and miraculously dealt with pagan invaders.

The Saxons and Picts were attacking and the Britons feared they would be defeated. Germanus, with his military experience, rushed to the rescue, preparing the Britons both spiritually and militarily for the battle, preaching to them and baptising them but also checking their defences. He formed a plan. The enemy would be approaching through a steep-sided valley and trying to ambush the Britons, so he drew up his men in the valley and waited for the raiders. As the attackers approached, thinking they were about to surprise the Britons, they were themselves surprised. Germanus got his men to scream 'Alleluia' repeatedly as a battle cry. The cry echoed off the slopes and the attackers, presumably thinking they were outnumbered, legged it rapidly, abandoning their booty. A delightfully saintly method of winning a battle. After this, Germanus returned to Gaul (though he may have had to make another journey later to Britain, when the Pelagians were once again on the rise). When Germanus died he was buried in his home town of Auxerre, and a shrine developed over the centuries there amid the still impressive architecture of the Abbey of Saint Germain d'Auxerre.

And now we come to St Gildas. Gildas was a cleric who probably lived in the late fifth or early sixth century AD. Little agreement exists about where he is likely to have lived. Two, often contradictory, medieval accounts of his life survive, both of which were written centuries after the period in question.

The earlier of the two versions, the Rhuys Life, among other things has him born into a royal family in the Clyde region of northern Britain, educated in Wales and working as a priest in Ireland before visiting Rome and Ravenna, eventually settling and dying in Brittany.

The later life, the Llancarfan Life, also has Gildas born into a royal family in northern Britain, though details differ, but then has Gildas travelling to Gaul to study before returning to Britain. It does have Gildas visiting Rome, and also a lot about King Arthur. Gildas' brothers, for instance, were said to have rebelled against Arthur. Arthur then allegedly killed Gildas' brother and, in the end, the story goes, Gildas visited Arthur and Arthur did penance for the death. And when Melvas carried off Guinevere (yep, Guinevere's in there too), Gildas had to intervene. Finally the Llancarfan Life has Gildas dying at Glastonbury.

In the end, it may well be that neither biography gives too much credible information about Gildas, who is mainly known as the author of the *De Excidio*, a book which describes the period before and after the end of Rome. Unfortunately, *De Excidio* gives few indications in the book about the life of its author. Instead, the writer spends most of his time discussing events in the south and west of Britain (no mention of King Arthur!). What is most significant about the *De Excidio* is that it continues Constantius' depiction of Britons battling invading Picts and Saxons. The *De Excidio* is in fact the first expression that we still have of some ideas that became the very bedrock of how many English and others viewed the beginnings of England. Gildas describes a process in which a British king in the post-Roman period invited pagan Saxons in to help him fight his enemies. The king then found that, with increasing numbers of the Saxons arriving on British shores, instead of being much help to him the Saxons rebelled and then ravaged Britain, slaughtering and burning, forcing Britons to flee to remote parts of the island or abroad. Gildas also tells of the growth of British resistance to the invaders, a successful British leader (still not Arthur) and a major victory at Mount Badon (a victory later to be attributed to Arthur). However, the *De Excidio* is not just a history; it is also an attack on assorted British leaders of the time, with assorted accusations of greed, murder and lust. Without the *De Excidio*, people's ideas over the centuries of the very beginnings of England might have been rather different.

St Gildas did not become as popular after his death as St Germanus and is now unknown to a lot of people. In the pretty little Breton town of St Gildas de Rhuys is a beautiful abbey, and inside the abbey are reliquaries of Gildas.

And then we have Saint Bede. Yep, the Venerable Bede himself. Bede is, of course, much more widely known than the other two saints in this chapter, so, this being *Unexpected Britain*, we're not going to spend as much time on him as on the other two saints.

He was born around the year 673 and died on 26 May 735. He spent time at the monastery at Wearmouth and then lived and worked at the monastery at Jarrow. He wrote many things, but he is now best known for his *Historia Ecclesiastica Gentis Anglorum* (*Ecclesiastical History of the English People*), in which he traced not just the spiritual but also the political history of England. In his history of the period after the end of Roman Britain Bede relies to some extent on Constantius' Life of St Germanus and on Gildas, but in Bede you will find more of those elements which became key to how English people viewed their origins.

In Bede's account of the arrival of the Saxons we now have the familiar names Hengest and Horsa (found in the *Anglo-Saxon Chronicle*) for the leaders of the invaders. We have

Bede dividing the new arrivals into Angles, Saxons and Jutes, and allotting to each group a part of England. So Bede says that from the Jutes came the people of Kent, the Isle of Wight and a bit of the mainland opposite the Isle of Wight. From the Saxons came the East Saxons, the South Saxons, and the West Saxons, and from the Angles came the East Angles, the Midland Angles, the Mercians and the Northumbrians.

And again, not all of the people who have heard of the Venerable Bede will know that his tomb is on display in Durham Cathedral. Another amazing stone link to England's earliest history.

Between them, the three saints have had a massive influence on how England's history has been viewed. For centuries, the dominant view of the origins of England was of Britons chased out of England by rampaging Angles, Saxons and Jutes. Today, many modern historians would argue that the process was much more complex; that many Britons were not chased out but stayed and adopted Anglo-Saxon culture as some of their ancestors had adopted Roman culture; that some of the Angle/Saxon/Jute newcomers cooperated with the Britons rather than fought them; that Britons fought Britons and Anglo-Saxons fought Anglo-Saxons (as well as Britons fighting Anglo-Saxons, of course), and that the distinctions in Britain between Angles, Saxons, Jutes and Britons were often not clear cut. Still, these three saints hold a huge place in the history of England and in the history of Britain.

4

The Welsh Conquest of Northern England

Many people, if asked about Anglo-Saxons and Welsh in the seventh century, would probably suggest a process of Anglo-Saxon warlords slowly pushing forward against the Welsh and the Welsh slowly retreating into what is now Wales.

The alliance of Cadwallon, King of Gwynedd, and Penda, King of Mercia, shows that it was often a little more complicated than that.

Little is certain about the early careers of either of the two characters. What is certain is that both must have felt threatened by the expansion of Northumbrian power. At some stage, in the late 620s or early 630s, the then King of Northumbria, Edwin, had extended his power westwards as far as Anglesey and the Isle of Man. Cadwallon may have ended up besieged on the small island of Priestholm off Anglesey. If so, Edwin's triumph was not to last.

In 633, Cadwallon and Penda teamed up. Cadwallon was Christian and British, Penda was pagan (the *Anglo-Saxon Chronicle* even contains a genealogical descent from Woden) and Anglo-Saxon, though ruler of a kingdom, Mercia, that probably included substantial numbers of Britons; indeed, some have even suggested Penda himself may have had some British roots. The two teamed up to tame the Anglo-Saxon and newly Christian (and about to become martyr and then saint as well) Edwin.

The result was the Battle of Hatfield Chase on 12 October

633, when the combined forces of Cadwallon and Penda smashed Edwin's army and killed the Northumbrian king and his son Osfrith. They weren't finished there. Not at all. Cadwallon went on to kill two more local royals. Cadwallon found himself besieged by Osric, but surprised him with a sortie and killed him. Cadwallon found Eanfrith coming to try to negotiate terms and killed him. For a year, Cadwallon, Welsh ruler of Gwynedd, ruled the Northumbrians.

Gildas has some very unflattering things to say about Maelgwn, Cadwallon's predecessor as ruler of Gwynedd, and Bede is clearly not a fan of Cadwallon either. He describes him as being like a beast, slaughtering women and children and wanting to wipe out the English race in Britain. This is extremely unlikely to be literally true, especially since he was allied with the Anglo-Saxon kingdom of Mercia, but it is at least an interesting counterbalance to Gildas' (also probably exaggerated) depiction of genocidal violence by Anglo-Saxons against Britons.

However, the Welsh conquest of much of northern England was not to last. Another local royal, Oswald, who had spent time in Ireland in exile, returned and defeated Cadwallon (even though the British king was said to have forces superior in number) near Hadrian's Wall at the Battle of Heavenfield.

Oswald's rule was not, however, to be a long one. Much to Bede's delight, Oswald seems to have gone to some lengths to help spread Christianity. The king also seems to have had widespread political and military influence during his reign, including, according to Bede, some over Picts and Scots to the north. However, even though Cadwallon had been killed at Heavenfield, his ally at the Battle of Hatfield Chase had not. Penda was still very much alive, and pretty soon Oswald wouldn't be.

It's not entirely clear what had been happening to Penda between 633 and 642, but on 5 August he was facing King Oswald at the Battle of Maserfelth. Oswald was killed. Once again Penda was victorious and once again the pagan Anglo-Saxon king may have had Christian British help against other

Anglo-Saxons. An early Welsh poem suggests a King of Powys fighting on Penda's side at the battle. The victory seems to have been perhaps even more of a boost to Penda's fortunes than Hatfield Chase had been. He went on to penetrate as far as Bamburgh on the North Sea coast. In Wessex he drove out the ruler Cenwalh after Cenwalh had repudiated his wife, who happened to be Penda's sister (Penda was clearly a brother-in-law it was unwise to antagonise). In East Anglia he killed two kings and an ex-king.

Today we tend to think of the chief problems of being a monarch as being constant scrutiny by the tabloid press and the rigours of endless speeches, shaking hands and opening things, but in the seventh century a very real and frequent risk of violent death was the counterbalance to the wealth and power of being a monarch. Probably in 655, Penda faced Oswiu of Northumbria at the Battle of the Winwæd. This time, even though he (allegedly) had vast superiority in numbers, Penda would not be victorious. He was defeated and killed, and so were large numbers of his men.

For King Oswald, though, things were starting to look up – or, at least, as much as they could considering he was dead. Bede was writing around 730, and by then he was already recounting stories of miracles connected with the spot where Oswald had been killed. Every year on the day before the anniversary of his death, monks made a pilgrimage to the cross that Oswald had erected before his victory at Heavenfield. King Oswald became Saint Oswald.

The story of Cadwallon and Penda and Oswald is both fascinating and important. This is partly because it demonstrates the ability of a Welsh king to send shock waves through one of the biggest and most powerful Anglo-Saxon kingdoms and partly because it illustrates how, amid the brutal politics of the seventh century, the search for power could create alliances that crossed both cultural and religious boundaries.

5

Life of a Warlord, from Vengeance to Vatican

Pretty much every Brit has heard of two Anglo-Saxon rulers, Alfred the Great and Harold II (the Battle of Hastings Harold). A host of other rulers also lived, fought and died during the Anglo-Saxon period. Many of them have jolly names and interesting, though not widely known, stories that say something about the wider history of Anglo-Saxon England. One such is Cædwalla, a king whose reign was short but action-packed and perhaps vital to the way England finally developed.

For a start, the name is interesting. Cædwalla is known to history as a Saxon king and yet his name seems much more British or Welsh, like the Cadwallon of Gwynedd in the previous chapter. It doesn't automatically mean he was of British or Welsh origin, but he may have been at least partly. It certainly suggests that personal senses of identity in the centuries following the arrival of the Anglo-Saxons in Britain could be more complex than people have sometimes thought, particularly in the more western parts of England.

Cædwalla was born in around 659 into the royal house of the kingdom that became Wessex, the Anglo-Saxon kingdom that would come to dominate Anglo-Saxon England and help unify it. However, the heartland of Wessex was in the west. This area was far from the eastern coast most easily reached by Angles, Saxons and Jutes crossing the North Sea and much closer to areas that either still then were, or until recently had been, beyond the reach of the Anglo-Saxon kingdoms – Cornwall and Wales, obviously, but also the area around Bath, Cirencester, Worcester and Gloucester. The royal house itself in Wessex traced its descent from a man called Cerdic, again identified as a Saxon king despite a name that looks rather British.

When we first hear of Cædwalla, he was in exile from Wessex (not, frankly, that unusual an experience for an Anglo-Saxon royal in a world where the competition to be king was often fierce and rather unsporting). Cædwalla's reaction to the experience was not all that uncommon either. He assembled himself an army in the Chilterns and the Weald, both regarded then by people as somewhat remote and wild. From here he set off to find himself a kingdom. Or steal somebody else's, anyway.

For whatever reason, his first target was not Wessex but the nearby kingdom of the South Saxons. He managed to kill the King of the South Saxons, Æthelwalh. Any hope of taking the kingdom at that point, however, was crushed by local commanders Andhun and Berhthun. Cædwalla does, however, seem to have retained something from his foray into Sussex, which was an association with St Wilfrid, who had been at the court of Æthelwalh. Cædwalla himself was not baptised at the time, and may have been a pagan. If so, he was among the last Anglo-Saxon royals to be pagan and, as we shall see, his later life saw a decisive switch to Christianity.

It would not be the last that the South Saxons would see of Cædwalla, not at all. In around 685, at the age of something like twenty-seven or twenty-eight, he took control of Wessex. It was bad news for Berhthun. Very bad news. In fact, it really couldn't have been much worse. The man he had previously defeated now returned to the kingdom of South Saxons as well, killed him and took control. It was bad news too for the South Saxons themselves, who seem to have been given something of a tough time by the invader. Things weren't looking too good for the people of the Isle of Wight either, because they were next to suffer Cædwalla's attentions. In

686 Cædwalla stormed ashore on the island with his forces and seized control, committing a major massacre to free up space to bring his own people into the land. Two brothers of the King of the Isle of Wight managed to escape the slaughter and make it to the mainland, where they were captured. Cædwalla allowed them to be baptised before they too were slaughtered. Apparently, though, Cædwalla had promised land and rewards to the Church if he managed to capture the Isle of Wight. Allegedly he did fulfil his promise, giving land to St Wilfrid.

Next it was Kent's turn. In the same year that he struck at the Isle of Wight, he hit Kent too. He seems to have taken control there and put his brother Mul on the throne. However, a rebellion broke out against Mul in Kent and the rebels killed Mul and twelve others by burning. It wasn't just Cædwalla who was capable of being brutal. Characteristically, though, Cædwalla's response was violent. He attacked Kent and ravaged the land, imposing his will and crushing the rebels. It is even possible that his power and influence extended further, into Surrey and Essex.

All in all, in the very brief time he had been king, Cædwalla had done a lot to expand Wessex's horizons and help begin the process whereby Wessex would eventually become the dominant force in Anglo-Saxon England and eventually help unify it. He had done it brutally, but he had done it.

Such concentrated brutality may have taken a heavy toll on Cædwalla, certainly physically but perhaps also spiritually. According to Bede, he had been wounded during the attack on the Isle of Wight and, as we shall see, he did not have much of his life left. Perhaps after two or three years of death and destruction, along with the loss of his brother, he had had enough. Maybe the teachings of St Wilfrid were starting to have an effect on him, or perhaps it was a combination of all three factors. For whatever reason, in 688 he suddenly abdicated and announced that he was going to Rome to be baptised.

Whatever his physical state, he set off on the long, long

journey to Rome. He may have been the first Anglo-Saxon king to have visited the city. On Easter Saturday 689, 10 April, the thirty-year-old Cædwalla was baptised and took the baptismal name Peter. He was baptised by Pope Sergius I himself. Pope Sergius was a man who'd seen a bit of drama in his life too. Sergius had ended up being elected pope only after a fierce struggle between factions supporting two other candidates for the papacy. Later in his life, Sergius would only manage to avoid being arrested by forces of the Byzantine Emperor because militiamen defended him. He was also the pope who sent the English Willibrord (see next chapter) to be bishop of the Frisians.

Cædwalla's life on earth, though, was now almost finished. Cædwalla, a man who had seen so much death and destruction and who had been responsible for much of it, died a few days later. He was buried in St Peter's, still clothed in his white baptismal garments. According to Bede, he had a tomb there with an epitaph on it commemorating how he had given up his position, his wealth, his crown and his kingdom in order, as a pilgrim king, to see St Peter's and the saint's shrine.

6

Britain Converts Germany

Sometimes we tend to think of early medieval Britain as a rather isolated place, or if there was contact with the mainland we tend to think that it was all incoming, with hordes of Angles, Saxons, Jutes, Frisians and eventually Vikings. However, movement was in fact pretty much always a two-way street, and one of our most influential exports was one Boniface.

Christianity survived beyond the end of Roman Britain in the west of the island, and there may have been some Christians in the Anglo-Saxon east as well, but St Augustine, on the orders of Pope Gregory the Great, began the official conversion of Saxon England at the end of the sixth century. He started in Kent with King Aethelberht, a pretty good place to start since it was handy for the Continent and the king had already married a Christian princess, Bertha. Aethelberht converted, as did hundreds of others, in a mass baptism on Christmas Day 597 and St Augustine became the first Archbishop of Canterbury.

At this time, the situation wasn't quite so rosy for Christianity in what is now the Netherlands and Germany. However, things were about to change big time, both politically and religiously, for the pagan inhabitants of the area. They were being threatened by the growing power of the princes of Francia, who wished to extend their control. From 718 it was Charles Martel, Prince of the Franks, who took on the role of bashing the locals into submission. His mission, to plug them into the European mainstream (whether they liked it or not), was aided by an apostle who wished to conquer souls. This is the story of Winfred, alias St Boniface, the English Saxon who became patron saint of Germany.

St Boniface was born as Winfred, perhaps somewhere near Exeter, sometime around the year 675. His family was wealthy and his father was allegedly bitterly disappointed when his son decided to become a monk and devote his life to God. Winfred began his theological training in a Benedictine monastery at Nursling, close to Winchester, under the leadership of an abbot named Winbert. Winfred was a gifted academic; he would write a book on Latin grammar, the *Ars Grammatica*, and he became a teacher in the abbey school. However, Winfred was not one for the easy life. He had his heart set on a missionary expedition to convert pagans to Christianity.

Things didn't get off to a great start. He boarded a ship in London and headed for the Continent, but when he reached Utrecht he found he was unable to make much further progress due to travel delays caused by an excess of slaughtering and maiming. Radbod, King of the Frisians, was busy fighting Charles Martel at the time. Winfred returned temporarily to Wessex.

However, he was not to be deterred forever. Two years later, he set forth on his missionary work. He went to London and took a ship for Quentvic, on the French side of the Channel. This time he headed to Rome to get support from the Pope. After chatting with Winfred and reviewing his credentials, Pope Gregory II gave him full authority to preach to the heathens in Germany. With his position strengthened by the support of the Pope, Winfred set off once again to convert the 'savage peoples of Germany', taking with him some holy relics which were bound to come in useful.

Winfred began his mission in Bavaria, where he found the church flourishing. Unneeded there, he pressed on into Thuringia. The Pope had this listed as Christian, so Winifred was somewhat shocked by what he found. Many Christians had reverted to paganism or practised some combination of Christian and pagan religion. The Christian rulers, Duke Gotzbert and his son Hethan (a perhaps unfortunate name for a Christian ruler), had both been killed by the pagans. Winfred set about preaching and converting, but found himself somewhat disappointed with the results.

So, when he learned that King Radbod had died, he wasted no time in meeting up with Willibrord (whom we have already met in the previous chapter; a Northumbrian missionary who had by this time, handily, become Bishop of Utrecht) and heading into Frisia. Their mission was to support those Christians who had survived Radbod's pagan rule and to convert the remaining pagans. Travelling in the wake of Charles Martel's army, the two clerics at last met with some success.

Encouraged by his missionary triumphs in Frisia, Winfred followed Martel south into Hesse and, once again, into Thuringia. This time he was much more successful in winning converts and he established a missionary centre at Amöneburg on the River Ohm.

Winfred reckoned he'd found a winning formula. After triumphs in Frisia, Hesse and Thuringia, Winfred sent off to Rome an account of what he'd been up to, only to find himself summoned south. He journeyed through Burgundy and France to tell the Pope about his work in Frisia in 723. Pope Gregory II must have liked what he heard, because he responded by making Winfred Bishop of Germania and giving him the job of converting even more pagans to Christianity. Somewhere along the line Winfred had also acquired a new name, Boniface, 'doer of good deeds', after the fourth-century martyr Boniface of Tarsus. And so, full of enthusiasm, Boniface returned to Hesse to see how things had been going while he had been in Rome. Not so well was the answer.

Boniface was shocked to find that in his absence there had been yet another pagan revival. This time he had really had enough. His decisive battle with the pagans of Hesse took place near the town of Fritzlar, where he helped his cause with a miracle.

He decided to fell a giant oak tree that the locals had dedicated to the pagan god Thor. The locals gathered to see what retribution Thor would claim for this insult, but Boniface was able to fell the tree with little difficulty, helped by a mighty and miraculous wind. The tree also split into four identical pieces.

The people of Hesse were so impressed by this miracle that they converted to Christianity and helped Boniface build a chapel dedicated to St Peter from the wood of the oak. Anyway, according to the near-contemporary *Vita Bonifatii auctore Willibaldi*, this was how Boniface accomplished his mission. The Abbey of Fritzlar was established on the site of the miracle.

To be fair, Boniface was not working alone on this mission. Much of the groundwork had already been done by Willibrord and Northumbrian monks. The leader of the Christian Franks, Charles Martel, was also keen to extend both Christianity and his political influence northwards to include the Saxons of northern Germany. Boniface's personal safety was to a large extent guaranteed by the protection of Charles Martel.

After his success in Hesse, Boniface headed off to tackle the less-than-perfect Christians of Thuringia once again. The Pope and Charles Martel provided valuable books to educate the clergy and helpers flocked in to boost Boniface's efforts. Some, like Lullus, came from Saxon England; others were recruited more locally in Germany.

Boniface was moving up the papal hierarchy. In 732, Pope Gregory III, who had succeeded Pope Gregory II, appointed Boniface Archbishop of Germany and gave him the authority to appoint new bishops throughout Germany as he saw fit. Five years later Boniface made his third and final visit to Rome, intending to resign his offices in order to devote himself to spreading the gospel among the Saxons. Boniface stayed a year in Rome, but instead of resigning he left Rome with even more papal authority. He had become a papal legate. Great title. He also came away with more relics.

To spread his missionary work, Boniface was going to need

both the spiritual authority of the Pope and the decidedly less spiritual – but also more powerful – political authority of Charles Martel. In 741, though, there was a change of personnel as first Charles Martel and then Pope Gregory III both died. Charles Martel was replaced by his sons Carloman and Pepin, while Pope Zachary became pontiff.

The personnel may have changed, but the new incumbents continued to support Boniface and his mission. In 742, with the backing of both Carloman and Pope Zachary, Boniface organised the first German synod. It is not known where this was held, but the following matters were agreed and they shed an interesting light on what was going on in Germany. There were to be very strict rules about the carnal sins of priests. Clergy and bishops were forbidden to take up arms or to take part in any wars. The clergy were not allowed to hunt. There were also rules preventing marriage within certain degrees of kindred to prevent incest. This was the first of several German synods held during Boniface's life.

In May 747, Boniface was appointed Archbishop of Mainz and Primate of Germany by Pope Zachary. His archdiocese included the dioceses of Cologne, Worms, Speyer, Utrecht, Buraburg, Eichstatt, Erfurt, Wurzburg, Augsburg, Coire and Constance. His authority stretched from Bavaria in the south to Cologne and Utrecht in the north. When Carloman resigned in order to become a monk, it was Boniface who was authorised by the Pope to crown Pepin, the first of the Carolingian rulers. It was Pepin's son Charlemagne who was to become the first Holy Roman Emperor. There is some dispute as to whether Boniface did actually crown Pepin, but he was trusted by the papacy and would have been in a position to perform this rite.

In 754, nearly forty years after his first attempt to convert the pagans of Frisia, Boniface set forth again to complete his mission. He baptised a large number of pagans and summoned a gathering of the converted to meet at Dokkum.

And that's pretty much where it all went wrong. Instead of enjoying another missionary triumph, they were attacked and killed by pagans looking to plunder the wealth of Boniface and his Christians. Boniface instructed his followers not to fight back, telling them, 'Cease fighting. Lay down your arms, for we are told in Scripture not to render evil for good but to overcome evil by good.' The pagans enjoyed drinking the wine of the Christians but were very disappointed that, rather than gold, Boniface's luggage contained sacred texts. They burnt the texts in disgust. In response to the massacre of Boniface and his followers, a small army of Christian warriors then assembled and in turn massacred a lot of the pagans responsible and seized their women, children and portable goods.

The body of Boniface, clutching a bloodstained copy of St Ambrose's *Advantage of Death*, was recovered by Lullus. It is said that he had held up the book in an attempt to ward off the blows of his assailants. The body was taken to the Abbey of Fulda, which had been built by Boniface and where he had said he wanted to be buried. The bloodstained text is one of the relics of the abbey.

For some Boniface is the 'greatest Englishman', for others he is the patron saint of brewers, but for most he is the Apostle of Germany and its patron saint. A rare achievement to be remembered both in England and Germany. His true genius was, in some sense, not so much in converting pagans in Germany but in organising the Church there and giving it a structure. He was in constant touch with the papacy and he worked well with the emerging political leaders, Charles Martel, Carloman and Pepin, who had their own interests in spreading Christianity. His martyrdom was first celebrated in England, but in 1874 Pope Pius IX extended the celebration to the entire world.

7

Three Battles for the North

While things had been getting pretty bloody across the south of Britain (see Cædwalla in Chapter 5), it wasn't exactly that peaceful in the north either. And soon those Vikings were going to get in on the fun as well.

We're all used to Braveheart and the battle for control of Scotland in the fourteenth century, but what's much less well known is that the battle for dominance between those living in what is now Scotland and those living in what is now England started many centuries earlier, and could have ended in English defeat not only in the north but further south as well. This is the story of three battles – Catreath, Dunnichen and Brunanburh, all little known (and sadly hard now to locate) but battles nonetheless – that would define the futures of both countries.

Just as what is now England was politically and culturally fragmented in the early medieval period, so was what is now Scotland. In central and eastern Scotland were the Picts with their beautiful stone memorials and jewellery. To the west were the Gaels of Dál Riata, who had cultural links across the Irish Sea with the Gaels of Ireland and who would eventually give Scotland its name (from a word, *Scotti*, used by the Romans). In the south of what is now Scotland were Britons, ethnically and cultural linked to the peoples who had dominated the south of the island before the arrival of the Anglo-Saxons. Soon added to this mix were the Angles, advancing north from Northumbria. On top of all this would come the Vikings as well.

It was the Angles of Northumbria who appeared to be the strongest power in the region by the end of the seventh century. The famous British poem 'The Battle of Catreath' records an expedition launched by the Britonic Gododdin sometime around the late sixth or early seventh century. An aside reference to Arthur in it is also (unless it's a later interpolation), incidentally, one of the bits of near-contemporary evidence referring to this elusive character or British myth or history. In the poem, after much feasting the expedition headed south from a base at Din Eidyn (widely identified with Edinburgh) into Angle territory to the south. At Catreath, thought by many to be Catterick in what is now north Yorkshire, the British war band was decisively defeated, marking a significant stage in the solidification of Angle power in what is now north-east England. It would not be long before things took an even better turn for the Angles.

In 638, Oswald took control of all land south of the River Forth. Northumbria stretched westwards to include Cumbria, Dumfries and Galloway and south to Yorkshire and the Humber estuary. It was the strongest of the Anglo-Saxon kingdoms.

However, in the late seventh century in the reign of Ecgfrith this Northumbrian hegemony was beginning to crumble. Further north, Bridei mac Billi, King of the Picts, set about expanding his kingdom by, for instance, capturing the Orkney Islands. Then he turned south, taking on the Northumbrians by attacking forts such as Dunnottar and Dundurn. He insulted Ecgfrith by refusing to pay tribute, so, as tended to happen in such situations, Ecgfrith reckoned it would be a good idea to head north with an army. It wasn't a good idea. At least not for Ecgfrith and his forces.

On 20 May 685, Bridei crushed Ecgfrith's army at a battle known as Dunnichen or Dun Nechtain or (Anglo-Saxon version) Nechtansmere. The Picts faced up to the Northumbrians and then retreated, luring them into a trap between what Bede calls 'inaccessible mountains', where Ecgfrith was 'slain with the greatest part of his forces'. The dead king's body was taken to Iona for burial. This victory ensured that the Picts were free from the control of the Angles of Northumbria, although the Northumbrians kept control of Edinburgh and Lothian. According to Bede, 'the Saxons never again reduced the Picts so as to exact tribute from them'. It meant the end of the possibility that Anglo-Saxon control would spread across the whole of northern Britain to the same extent that it was spreading across what is now England.

While there is broad agreement among Scottish historians as to the importance of the battle, there is no certainty about where it was fought or what to call it. These historical debates show how little the sources actually say about these events and also the problem that none of the sources were written by the Picts. In Old English this was the Battle of Nechtansmere; in Old Welsh, the language of the Britons and probably of Bridei and his Picts, it was Linn Garan; in Old Irish it turns into Dun Nechtain; in Scottish Gaelic Blar Dhun Neachdain. It is ironic that, on this occasion, the victor did not get to name the battle or write the history.

The location of the battle may have been Dunnichen near Forfar in Angus, which has the name but not the inaccessible mountains described by Bede, or it may be the Pictish settlement of Dunachton on the shores of Loch Insh, which does have suitable mountains. Whatever the battle is called and wherever it was fought, it ensured that the Picts survived until the closing years of the ninth century, where they disappear and Pictland is transformed into Alba, or Scotland.

One of the candidates as the first King of Scotland was Kenneth Macalpin, but Kenneth, who ruled between 810 and 858, was perhaps in reality more a Pictish king. However, his grandson Constantine II assumed the title of King of Alba in 900. The name change was symbolic of a new Gaelic and Pictish alliance to create a new kingdom, Scotland. The name Alba appears for the first time in the *Chronicle of Alba*, where for the first time the Scots were able to record their own history.

Anyone expecting Constantine to reassert Pictish culture and favour Picts in his new kingdom would have been disappointed. Having been brought up by a Gaelic prince in Ireland, Constantine continued with combining the two cultures. In 904, he defeated the Viking King Ivar the Younger of Dublin at Strathcarron and massacred his army. He then turned his attentions to the south and defeated Ragnall, the Viking King of York at the Battle of Corbridge. This meant that the new kingdom stretched south of the River Forth and included the Edinburgh area. The new kingdom was beginning to resemble the territory of modern Scotland.

However, it was not just in Scotland that Viking power was waning at the start of the tenth century. In Anglo-Saxon England, Athelstan had also succeeded in defeating the Viking King of York and had incorporated York into his territory. In 934, Athelstan headed further north into Alba with a huge army. He forced the King of Strathclyde and the Earl of Northumbria to submit to him. King Constantine knew that he could not compete in a direct battle with Athelstan, so in 934 he took shelter in the coastal fort of Dunnotar, close to Stonehaven. The fortress was too strong for Athelstan, but Athelstan forced Constantine to accept him as some form of overlord. Content with Constantine's submission, Athelstan withdrew south, allowing Constantine to regain face with his supporters by immediately withdrawing his allegiance to Athelstan.

Instead, King Constantine set about building a diplomatic alliance to settle the dispute with Athelstan. He married his daughter to Olaf Guthfrithsson, the pagan Viking King of Dublin, and persuaded Owein of Strathclyde to support him. Therefore, the army which Constantine led south against Athelstan in 937 represented the combined might of the Viking, Gaelic, Britonic, Pictish north, as represented by the Kingdom of Alba. When the two sides met at Brunanburh, it was to decide who would be the dominant power in the island – the Anglo-Saxons or a Celtic alliance led by Alba. As with Catraeth and Dunnichen, it is hard to be exactly sure where the Battle of Brunanburh was fought (one suggestion is on the Wirral), but it does seem to have been a very major clash.

The Battle of Brunanburh was one of the largest and bloodiest of the so-called Dark Ages. According to an Anglo-Saxon poem, 'the field flowed with blood of warriors'. The *Anglo-Saxon Chronicle* gleefully recorded that Constantine 'left his son on the place of slaughter, mangled by wounds'. Owein of Strathclyde was also killed. The battle was a victory for Athelstan and the Anglo-Saxons, but its consequences ultimately did little to strengthen Athelstan's position in the north. Olaf Guthfrithsson restored Viking rule in York, Strathclyde remained free of Anglo-Saxon interference and the King of Alba was subservient to nobody. This island was to be ruled not by one single, dominating power block but by competing power blocks.

In the end, after in many senses creating a nation, Constantine returned to Scotland and retired six years later to spend the last decade of his life as a monk at St Andrews. Well, at least he got to enjoy a longer retirement than Cædwalla had.

8

Plots and Passions of a Saxon Queen

Meanwhile, down south, the defenders of England had also been having a busy time of it against the Vikings, eventually achieving some notable successes, particularly under Alfred the Great, who wasn't called the Great for nothing.

Some Anglo-Saxon names we still use and still give to our children. Alfred and Harold are obvious examples. Partly because of that, the original people who made those names famous still seem somehow accessible and understandable. However, some Anglo-Saxon names have long fallen out of use, making the people who first made them famous seem more distant. One such name is the female name Ælfthryth. Even though it apparently means 'Elf-strength', which is rather fun, it's hard to see people rushing out to name their daughters Ælfthryth after reading this book – or perhaps especially after reading this book, as perhaps the most famous Ælfthryth became, to put it mildly, a controversial character. Yes, other Ælfthryths existed, including a daughter of King Alfred. (One of her daughters was called Eormenthryth, another name unlikely to be fashionable for girls again any time soon, although her husband's name, Baudouin/Baldwin, has done rather better. One Baudouin was Count of Flanders and another was King of the Belgians until 1993.) But this Ælfthryth is one of the most intriguing characters in English history, which makes it all the more surprising so few people have actually heard of her. It's sometimes hard to know how much of what was later written about her is actually true, so we have to be slightly careful, but some great stories have been told about her and those around her, if nothing else.

Ælfthryth was born late in the first half of the tenth century. We know she died around 1000, but the date of her birth is rather more obscure. She was born into power and wealth. Her mother had blood ties with the royal family of Wessex and her father, Ordgar, was a powerful ealdorman somewhere in the west of Wessex. She was apparently very beautiful and it wasn't long before a powerful man took her for his bride. This was apparently one Æthelwald, also an ealdorman, though this time of East Anglia. Soon, however, she would be married to an even more powerful man, and William of Malmesbury, writing in the early twelfth century, has a rather juicy story about how he reckons this all came about.

According to William, King Edgar was a man who liked a pretty face, and indeed not just a face. He tells one scandalous story of Edgar carrying off a nun and bedding her repeatedly before being told by St Dunstan to do a seven-year penance. He tells another story about how Edgar turned up in Andover, saw an aristocratic young lady he fancied and ordered her to be brought to his bed. The young lady's mother might have been interested in a marriage proposal, but a one-night stand, even with Edgar, was not what she had in mind for her daughter. However, she wasn't quite so fussy about her maidservant. So, according to William, she sent the maidservant, apparently also a looker, into Edgar's bed instead. In the morning, the maid tried to escape before daylight allowed Edgar to see that the girl in his bed wasn't the girl he'd ordered. The maidservant didn't quite manage her escape, and when Edgar caught her she explained and begged him to free her from the house. Edgar seems to have enjoyed his night, because he freed the girl and made her his mistress.

According to William, the king had heard tales of Ælfthryth's beauty and, being in the market for a queen but also being a busy man, he sent a certain Æthelwald to check her out. Æthelwald took one look at her and decided that he'd have her instead. So he married her, while telling Edgar that she wasn't suitable for him. Bad mistake for Æthelwald as it turned out, because Edgar, finding out what had happened, decided to pay Æthelwald's new wife a visit in person. Æthelwald panicked and told his wife to make herself look ugly. Not Ælfthryth. According to William, she decided instead to 'call up every charm by art, and to omit nothing which could stimulate the desire of a young and powerful man'. Saucy. And it worked. Edgar was so smitten that he decided Æthelwald was about to have a 'hunting accident'. Æthelwald did indeed have a 'hunting accident', a nasty and fatal experience with a javelin, and suddenly Ælfthryth was free to marry Edgar. Handy. Now obviously all these stories about Edgar and Ælfthryth are thoroughly scandalous and could well contain elements that are untrue, but they are great fun.

However she got to be queen, once she made it there she began to make her mark. She married Edgar in about 964. Already by 966 she had given Edgar a son, Edmund, and just two years later they had a second son, Æthelred. Ælfthryth had obviously been busy in the bedroom with Edgar, but in her career, both during Edgar's life and after, she would do plenty outside as well. She took a special interest in nunneries (for instance, she would make a foundation at Wherwell) and was a benefactress at Ely and Peterborough. She became a legal *forespeca*, an advocate helping mediate between people and the Crown. In 973 she was anointed and crowned as queen, and afterwards she is said to have feasted in a silken gown adorned with gems and pearls. In fact, Ælfthryth was doing pretty well for herself except for one problem. A big problem, and one that was quite literally growing: a boy called Edward. Edward is also now known as Edward the Martyr. He wasn't then, obviously, but he soon would be.

Edward was Edgar's son from a woman who came before Ælfthryth. He was therefore older than Ælfthryth's two sons. Edward does not seem to have been officially Edgar's heir, but he was a definite threat to Ælfthryth's boys succeeding to the throne. In 970, Edgar and Ælfthryth's eldest son,

Edmund, died, which meant that the two main contenders for the throne would be Edmund and Ælfthryth's younger son, Æthelred. They wouldn't have that long to wait.

In 975, Edgar himself died. With Æthelred still a small child, support grew among influential figures in the kingdom for the idea of putting Edward on the throne. Among the supporters of Edward was, interestingly and perhaps not surprisingly, the brother of Ælfthryth's first husband. Perhaps not a big Ælfthryth fan, then.

So Edward became king. But not for long. On 18 March 978, Edward was visiting Ælfthryth and Æthelred at Corfe Castle when he was murdered. It is generally agreed that he died at Corfe Castle and that he was buried afterwards at nearby Wareham, but the question of who actually killed Edward is much more challenging.

One source described Edward being killed by followers of Ælfthryth as he dismounted. It is clear that Edward increasingly came to be viewed as a martyr (his body was moved to Shaftesbury Abbey) and Ælfthryth was accused of being linked to the killing, either planning it or even being present. The twelfth-century *Book of Ely* even accuses Ælfthryth of being a witch and killing the Abbot of Ely as well. It is impossible now to find out the truth about what happened to Edward and whether stories of Ælfthryth's involvement should be placed in a similar category as the dubious ones about Edgar and Ælfthryth's love lives. However, she did have a motive and she was close to the scene when he died.

With Edward dead, Ælfthryth probably became regent until Æthelred came of age in 984. Æthelred is, of course, much better known than his mother, known by the rather unfortunate name Æthelred the Unready. Æthelred's original nickname didn't really mean he was unready. It really meant rather more that he was 'without counsel'. Still not great, though.

When Æthelred had children, Ælfthryth took care of bringing up these heirs to the throne and her brother Ordulf became one of Æthelred's major advisers. Finally, in about the year 1000, she died at her foundation at Wherwell and was buried there. Ælfthryth is always going to be a controversial figure, but at least she's an interesting one. If nothing else, she deserves to be better known. Perhaps if she was referred to not as Ælfthryth but by a derivative of her name, Elfrida, she would be. Elfrida somehow sounds so much more accessible.

9

The Man Who United Wales

Both England and Scotland were once lands divided into different territories, and both went through a long, painful process whereby power was gradually centralised and extended until unified countries were eventually created under one monarch, a king or queen of England and a king or queen of Scotland. But what about Wales?

This is the story of Gruffudd ap Llywelyn, a major character of Welsh history who deserves to be better known outside Wales today. This is the man who united Wales for a brief eight years before conflict with an Anglo-Saxon lord set the scene for his death and the Welsh territories he had united were once again split apart. That Anglo-Saxon lord was one Harold, soon to be King Harold and, soon after Gruffudd's death, to be dead as well, as the Normans arrived and changed the futures of both England and Wales.

Gruffudd's father, Llywelyn ap Seisyll, had been a powerful ruler, but when Llywelyn died in 1023 Gruffudd was still young. Iago ab Idwal took control of the mighty kingdom of Gwynedd that Gruffudd's father had once ruled.

Things had not started well for Gruffudd, and they didn't immediately get much better. According to one story, it reached the stage where he was so demoralised and so unable to decide how to proceed that his sister had a go at him for not being a worthy son and heir to his father. Whether or not the story is true, things were about to change big time for Gruffudd. And for Iago.

Iago took control of Powys and then, in 1039, was killed. It's impossible to know now exactly how it happened, but Gruffudd's involvement has been suspected and alleged. Gruffudd took control of Gwynedd as well. By the standards of previous Welsh rulers he was now a powerful figure, but for Gruffudd it was not to be enough. Perhaps he was haunted by his sister's words.

Soon after becoming King of Gwynedd, Gruffudd clashed with a Mercian army at Rhyd-y-groes on the Severn and smashed it. Then he turned his eyes towards the south, towards the southern Welsh lands of Deheubarth. In 1039 he targeted Hywel ab Edwin. The conflict between the two would last for years. In 1041, Gruffudd defeated Hywel at the Battle of Pencader and captured his wife. Hywel was not finished. He returned with Vikings from Dublin to aid him against Gruffudd. However, after a fierce battle, Hywel was once again defeated and this time killed.

But Gruffudd's battle to take control of Deheubarth wasn't over. A different Gruffudd, Gruffudd ap Rhydderch of Gwent, along with his brother Rhys, became new obstacles to Gruffudd ap Llywelyn's efforts to seize total control. The warriors of Ystrad Tywi launched an attack and killed 140 of the men of Gruffudd ap Llywelyn's bodyguard. It was a huge blow, but not the end for Gruffudd ap Llywelyn. He did not give up. In 1055, Gruffudd ap Rhydderch was killed and Gruffudd ap Llywelyn finally took control of Deheubarth. He also took control of Gwent and Morgannwg that year, and soon he was the ruler of all Wales, with a residence at Rhuddlan.

He wasn't just interested in Wales. Gruffudd ap Llywelyn's story throws an interesting light on power politics among the Welsh and English (and others) in the years just before 1066. In England, things were tense between the earls of Mercia and Wessex. In 1055, Ælfgar, son of the Earl of Mercia, was forced to flee into exile. But he wasn't gone for long. He soon returned with Vikings from Ireland and with Gruffudd ap Llywelyn. The attackers advanced into England and found themselves up against Ralph de Mantes, Earl of Hereford.

Since this is before the Norman invasion, it's interesting to note Ralph de Mantes' French name. This is down to the fact that his father was from France, from, not hugely surprisingly, Mantes. But his mother was English and the daughter of King Æthelred.

Ralph was in charge of defending the frontier. It didn't go well. Not for Ralph, nor his fighters, nor the unfortunate inhabitants of Hereford. Ralph's army was smashed, Hereford was captured, and Gruffudd ap Llywelyn got lots of lovely loot. He would also soon after that get a lovely Mercian wife, Ealdgyth, Edith, the daughter of Earl Ælfgar.

And this is where Harold, Earl of Wessex, comes into the story. He raced to the area with reinforcements. One of Harold's supporters, the Bishop of Hereford, had a go at Gruffudd and was defeated. Calm was eventually restored and deals were done. However, Harold had not yet finished with Gruffudd. At Christmas 1062, Harold suddenly attacked, surprising Gruffudd at Rhuddlan. Gruffudd managed to escape by sea from the attack, but not for long. Harold followed up with another campaign in 1063 which forced Gruffudd inland into the mountains. Finally he was killed, perhaps by Welshmen with a grudge against him, and his head was cut off and delivered to Earl Harold. Gruffudd had lost his life and his head, and now Harold took his wife as well, marrying her. Ealdgyth had been Queen of Wales, but not for long. Soon she would be Queen of England, but not for long either.

After Gruffudd's death Wales was once again divided, with different parts of his realms being given to different new rulers. Gruffudd had managed to unite Wales for just eight years.

Harold, of course, would soon be dead at the Battle of Hastings, and a new force would arrive on the borders of Wales; yes, William's Normans.

10

A Very English Democracy

In this country we like to think that we played a key role in the development of parliamentary democracy, but many Brits know comparatively little about the actual earliest origins of democracy in England.

The Anglo-Saxon system of local government originated in many senses from the well-developed systems which the original Angle and Saxon settlers brought with them from northern Germany. This was supplemented in the later period by innovations drawn from the Vikings, who settled in Scotland and what is known as the Danelaw.

Freemen were divided into groups of ten, known as a 'tithing'. Tithings were expected to meet regularly to discuss and decide any local business which needed managing. Members of the tithing were responsible for each other's behaviour and good conduct. The tithings elected a leader known as a tithingsman, who represented the tithing. Ten tithings were gathered together to form a 'hundred', led by, you guessed it, a hundredman. Nice and logical.

There was a meeting of the hundred every four weeks, where the hundredman, his ten tithingsmen and a clerk would gather in public to do business. This meeting was called a hundred moot. The hundred was in charge of encouraging legitimate trade and discouraging cattle theft. It was also the first port of call for any victim of crime looking for justice.

Hundreds were grouped into shires organised by the shire reeve, or, yes, sheriff. These meetings were known as shire moots. The Church was represented by bishops at the shire moots and this injected an important religious element into proceedings. In the Danelaw, the shires were known as wapentakes. Wapentake means literally 'weapon touch', and signifies the importance of arms in society at the time.

Edward the Elder and Athelstan were responsible for replacing the wapentakes with shires in the Danelaw. The shire reeve would represent his shire in front of the king at the witan or king's council. As the population expanded, the scale of tithings and hundreds expanded from being based on the number of freemen to being based on the number of families, and in the case of hundreds it seems ultimately to have become used to designate a specific measure of land based in hides.

The system grew from the bottom up, with local freemen electing their own representatives to take care of local matters. If local bodies could not resolve the issue it was referred up the chain. As such, it provides a contrast with the more centralised king-down model of law enforcement that some would like to blame on the Normans. It also contrasts with our own current system, where large numbers of people feel they have little involvement in, and influence over, politics and justice at all.

However, by the end of the Anglo-Saxon period the system could be and was being used by the king to assert his own authority. Athelstan reinforced the role of the hundredman in enforcing law and order. The hundredman was encouraged to gather one or two men from each tithing and use them to hunt down lawbreakers by forming a posse and giving chase to cattle thieves. He was empowered to flog those in his hundred who did not inform him of suspicious cattle movements. Æthelred also gave instructions to hundredmen to support his shire reeves.

The system gave Anglo-Saxon kings an efficient way of passing on instructions. The king and his witan spoke to the shire reeve, who in turn contacted the hundredman, who then told the tithesmen. This was about as efficient as early medieval government could be. It was one of the reasons why Anglo-Saxon England was so wealthy and such an attractive proposition for William the Conqueror. The moots, shires and wapentakes provided a way for local people to make their views known to their leaders but in return were a crucial link in passing messages down from the king. By contrast, many people today seem to feel that our governments talk at us and people often then try to ignore them. In the opposite direction, people sometimes, when they feel really strongly, contact our governments to express their own views and then also often seem to feel that they are being ignored.

At the top of the Anglo-Saxon system was the witan. This comprised the leading earls and bishops in the country. They could be summoned by the king to give advice, but he had no obligation either to consult them or to listen to their advice. They were summoned so that the king could pass on his instructions and they could trickle down through moots to the rest of the population. The witans recognised the basic facts that without the support of the most powerful earls and the Church, the king's power was much weakened. They also had power in their own right; one of the methods by which Anglo-Saxon kings could claim the throne was through the assent of the witan. Harold Godwineson claimed the throne through the support of the witan on the death of Edward the Confessor in 1066.

In the Danelaw, this system was supplemented by a system of open-air meetings of all freemen, known as things or tings from the Old Norse for meeting or parliament. The most famous of these is Tynwald on the Isle of Man, which claims to be the oldest continuously sitting parliament. It meets at St John's on 5 July each year. Its origins go back to the Viking invasions of AD 800.

Tings were not confined to the Isle of Man, though. In fact, Tynwald's claim to be the first parliament is disputed by residents of Alpingi in Iceland and Jamtamot in Sweden. Both towns claim that their parliaments started earlier than in the Isle of Man. There was also a Tingwall and a Law Ting Holm in Shetland and a Dingwall in Eastern Ross in Scotland, just north of Inverness. Further south there was another Thingwall on the Wirral peninsula. While the documentary evidence is slim, the place names suggest that there was a widespread tradition of Norse settlers attending open meetings with their jarls and that the Vikings engaged in some form of early democracy.

Anglo-Saxon law consisted of an unwritten collection of laws which were observed by the local communities. Each hundred may have had its own rules and laws. There were certainly differences in the laws used in Mercia, Wessex and Northumberland, which grew from separate local traditions. There was also a series of written law codes produced by different kings. The earliest of these was the dooms of Æthelberht, King of Kent (560–616), but there were also collections of dooms attributed to Alfred the Great and King Cnut. These collections were usually a mixture of restating existing laws and unifying the punishments.

Alfred's law code made great play of being based on the justice described in the Bible. He was clear that he thought his laws were doing God's will and bringing Wessex closer to God. In the preface, Alfred cited the Ten Commandments. This religious foundation of Anglo-Saxon law had a practical implication for those who threw themselves on God's mercy and opted for trial by ordeal.

The hundred court was the starting point for most disputes. The procedure was very formal and, just as today, if the rules were not followed precisely then the case was lost. The first hurdle for any plaintiff was to convince the hundred court that he had a case to make. Some Norsemen apparently had a reputation for being quick to resort to using the courts with dubious claims. The plaintiff had to make his charge under oath and in front of witnesses. The hundred court could then decide if it was worth its time to investigate the case or whether it needed to be passed up to a superior court like the shire court for a judgement. If the hundred court accepted the case then it set a date for the accused to appear.

If the accused did not appear on the appointed date, then the plaintiff had to repeat the accusation under oath and in front witnesses. It was possible for the accused to delay justice for some time by refusing to appear before the court, but in the end the court had the power to assume that his absence indicated guilt.

If the accused did appear before the court he was required to take an oath declaring his innocence. The defendant could also bring oath-helpers to take an oath confirming that the defendant was telling the truth. The more serious the crime, the more oath-helpers were required to support the defendant. The basic principle was that the denial was always stronger than the charge, so in most cases this was where the trial ended and the defendant walked away.

While the system appears open to all sorts of abuse, it worked on the principle that the hundred was quite a small unit, where most people knew each other and those who were suspected of being guilty may have had a difficult time summoning sufficient oath-helpers to support them. Some defendants were not considered 'oath worthy'. If they had already been found guilty of many crimes or had been caught red-handed with stolen goods, then the advantage lay with the plaintiff. The plaintiff had to gather witnesses prepared to take an oath declaring, 'In the name of Almighty God, I saw with my eyes and heard with ears that which I pronounce.' The Anglo-Saxon system was based more on establishing the good character of the defendant and his contribution to the local community than the specifics of a particular case. As such it is very different from the present system.

If the defendant had failed to muster sufficient oath-helpers or was not considered 'oath worthy', then he had the option of trial by ordeal and leaving his fate up to God. Trial by ordeal was not compulsory. It was an option for those who were unable to clear their name through oaths. There were three forms of ordeal used by the Anglo-Saxons. These were trial by iron, trial by hot water and trial by cold water.

In the trial by hot water the defendant had to lift a stone

from a pot of boiling water. The badly scalded hand was given three days to heal. After three days, if the hand was healing cleanly and without infection, then the defendant was innocent; if there was infection, then God was viewed as declaring the defendant guilty.

Trial by iron was similar, except that in the place of the stone and hot water, the defendant had to grasp a bar of glowing iron from a fire and carry it three paces. Again, the absence of infection was seen as God wishing to save the accused.

Trial by cold water involved being bound and thrown into a deep pond. Floating was considered evidence of guilt. Sinking was considered evidence of innocence. Though you can see a fairly obvious problem with this approach.

A fourth form of trial by ordeal, trial by combat, where the defendant and the plaintiff could fight it out between them, was not part of the Anglo-Saxon system. It was introduced later by the Normans.

Trial by jury was not a part of the Anglo-Saxon system. However, as the business of both shire and hundred courts increased to cover administration and more local government, it became necessary to select a dozen men to specialise in the judicial business of the court rather than its administrative and executive functions. Cases began to be heard in front of these selected members of the hundred court rather than in open court. These twelve legal specialists may have been the origins of the jury.

Once guilt was established, the hundred court had to decide on punishment. Here they could consult the relevant legal code and see what was recommended. A custodial sentence was impossible as there were no prisons.

The most common penalty was fines. All forms of assault up to and including killing were punished by fines under a system known as weregild. The size of the fine depended both on the nature of the injury and the status of the victim. Damage to an eye required a payment of 50 shillings, while damage to an ear required a payment of only 3 shillings. The payments were listed in incredible detail. Damage to front teeth had a higher fine than damage to back teeth. Obviously a lot of teeth were getting damaged. There is a payment for damage to nails and even a specific price for a wedding finger.

Earls and thanes received greater compensation than churls or freemen. Sleeping with one of the king's maidens incurred a weregild of 50 shillings, but if she was the lowest level of slave the payment was reduced to just 12 shillings, according to Æthelberht, King of Kent. The money was paid either to the victim or his kin. Kin included not just family but also other members of the tithing.

The Anglo-Saxons opted for this system of weregild to bring an end to the older system of blood feuds. Under this system it was the duty of the family and the tithing to seek revenge for the assault. Weregild may have done something to put an end to these feuds.

The guilty were also required to pay some of the costs involved if the hue (volunteers from each tithing) had been called to apprehend him.

If the guilty party had insufficient funds to pay weregild and his kin and tithing were unable to afford the payment, the court had the option of making the criminal a slave to his victim's family. The length of slavery depended on the severity of the crime. When the sentence had been served the prisoner was once again a free man. A novel take on community service.

Some crimes, like housebreaking, arson, treason, open theft and murder, were called 'bootless crimes'. The term 'bootless crimes' does not refer to some horrific avalanche of crimes by people who'd left their footwear at home but instead refers to crimes that could not be dealt with just by 'bot', compensation. The punishment for these 'bootless crimes' was usually the death penalty. Criminals were usually hanged, but there are also examples of beheading and drowning. The Church disapproved of capital punishment and advocated mutilating the guilty. This gave the guilty time to reflect on their sins and save their souls.

This was the system of justice the Normans discovered when they arrived in 1066. They then introduced the feudal system and with it came manorial courts, where the lord of the manor sat in judgement on his villeins. They added a royal council made up of tenants-in-chief, who sat on a more permanent basis than the witan. They introduced the crime of 'murther', or murder, for the killing of a Norman by a Saxon. The personnel changed but the basic administrative and legal structure of Anglo-Saxon England was preserved.

11

The Last Lord of the Saxons

Pretty much everyone knows that Harold (in strict terms Harold II, though Harold Harefoot, the other Harold, doesn't exactly have a high public profile these days) was the last Saxon king and that the Saxon line of kings died out when Harold met his death at the Battle of Hastings and Duke William of Normandy took over as William the Conqueror, William I, commencing the Norman age in Britain, etc. etc.

It may, therefore, come as something of a shock to some to find out that in a sense Harold wasn't actually the last Saxon king at all. Between his death on 14 October and Christmas Day 1066, when William was crowned King of England, the country was ruled – in name at least – by Edgar Atheling, or Edgar II, a Saxon claimant who had in many ways a stronger claim to the kingship than Harold himself.

Edgar did not succeed in stopping William, but he did spend the following sixty years scheming and trying to mastermind a return to power and influence. These schemes saw him travel from Hungary to Scotland, Sicily and Jerusalem before ending his days in northern England.

Edgar Atheling (Atheling means simply that he was a royal prince and potential heir) owed his claim to the throne to his grandfather Edmund Ironside, who was the third son of the Saxon king Æthelred the Unready. After the deaths of his elder brothers Athelstan and Egbert, Edmund was crowned King of England after the death of Æthelred the Unready in 1015. However, he had only ruled England for a mere six months, from 23 April to 18 October 1016, when he was defeated by the Danish leader Cnut at the Battle of Assundun.

After this battle the country was divided, with Edmund being left in control of Wessex while Cnut claimed the remainder. It hadn't been a good year for Edmund and it wasn't about to get any better. He proceeded to die later that year and Cnut became ruler of all of England.

Cnut remained nervous about competition, and wasn't shy about using opportunistic conspiracy and murder. He allegedly sent Edmund's son, Edward, to the King of Sweden with instructions that Edward should be killed. The King of Sweden instead decided to send him to the Holy Roman Emperor in Hungary. It was here that Edward (at this point not very imaginatively called Edward the Exile), married Agatha, who was a member of the imperial family. Edgar Atheling was their eldest child, and was born and brought up in Hungary. Followed all that so far? Good.

In 1057, Edward the Confessor summoned Edward the Exile and his family back to England, at which stage he would have presumably had to find a new nickname. Edward the Confessor, the seventh son of Æthelred the Unready (someone had been a busy lad) and the first by his second wife Emma, had become King of England on the death of Cnut's son Harthacnut in 1042.

It seems that the Confessor may have initially been unaware that Edward had survived being sent to the King of Sweden (news didn't travel so far or so fast in those days). However, the king began to see in Edward the Exile a possible heir, who would allow the Confessor to escape from the influence of the Godwines, a powerful Anglo-Saxon family. Edward the Exile certainly had the pedigree and only time would tell whether he had the skills to be a king. Time, though, was one thing that Edward the ex-Exile did not have. No sooner had Edward been proclaimed heir to the throne than he died. This may have been an accident, but, frankly, the timing is pretty suspicious. It may have been the work of the Godwines, who had the most to gain from his demise.

The stage was set for big problems when Edward the Confessor finally died in 1066 with no undisputed heir. Edgar was grandson of a King of England and his youth did not automatically rule him out as a successor to Edward the Confessor. What did rule him out were his lack of powerful friends at court and Edward the Confessor's indecisiveness. Edward the Confessor appears to have promised the throne to at least three different people – maybe four if his proclaiming Edgar as the Atheling was hinting at a possible desire for him to inherit the throne. Edward promised the throne to William of Normandy according, not surprisingly, to the Norman sources. Harold Godwineson claimed that Edward had changed his mind about William and as he lay on his deathbed he had promised Harold the throne. For Harold Hardrada his claim lay in being a descendent of Cnut.

When Edward the Confessor died in January 1066, it was the Earl of Wessex, Harold Godwineson, who was first off the mark, getting the witan to support his claim to the throne. Archbishop Stigand promptly arranged for his coronation as Harold II. As we all know though, Harold was not destined to have a long and happy reign. In fact, it was a pretty short and unhappy one, terminated rather abruptly by his death at Hastings.

Edgar's time had come. Sort of. While William was still in Hastings, in London the witan was quick to react by proclaiming Edgar as the new king. Stigand, the Archbishop of Canterbury who had crowned Harold, now switched his allegiance to Edgar. He was joined by Ealdred, Archbishop of York, and the brothers Edwin, Earl of Mercia, and Morcar, Earl of Northumbria.

Realistically, though, things weren't looking great for the new king. In fact, they were looking pretty desperate. As William's victorious army approached London, Edgar's support crumbled. William was turned away when he approached the city at Southwark but he then proceeded to move around the west of the city, burning villages as he went in an attempt to intimidate the locals. By the time William crossed the Thames at Wallingford, Archbishop Stigand had changed his mind again and decided to abandon Edgar and submit to William. The remaining members of the witan did not resist much longer and by early December they had abandoned Edgar and submitted to William at Berkhamsted. William went on to be crowned King of England on Christmas Day 1066 and Edgar was William's prisoner. His rule had lasted a mere two months – even less than the six months of his grandfather – but at least he had been made king, unlike his father, Edward the ex-Exile. And, to be fair to him, despite his youth and lack of support, Edgar did not give up campaigning to reclaim the throne.

William decided to keep Edgar alive, probably because he feared causing further rebellions and therefore felt that Edgar was less of a threat alive and a prisoner than dead and a martyr. But Edgar wasn't to be a prisoner for long. In 1068 he escaped from William's control and along with his mother and sisters he headed north to Scotland, where he launched an attempt to regain his throne.

His sister Margaret married the Scottish king Malcolm III Canmore of Scotland, and in 1069 he returned to northern England as the figurehead of an anti-William group of Northumbrians, supported by a Danish fleet sent by King Sweyn of Denmark. Despite capturing York, the rebellion was savagely suppressed in 1070 when William marched north. In a scorched earth policy, remembered by the chroniclers as 'the Harrying' of the North, he caused the deaths of something like 100,000 people. Edgar fled back to Scotland, but even there he was not safe. In 1072 William invaded Scotland, defeated Malcolm III and forced Edgar to flee once again. Edgar, the son of Edward the ex-Exile, was now leading the life of a royal exile himself, wandering the courts of Europe looking for a home and shelter.

Fortunately for Edgar, William had many enemies in Europe who were more than happy to help Edgar cause a few problems for him. Count Robert of Flanders was the first to offer Edgar assistance, and Philip I of France offered Edgar a castle near the border with Normandy so that he could raid

William's territory. These plans came to nothing, however, after a rather inconvenient shipwreck off the coast of England left Edgar and his supporters being hunted down in William's England.

Edgar had had enough. He decided at this point to submit to what perhaps now seemed inevitable. He accepted William as King of England, giving up his own claim to the throne. In return he was allowed to take up residence in England, and he was given a modest amount of land according to William's great bureaucratic triumph, the Domesday Book.

In some ways, Edgar was to have the last laugh in his dispute with the Conqueror; because he was so much younger than William, he was able to outlive the Conqueror and cause problems in the Norman succession.

When William died in 1087 he divided his inheritance, with his eldest son, Robert Curthose (or 'short pants'), being put in charge in Normandy and William Rufus becoming the new King of England. Edgar threw in his lot with Robert Curthose and became one of his principal advisers. Presumably Robert thought he'd benefit from Edgar's English supporters and his royal Saxon name, and Edgar thought he'd benefit from having a Norman royal pal. Not for the first time in his life, Edgar was wrong. He found that he'd supported the loser in this power struggle. In 1091, when William Rufus defeated Robert, Edgar found that he had to return the estates in Normandy which had been given to him by Robert. Once again, Edgar headed north to Scotland to lick his wounds.

To be fair to Edgar, he was still trying. Between 1091 and 1098 he seems to have managed to establish himself as something of a peace broker between the Scots and the Normans. On the one hand, he had good knowledge of the Scottish court through his sister Margaret, the wife of Malcolm III, and on the other hand he had worked with Robert Curthose, who by now had settled his differences with William Rufus. After a series of wars and negotiations, Edgar was even able to help install his namesake and nephew Edgar, the son of Margaret and Malcolm, as King of Scotland.

And he didn't stop there. Edgar then turned his attention to Europe and the First Crusade, which was launched in 1096 by Pope Urban II. The chronicler Orderic has Edgar leading an English fleet off the coast of Syria before abandoning the fleet and joining the march on Jerusalem. Some historians have suggested that Edgar joined the Varangian Guard of the Byzantine Emperor. This was the elite bodyguard unit of the Byzantines, which seems to have been a magnet for Saxons and nobles from northern Europe who had fallen out with the Normans (see next chapter).

While it is not clear that he did serve the emperor, it is likely that he was in the area as he was also recorded by William of Malmesbury as being on pilgrimage to Jerusalem in 1102. After the Crusade (or pilgrimage), Edgar was offered places at either the Byzantine or German Courts but declined both and returned north to re-engage in royal power politics. You'd have thought he'd had enough of it by now, but apparently not.

When Henry I took over from William Rufus (after an unfortunate incident in the New Forest), Edgar once again threw in his lot with Robert Curthose. Again Edgar was on the losing side, this time at the Battle of Tinchebray in Normandy in 1106, where he was taken prisoner. While Robert was kept prisoner for the rest of his life, Edgar was allowed to remain free. This may have been down to the fact that his niece Edith, the daughter of Malcolm III and Margaret, had married King Henry.

Edgar travelled north to Scotland one final time in 1120 and is thought to have died in 1125, nearly sixty years after William's victory at Hastings and his own few weeks in power. It is not known where he was buried, but, being childless and unmarried, when he died it was truly the end of the line.

12

English Warriors of Byzantium

Edgar may or may not himself have joined the Varangian Guard, but he wasn't the only English warrior looking for a new career in the years after 1066. And some of those certainly did like the look of the Byzantine Emperor's gold.

The word Varangian was originally used not to describe Viking warriors in Byzantium but to describe Viking mercenaries in the pay of the rulers of Kievan Rus', and the origins of the Varangian Guard are inextricably linked with Kievan Rus' as well as Constantinople. Kievan Rus' was a state originally formed by Vikings heading south from Sweden and Finland along rivers like the Dnieper either to trade or to raid. The Viking Oleg, ruler of Novgorod from around 879, captured Kiev in 882 and extended his rule over the local Slavs to establish an eastern Slavic state. This is about the same time that Alfred was fighting the Vikings in England and agreeing to the division of the country into Wessex and Danelaw.

The Slavs called the Vikings the Rus', and Varangians were men who had taken military service. Rus' and Varangian were to some extent interchangeable at this stage. Kievan Rus' was ruled by a small elite, which intermarried with the leaders of local Slavonic tribes. These princes preferred to use hired Varangians to fight their power struggles and to extend their trade routes and conquests southwards towards Byzantium. Consequently, through these adventures, the Varangians had become well known in Constantinople even before the official forming of the Imperial Varangian Guard.

While Varangians were already fighting for the emperor against the Arabs in Syria in 955, the formation of the Varangian Guard is usually seen as being the work of Emperor Basil II in 988. He asked Vladimir I of Kiev, who had recently converted to Christianity (the 1025th anniversary was celebrated in 2013), for help. He was sent a troop of Varangians in response, and in return he offered his daughter Anna to Vladimir in marriage – an exchange rate of one imperial princess to 6,000 burly warriors.

The Byzantine Empire was one of the few tenth-century countries which had a tax system capable of supporting a mercenary army over a long period of time, and the role of the Varangians was to act as both the emperor's bodyguard and his elite fighting unit. Their duties ranged from ceremonial roles and the guarding of palaces to being at the critical, most bloody, points in battle. The Varangians were prized by the Byzantine emperors for their loyalty, their effectiveness and their willingness to fulfil the terms of their oath rather than change sides when they got a better offer. According to the Byzantine sources, they were 'frightening both in appearance and in equipment, they attacked with reckless rage and neither cared about losing blood nor their wounds'.

The Varangians saw action for the emperor at Cannae in Italy (the same site as Hannibal's 216 BC destruction of a Roman army, but rather less well known) in 1018 and in Sicily in 1038.

Long after the arrival of the original 6,000, a steady stream of Viking warriors headed south to join the Varangian Guard. In fact, they came in such quantities that laws were even changed in Scandinavia to prevent anyone who had left for 'Greece', as Constantinople was known to the Vikings, from claiming his inheritance while he was still in the south. The Sagas record the names of many men who served in the Varangian Guard and their names also crop up in the legal records.

The appeal for the Vikings is fairly easily understood – it lay in the huge amount of wealth which could be amassed. The Guard were allowed first access to pillaging after a battle, and, as they were royal guards, they had access to the emperor and those who visited him. When he died they were allowed to take as much gold and silver from his palace as they could carry. In fact, the opportunities for profit became so large that the supply of willing volunteers exceeded demand. Vikings who could not afford the sizable entry fee were turned away.

Among the most famous members of the Varangian Guard was Harald Hardrada, the Varangian who was to go on to be King of Norway and make a claim to be King of England in 1066 before being killed by King Harold at Stamford Bridge. He had left Norway for Constantinople after the defeat of his half-brother King Olaf II at Stiklestad in 1030. Although originally too poor to join the guard, he quickly established himself as a warrior for hire and when he did join the guard he made a fortune – not all of it, perhaps, in a conventional manner. Despite being accused of – and, indeed, being imprisoned for – embezzlement, he was released and able to send his fortune to Kiev for safe keeping. He then visited Kiev on his return journey to Norway, picking up both his fortune and a new wife, the daughter of Prince Jaroslav of Kiev.

The Anglo-Saxon equivalent of the Varangian Guard were the huscarls established by King Cnut in the early eleventh century. The price of entry into his guard was a two-edged sword with a gold-inlaid hilt. King Cnut had no difficulty in raising an army of 3,000–4,000 willing to serve him. These were professional soldiers, who were expected to equip themselves with the finest chainmail, a metal helmet, a giant two-handed fighting axe and a horse so that they could be mobile. Although they travelled by horse, they fought on foot and the mighty axe was more feared than the gold-inlaid sword. They were paid monthly in cash by the king and were proud of their status. There was considerable discipline as their financial future depended on their employer, and the greatest threat they faced was being called a coward and forced to leave the king's service. When Cnut died in 1035, some huscarls made their way south to Byzantium and entered the Varangian Guard. Others sought employment with the new king and the leading members of the Anglo-Saxon elite.

When he seized the crown in 1066, Harold Godwinson is thought to have had about 3,000 huscarls. Some of these died in Harold's victory over Harald Hardrada at the Battle of Stamford Bridge, and many more died with the king on Senlac Hill at the Battle of Hastings. Twenty years later, the Domesday Book records only thirty-three huscarls as landowners in Norman England.

The members of the Anglo-Saxon elite who weren't wiped out at the Battle of Hastings tried to organise a defence of London and, with the help of the Scots and the Vikings, campaigned against William in the north of the country. However, after William's scorched earth policy in 1070 (see previous chapter), there is no further mention of the old Anglo-Saxon elite – not over here, that is. In Byzantium it was something of a different situation.

The Varangian Guard appears to have become somewhat anglicised and the sources refer to Saxons and Varangians fighting together for the emperor. Some historians think it was Saxon émigrés who dominated the Varangian Guard in the eleventh and twelfth centuries.

According to an Icelandic saga written in the fourteenth century, Siward, the Earl of Gloucester, led a troop of three earls and eight barons south, away from the tyranny of William. They travelled in 350 ships via Mont St Michelle, Galicia and the Strait of Gibraltar to arrive in Constantinople in time to rescue the emperor, Alexius I Comnenus, in 1075 and be rewarded with places in the Varangian Guard. The *Chronicon Universale Anonymi Laudunensis*, written by an English monk in Picardy in the thirteenth century, confirms the essentials of the story, although he doesn't mention the route taken. Some historians feel the Saxon exiles are more likely to have arrived at Byzantium by heading to Denmark and making use of the Viking trade routes south through Kievan Rus' to Byzantium. Although there is a doubt about the accuracy of both sources and the details of how the Anglo-Saxons came to be in the Varangian Guard, there is little doubt that many huscarls and Saxon exiles did find their way south to Byzantium.

After they arrived and Emperor Alexius offered them places in the Varangian Guard, the Saxons split, according to the two written sources. Some were happy to stay in Constantinople and serve in the emperor's bodyguard, as the similarities between the Varangian Guard and the huscarls made them feel right at home. Others were looking for more freedom and a chance to preserve their old life. Alexius gave land six days' journey to the north of the city to those who wanted to leave Constantinople.

Here Siward, their Saxon leader, set up a New England, with towns even named London and York for the homesick. This new territory did not accept the Eastern Church and brought in bishops from Hungary. Hungary was where the closest blood relative to the English throne lived in 1066; Edward Atheling had been brought up there and there may have been links between the Hungary and the Saxon exiles. While there is no archaeological evidence for this New England (as opposed to the one to be set up six hundred years later), and its existence relies on the written sources, it may help to explain why the Saxon influence on the Varangian Guard was to last long beyond the eleventh century.

'The English groaned aloud for their lost liberty and plotted ceaselessly to find some way of shaking off a yoke that was so intolerable and unaccustomed,' claimed the chronicler Orderic Vitalis in the late eleventh century. The Saxons in the Varangian Guard chose to take out their frustrations on the Normans of Robert of Guiscard, Duke of Apulia in Sicily, who had upset the emperor. To some extent this was a new battle against the same old enemy. Unfortunately for the Saxons (though obviously not for the Normans), the results showed no sign of improvement.

In the Battle of Dyrrhachium (now Durrës, Albania's main port – the Normans certainly got around, as did the Varangians) in 1081, where Alexius put an army of 20,000 (including 1,000 Varangian Guard) into action against Guiscard's Normans, it was a familiar result. The Varangians fought on foot with their double-handed axes, and, just as at Hastings, they had the better of the early encounters against the Norman cavalry. However, as the Saxons of the Varangian Guard thought they had made the decisive thrust in the battle, they headed too far, becoming separated from the remainder of the Imperial forces, and the battle ended with the Varangians wiped out as the church in which they had sought shelter was set on fire by the Normans.

Perhaps there is an element of truth in the tale that the Saxon Varangians never got used to fighting in the saddle. The story goes that they were given horses when they joined the Guard but, instead of using them as cavalry might, they simply used the horses to reach the enemy before killing them with a blow of their axe in order to facilitate fighting on foot. Whatever the truth of the tale, the Saxons in the Varangian Guard lost at Dyrrhachium, but the emperors continued to value their loyalty and bravery.

The Saxons played a leading role in the Varangian Guard and are identified as a specific contingent of the guard up until the fall of Constantinople in 1204 during the Fourth Crusade. They led the defence of the city against the Crusade of Innocent III and, although they were unable to prevent the fall of the city, served with distinction.

The fact that, over one hundred years after they were eliminated by the Normans in England, the Saxon elite had managed to carve (literally, with those axes) out a distinct identity in Constantinople and the Varangian Guard suggests either that New England did indeed exist or that successive waves of emigration took place from Norman England, even though no mention in written records exists of such a major outflow.

13

An Englishman in St Peter's

The first half of the twelfth century was a busy time in Britain. In Scotland, David I had managed to take control with the support of Henry I of England, and had then introduced a bunch of Anglo-Norman-type measures into Scotland. In Wales, Owain Gwynedd, Cadwaladr ap Gruffydd and Gruffydd ap Rhys of Deheubarth teamed up to defeat a Norman army in 1136 at the Battle of Crug Mawr. In England, Stephen and Matilda had been beating each other up in a civil war after Henry I's death. But big news of a more peaceful nature was soon to hit England.

In 2013, a new pope was elected. It was a surprise to some that the new pope was Argentine; it was a surprise to almost nobody that he wasn't English. It is true that Catholicism ceased to the be faith of the majority of Britons over 400 years ago, but Britain had had many distinguished Catholics in the time up to then, and it has had many in the period since then as well. Nevertheless, we have got used to the idea that Britons just don't end up as pope. The vast majority of popes have, of course, been Italian, though the Germans and French have had a few as well. But, in fact, we have had one pope – England's very own Adrian IV.

Yep, Adrian IV; not exactly a name on the lips of many Britons today, and he is only slightly better known by his original name, which was Nicholas Breakspear. How many who even know his name know anything about who he actually was and what he actually did?

Nicholas was born somewhere near beautiful St Albans. He seems actually to have been born in Abbots Langley. Perhaps they should rename it Popes Langley (they already have a Popes Road). Little is known for sure about his early life. His father may have been a monk at St Albans and it is alleged that the abbot of the monastery rejected Nicholas himself, telling him that he'd be more suitable if he stayed at school longer. But it was soon goodbye to St Albans for Nicholas. He was off to sunny Arles in the south of France, and eventually he became abbot of St Ruf near Avignon. In 1149 he was made cardinal-bishop of Albano by Pope Eugenius III.

For his next step he was off on his travels again, this time north to Scandinavia. Between 1152 and 1154 he was papal legate there, and he seems to have been quite a busy papal legate at that. He attended councils of the Church; he reorganised the Swedish Church; he gave the Scandinavian Church more freedom from German control; he reformed abuses; and at Trondheim he set up an independent archiepiscopal see for Norway. Busy lad, and for his work he was hailed as the Apostle of the North.

In 1154, Nicholas returned to Rome. Pope Eugenius III had died the previous year, being succeeded by Anastasius IV; not for long, though, because Anastasius himself died in December 1154. It's hard to know how much Nicholas wanted to be pope. Later in life he would tell John of Salisbury that the job of being pope was a tough one and that he wished he'd either stayed in England or lived quietly in the cloisters of St Ruf. He had accepted the papacy because it was God's will. However he originally felt about it, the day after Anastasius's death, Nicholas was pope. He was not actually Pope Nicholas, because he had taken the new name Adrian, and it was as Adrian IV that he would be known (not hugely well known, admittedly, but known nonetheless) to history.

He wasn't to have that easy a time of it as pope, which is probably one reason for expressing his longing for the quiet cloisters. First of all he had to face Arnold of Brescia. Arnold was a priest who had become to be a bit of a problem for the popes. He'd even at one stage forced Eugenius III out of Rome and got himself excommunicated for it. Arnold was a big fan of apostolic poverty and not a big fan of a wealthy Church. Arnold was also linked with the Commune of Rome, an attempt to create a free republic in the city. Adrian was forced to retreat from Rome to Viterbo. Fortunately for Adrian (though clearly unfortunately for Arnold), Adrian had found another newcomer who was prepared to remove Arnold. Meet the new emperor, Frederick I Barbarossa. Frederick took Rome in 1155, and shortly afterwards Arnold was captured and shortly after that he was dead, being hanged and having his ashes thrown into the Tiber.

However, this was not to be the start of some close alliance between the two. Emperor and pope would compete for power. Even at Frederick's coronation by Adrian, Frederick at first refused to lead the Pope's horse as was traditional and Adrian initially refused him the kiss of peace. Eventually it was all patched up, and Adrian got Frederick leading his horse and Frederick got crowned, but with William I of Sicily causing trouble in the south Adrian was going to have to look elsewhere for help.

Fortunately for him (or that's what it seemed at the time) help was at hand, coming from the east: the Byzantines were in town, or at least they were in the south of Italy. In 1155, Byzantine Emperor Manuel Comnenus had landed in Apulia to link up with local rebel nobles, and Adrian decided to join in too. An alliance was formed, and talk even began of rebuilding a Roman Empire and reuniting Eastern and Western churches. Could the Manuel-and-Adrian team be like a second Constantine the Great, re-establishing a united Roman Empire and Church? Well, no, they couldn't.

Manuel managed to upset some of his local allies, and then had to disappear off to Constantinople. In his absence, the Byzantines were comprehensively defeated at Brindisi and their commander captured. Soon they were gone again from Italy, and Adrian had to patch things up with William.

One of the great controversies of Adrian's papacy, however,

concerns a land far distant from sunny southern Italy. Adrian is said to have granted Ireland to Henry II of England in the context of a visit to the Pope by John of Salisbury. This is linked to the text of a papal bull known as *Laudabiliter*. Many have suspected that *Lauabiliter* itself is a forgery, but it is possible that Adrian did give some form of encouragement to Norman ideas of invading Ireland. Norman knights did land on the Emerald Isle in 1169, followed by Henry II himself in 1171, in moves that would have huge consequences for the futures of both Ireland and Britain.

Whatever his connection to the English invasion of Ireland, however, Adrian would not be around to see it (or even hear of it). The only English pope was to last for less than five years. A growing rift with Emperor Frederick soured his last years, and in 1159 he died. He may have choked on a fly while drinking a glass of wine. Not the most dignified way to go.

The boy from St Albans and Abbots Langley always seems to have remained fond of his English home, bestowing assorted privileges on St Albans Abbey. However, it was in Italy – at Anagni on 1 September – that he was to die, and it was in St Peter's in Rome that he was to be buried.

Adrian IV's tomb, a reused Roman sarcophagus (which seems somehow appropriate for a boy from St Albans), is now located in the Vatican Grottoes, and near Abbots Langley, on the site of what used to be Breakspear Farm, is a little plaque commemorating the English pope.

14

John Softsword Takes on Louis the Lion

Of course, a few years after Adrian IV's death, Henry II was going to have a few problems with a clergyman called Becket. And things weren't going to go too smoothly after Henry's death, either. First, Henry's son Richard took the throne and spent basically all of his reign out of the country fighting (including, of course, on the Third Crusade). Then we come to Richard's brother John. Yes, that John.

Wouldn't it be unexpected to find out that King John wasn't the useless king we all think but instead was a genuine hero and an innocent victim? Well, don't worry, we're not about to discover that. John was fairly useless. What will be unexpected to some, however, is the French invasion that occurred during his reign and almost gave England a King Louis.

The image of 'Bad King John' was pretty well established already in his own lifetime. The Barnwell chronicler called him 'a pillager of his own people'. He is alleged to have done thing likes starve to death the wife and son of the royal debtor William of Briouse. And he wasn't always exactly pleasant to his own family, either. He murdered, probably by drowning, his nephew Arthur of Brittany.

His allegedly voracious sexual appetite also didn't win him that many fans. He was accused of sleeping with the wives and daughters of his barons and being more interested in spending time with his young wife than protecting his territory in Normandy and England. That last accusation brings us to one of the key problems with John. In the days before mass public scrutiny of royals' private lives through the media, people could (and did) put up with a lot from medieval monarchs in terms of extrajudicial slaughtering and extramarital sexual activity. However, they were a lot more reluctant to put up with a monarch who lost large chunks of territory. For his efforts in this department, John managed to acquire the nicknames Lackland and Softsword, neither of which is particularly flattering.

The Norman invasion of 1066 had instituted a period of cross-Channel property ownership rather more extensive than owning a few holiday homes in the Dordogne. When King John succeeded Richard I in 1199, he inherited control not only of England but also of Normandy, Maine, Anjou, Touraine and Aquitaine. Many barons also controlled land both in England and France.

However, the French king wasn't hugely happy about having large parts of what he regarded as his kingdom controlled by a bunch of English people. King Philip Augustus was intent on strengthening the power of the Capetian dynasty by bringing more of France under his royal control, and King John inevitably came into conflict with him over his French lands. John got off to an uncharacteristically good start with a victory against the French at Mirebeau in 1202, but, rather more characteristically, by 1204 had been driven out of Normandy by Philip. A decisive French victory at Bouvine in 1214 finally proved to a lot of English barons that John was unlikely to do much to help them regain their Norman lands and wealth.

With no prospect of military success, the barons were unwilling to fund, through so-called scutage (from the Latin word for shield, *scutum*), King John's attempts to regain his lost lands. This was a payment made by barons in lieu of providing knights for the king's army, which had been their duty under the feudal system introduced by William the Conqueror. King John had, however, effectively made scutage a heavy and regular tax rather than a rare, one-off payment.

Some of the barons were very unhappy, and they happened to be very heavily armed as well. They rebelled in 1215, renouncing their feudal allegiance to King John at Northampton, and went on to take control of Lincoln and, most importantly, London. As so often, things weren't looking good for John. Tensions between John and his barons, who took the name 'Army of God', were temporarily lessened by the agreement of the famous Magna Carta, signed at Runnymede in 1215. However, Magna Carta – which included the promise of freedom from arbitrary arrest, the stipulation that taxes like scutage required some form of assent from those paying the tax, and the forming of a council of twenty-five barons to monitor the behaviour of the king – was never fully going to end the dispute between John and the 'Army of God' because John didn't intend to abide by its terms.

Both the barons and King John had similar amounts of support. About a quarter of the barons stayed loyal to the king, while a further quarter supported the 'Army of God' and the remaining half just wanted to be left in peace. King John was able to persuade the Pope, Innocent III, to take his side and condemn Magna Carta. The barons, however, were able to get the support of Prince Louis (the Lion), heir to the French throne, and Alexander II, King of Scotland. Thus, there was to be a battle between John Softsword and Louis the Lion, with the barons split between the opposing sides. If only on nicknames alone, you probably wouldn't fancy the chances of a Softsword against a Lion.

Prince Louis wasn't just making trouble for the fun of it. He was married to Blanche of Castile, who was a granddaughter of King Henry II. John was the last surviving son of Henry II, so if John died without an heir then Louis would have had a strong claim to John's throne. The problem for Louis, though, was that John did have an heir, with the future Henry III having been born in 1207.

In the autumn and winter of 1215, Louis could do no more than send knights to London to help the barons who held the city. It is not clear how much help these knights provided, but we do know that they complained about the quality and quantity of wine available for them and were unhappy at being forced to drink English ale. Somehow one imagines this is unlikely to have made them hugely popular with Londoners.

To the east of London, John occupied himself by attacking Rochester. John was a fairly useless king, and he could also be an unlucky one. Really not a great combination. He had actually strengthened Rochester Castle earlier in his reign, and thus he had made it even harder for himself to capture it now. He did, however, eventually succeed in mining under one of the towers and causing it to collapse. However, even with one tower down, the defenders held out on a diet of horsemeat and water. By the end of November 1215, they were starved into submission. John wanted to chop off the hands and feet of all those who had defied him and felt that he had a legal right to do so as they had not surrendered.

His advisers urged a more cautious approach, worrying about reprisals when John's castles were captured. Caution won the day, and the only prisoner executed was an archer who had the misfortune to have served with John earlier in the king's reign. John chose to stable his royal horses in Rochester Cathedral as a calculated insult to William Langton, Archbishop of Canterbury, who was one of his critics.

Having dealt very messily with Rochester, John turned his attention north to try to deal with Alexander II in Scotland. John wasn't very effective, but he could be very vicious, as described by Roger of Wendover:

> The whole land was covered with these limbs of the devil like locusts, who assembled to blot out everything from the face of the earth; for, running about with drawn swords and knives, they ransacked towns, houses, cemeteries, and churches, robbing everyone, sparing neither women nor children.

Despite the carnage, however, John's campaign did not prevent Alexander marching south in 1216 and swearing an oath of loyalty to Louis in London.

Louis landed in Kent in May 1216 and headed for London,

where he was proclaimed king in St Paul's Cathedral, though King John remained the crowned king. However, Louis quickly recaptured Rochester and captured Canterbury and Winchester as well. By the summer of 1216 he controlled about a third of the country, and many barons had unsurprisingly realised that John's fortunes were waning. The chronicler Gerald of Wales remarked, 'The madness of slavery is over, the time of liberty has been granted, English necks are free from the yoke.' Not a fan of John, then.

Louis, however, was still having a few problems at Dover, or actually quite a lot of problems. Here a group of archers led by William of Cassingham were waging guerrilla war on Louis's supply lines, and the castle constable, Hubert de Burgh, was organising their defence.

At the end of July, Louis decided to tackle the irritant of Dover head-on by attacking the castle. This may have been just strategic common sense, or he may have been spurred on by criticism from his father. Louis began the siege by using his ships to seal the castle from supplies reaching it by sea. From the land he used mangonels and heavy siege engines brought from France to bombard the castle. A chronicler, with a British sense of understatement, nicknamed one of the machines 'the evil neighbour' and underground Louis's forces set about constructing tunnels to undermine the tower. The tunnels did indeed bring down the gates of the barbican, but Hubert de Burgh led a heroic defence and Louis failed to take the castle. Even tempting De Burgh's soldiers with displays of fresh food failed to persuade them to surrender. By October Louis had become tired of the siege and a truce was negotiated, allowing Louis to concentrate on subduing the smaller castles while Dover agreed not to disrupt his supply lines.

In October 1216, fortune turned decisively against Louis. King John, after losing his baggage and some of the crown jewels in the Wash, died of dysentery at Newark Castle. With the main cause of the disagreements between king and barons out of the way, it was time for the barons to consider where their long-term interests lay.

Henry, King John's nine-year-old son, became king and the ageing William Marshal was made his protector. Henry III had to be crowned in Gloucester Abbey as Louis and the barons controlled London, but that didn't alter the fact that the unlamented departure of John Lackland/Softsword had fundamentally changed the political situation in England.

William Marshal promptly had Magna Carta reissued and set about persuading the barons that the time had come to change sides, encouraging them not to lay the blame for King John's mistakes on his young son. William Marshal had some success, and in the end many barons seem to have felt more secure with another Plantagenet on the throne rather than facing the possibility of being swallowed up in a Capetian empire.

The year 1217 was to see a decisive shift in fortunes in favour of William Marshal and Henry III and against Prince Louis. The two decisive engagements were the siege of Lincoln and the naval battles off Dover and Sandwich in the early summer of 1217.

Inspired by a sense that the tide had turned and that the young Henry III deserved a chance at his inheritance, the people of Dover began once again to threaten Louis's supply lines. While he diverted forces south to begin another siege of Dover Castle and to secure reinforcements from France, William Marshal was able to besiege and capture Lincoln. The locals made it very clear what they thought of the French troops as they retreated towards London; Roger of Wendover records that 'the inhabitants of the towns through which they passed in their flight went to meet them with swords and clubs, and, laying ambushes for them, killed many'.

Louis began to realise that he did not have sufficient resources to secure his control of England and so he called for reinforcements from France. His wife, Blanche of Castile, helped to organise a huge relief mission. She gathered together almost 100 ships heavily laden with knights and siege equipment. The size of force might well have tipped the balance of power within England and enabled Louis to seize the throne, but that wasn't how it was going to turn out.

The fleet was led by Eustace the Monk. Eustace had – unsurprisingly, given his nickname –been a monk before deciding that life as a pirate was more profitable and, in his opinion, more fun. He had served King John and captured the Channel Islands for the English king. However, by 1217 he had decided that his skills were better employed by Prince Louis and he was made commander of the French fleet.

The smaller English fleet, opposing the French reinforcements, numbered about forty boats and was commanded by Hubert de Burgh. The English fleet, however, was faster and more manoeuvrable than the heavily loaded French ships. In some sense, it was a bit of a portent of what was to come later in the Spanish Armada, with a small, mobile English fleet holding off a larger, more heavily equipped foreign invasion force. The English surprised the French and, by a combination of accurate crossbow fire and the use of lime powder to blind their enemies, were able to board and capture Eustace's flagship, *The Great Ship of Bayonne*. Eustace the Monk was found hiding in the bilges of his ship (no doubt wishing he'd stayed a monk) and, despite him offering 10,000 marks as a ransom, Stephen Crabbe chopped off his head with a single stroke of his sword.

The naval defeat at Sandwich and the defeat at Lincoln had made Prince Louis's position in England irretrievable. Peace was made on 12 September 1217, and the French invasion was brought to an end. We never did have a King Louis.

15

The English King of Germany

The medieval period in England is long and complex, and people trying to understand it often tend to focus on the monarchs involved. This at least makes things a little simpler to categorise, but unfortunately it can also lead to people ignoring some of the other fascinating, major figures involved and their careers.

One such is Richard, Duke of Cornwall, who was never King of England but may have come close to ending up as King of Sicily and actually did end up as King of Germany, which would look good on any CV. His fascinating life also illustrates another fact that will come as a surprise to some – just how international the life of some English aristocrats of the time could be.

Okay, so it didn't start off very international. He was born in 1209 at Winchester, the second son of King John. Having said that, his mother, Isabella, was French and was the niece of Peter, Latin Emperor of Constantinople. Already by 1214 he was off to France with his father; not, of course, on a family holiday, like a small boy today. His father being King John, they were off to fight in Poitou. After that it was time for a bit of schooling, though, again, not quite today's typical schooling. Richard was sent to Corfe Castle, not a large, exclusive boarding school for rich thirteenth-century children but in fact a large, exclusive castle. It is still very impressive today.

In 1216, John died and Richard's elder brother, Henry,

became King Henry III. Some brothers compete with each other, and obviously an elder brother who also happens to be king has something of an advantage on the competition front. Having said all that, Henry did knight Richard in 1225, soon after his sixteenth birthday, and a few days later he gave him his present. Not a computer or DVDs or a new phone; Henry had got him Cornwall instead. Impressive, though hard to wrap.

Soon Richard was hard at work. Not the average work, obviously. He was off to France, as joint leader of an expedition to try to regain Poitou and to defend Gascony. He had a bit of success in Gascony, but not much in Poitou. In 1227 he returned to England, and things began to get a little difficult between him and his elder brother. Richard had decided he wanted a particular person out of one of the manors of the earldom of Cornwall. Henry decided he wanted the person to stay. With normal brothers it might all have ended with some sharp words and the buying of an eventual peacemaking pint at the pub, but with these two it was all on a rather grander scale. Richard teamed up with assorted other earls who were upset with Henry and rose in arms against him until Henry bought Richard off by giving him assorted chunks of land.

More fighting in France in 1230 was all of a bit of a waste of time and money. Then things began to get difficult for Richard with his elder brother again. This time they fell out over Richard's choice of bride. Now, not everybody gets on with their siblings' spouses, but in this instance politics were also involved. Richard married Isabella Marshal (daughter of William Marshal, see last chapter), who happened to belong to one of the most powerful families opposed to the king. In the end, though, Richard was once again bought off with more land and some changes at court. Richard was getting richer and richer, and less and less trusted by all sides. In 1238, he was at it once more. Again it was trouble with the in-laws. Henry secretly married off their sister Eleanor to Simon de Montfort. Richard rose in arms alongside his own in-laws, the Marshals, but once again made peace with his brother in the end.

Richard's wife Isabella died in 1240 and, probably much to the relief of plenty of people in England, Richard left for the Med. No, he wasn't recuperating in a villa in the south of France; he was off on Crusade. He did, it's true, head first for Marseille, but only because from there he was going to sail to Acre in the Holy Land. He found a chaotic political and military situation, and, as had happened before, Richard here managed to achieve rather more off the battlefield than actually on it. That wasn't a huge amount, it's true, but he did have one or two diplomatic triumphs and at least he managed to return to England in 1242 without having suffered any of the military disasters that many Crusaders suffered. He also got to see an elephant in Cremona in Italy as he was returning.

The year 1242 turned into a bit of a mixed one for Richard. On the one hand, he ended up yet again in France, yet again fighting a failed campaign in Poitou and yet again falling out with his brother Henry, who was on the expedition this time. On the other hand, he did get to marry the apparently beautiful Sanchia, sister of Henry's wife, Eleanor. So two brothers married to two sisters. And actually the two sisters had two more sisters, one of whom was married to Louis IX, King of France, and the other was married to Charles I of Sicily. Allegedly, when all four sisters met up, Margaret and Eleanor, who were married to the King of France and King of England respectively, insisted on the other two sisters sitting on stools in their presence because their husbands were less important. This can't have done much for sisterly harmony.

Things were looking up for Richard. Not only did he have a beautiful young bride, but he was now so hugely rich that he was in a position to start lending money to his now rather impoverished brother, the king. Sometime around here, the Pope also seems to have offered Richard the crown of Sicily, which Richard, probably wisely, refused on the grounds that he was happy where he was. True to his track-record of achieving rather more off the battlefield, he was also acquiring something of a reputation as a mediator, stepping in to negotiate a deal with Scotland and calm things down between barons and king. In 1253, when Henry set off for more fighting in France, Richard stayed behind to help Henry's wife rule England.

He seems to have turned down Sicily, but in 1256 a title came up for grabs that Richard just could not resist. To be fair, King of the Romans is a pretty impressive title, though, slightly confusingly, the actual job was King of Germany, which, again slightly confusingly, didn't necessarily mean he got to rule Germany much as the Germans had a lot of powerful rulers of their own. Nonetheless, Richard wanted the title and, fortunately for him, had the money necessary to get it. Seven electoral princes would decide who would be the next king. Even though some of them wanted King Alfonso of Castile instead, Richard's massive bribes allowed him to claim the title. Despite some continued opposition to his claim (opposition which never entirely ceased), Richard was crowned king by the Archbishop of Cologne on 17 May 1257. He held his first royal parliament at Mainz in September. He never really achieved very much in Germany, but still it was a great title. In 1261, his wife Isabella died.

In 1264, he was in England again and having major, major problems with the in-laws. The in-law in question this time was his sister's husband, Simon de Montfort, who had a bunch of very discontented barons at his side. Richard this time sided with his brother, and in the massive Royalist defeat at the Battle of Lewes he ended up, rather ingloriously for a King of the Romans, being captured in a windmill. However, in 1265 it was the turn of the rebels to suffer massive defeat and Simon de Montfort to suffer death and mutilation, this time at the Battle of Evesham. Richard was a free, and powerful, man once again.

In 1269, at the age of sixty, at Kaiserslautern in Germany he married the sixteen-year-old Beatrice of Falkenberg. Richard now had little time left. In 1271, Simon de Montfort's son Guy murdered Richard's eldest son, Henry, at Viterbo.

In December of that year Richard suffered a seizure at Berkhamsted, outside London, and in April 1272 he died there.

After his death, a battle for power took place in Germany and the eventual victor was a man with a family name that came to play quite a role in European history. He was Rudolf von Habsburg.

16

The Maid of Norway and a Union Unmade

When looking at the course of history in one period, it is sometimes too easy to assume that there is an inevitability about what happened and how things developed. It is a trick of the mind that, because we can see where the path of history led to, we subconsciously assume that somehow it was always going to end up there.

Yet there are also times in history when it is clear that events could have taken a completely different direction, one that could have left us today in perhaps a very different place. One such is the story of Alexander III and the Maid of Norway, a story not so well known outside Scotland and one that could so easily have led to the crowns of Scotland and England being united more than 300 years before they actually were, perhaps avoiding so much bloodshed in wars between the two kingdoms.

Alexander III was born in 1241. By 1249, with his father Alexander II dead, the young boy was king. Now, obviously at that age it's unlikely that you're really going to be able to handle the many challenges of running a medieval kingdom, and what followed was a battle for power with the young king at the centre of it. The poor little lad even ended up being kidnapped at one point.

Christmas Day is a big day for most ten-year-olds. Christmas Day 1251, however, was big for Alexander for reasons far removed from computer games under the Christmas tree. On that Christmas Day, Henry III of England knighted Alexander at York, and the next day Alexander was married to Henry's daughter Princess Margaret. The proud father-in-law, however, was after something more than a boy who would grow up to look after his daughter. He wanted Alexander to recognise Henry as overlord of Scotland. Alexander, however, was having none of it. Arguing with the in-laws, it seem, is not a new thing.

In 1262, Alexander took control of his own kingdom and decided to make his mark. We're used these days to seeing Scotland as a unified country, but when Alexander came to the throne, significant parts of it were outside his control. In the Western Isles, for instance, in 1262, it was the King of Norway rather than the King of Scotland who was the royal power. Alexander set out to change all that.

Alexander formally claimed the Western Isles and launched an attack on the Isle of Skye. It wasn't long before King Haakon of Norway reacted. In 1263, he arrived with a large fleet. Things looked bleak for Alexander, but then the weather intervened as a storm smashed into Haakon's fleet, and in the ensuing Battle of Largs in Ayrshire Haakon suffered serious losses. He headed for home, but died at Kirkwall before he could get there. In 1266, after money changed hands, Alexander formally took control of the Western Isles from the Norwegians. Well, sort of. Angus Mor MacDonald had fought for Haakon at Largs but kept his lands in the Isles when he accepted Alexander as king. However, the Lords of the Isles would retain much of their independence and go on to challenge the authority of the kings of Scotland. That, as they say, is another story.

A lot went right with Alexander's reign, but one area where he was to have major problems was with the question of an heir. Since his initial marriage problems, things had been going better with the in-laws. In 1274, Alexander and Margaret popped down to London for the coronation of Margaret's brother, Edward I of England. But things were about to take a bad turn for Alexander; a very bad one indeed.

Just six months after the coronation, his wife died. And that was just the start of it. He had had three children with Margaret: a daughter who was married to Eric, the new King of Norway, and two sons. In 1281, the younger son, David, died. In 1283, his daughter, also called Margaret, died during childbirth. In 1284, his elder son, another Alexander, also died.

The grieving Alexander was left with no children and, as heir, the tiny young daughter of Margaret and Eric, another Margaret – Margaret, the Maid of Norway.

Alexander was only forty-four, not a young man by any means in an age of much shorter life expectancies but still young enough to hope for more children of his own. In 1285 he married again, being wed to Yolande, Comtesse de Montfort, daughter of the Comte de Dreux. It was not to be a long marriage. Just five months later, on 19 March 1286, Alexander was riding in bad weather from Edinburgh Castle to visit his new wife at Fife. The details of exactly what happened are unclear, but Alexander disappeared into the night at some stage and was found dead on the beach at Kinghorn in the morning. He probably fell from his horse.

And so, with Alexander dead, the Maid of Norway was in line for the throne. Perhaps inevitably, it was not long before the jockeying for power started in Scotland as nobles clashed. Nevertheless the Guardians of Scotland agreed with Edward that the Maid of Norway should travel to Scotland. Not only that, but it was agreed that she would marry Edward's son, the young Prince Edward, the future King of England. The King of England and the Queen of Scotland would be husband and wife.

For a brief time, at an age when most little girls have other things to concentrate on, like friends and fun and school, a little girl was key to the futures of two great kingdoms. But it was not to last. The little Maid of Norway fell ill on the journey to Scotland, and when her ship was hit by a storm it headed for the Orkney Islands. There the little girl died, and with her died any certainty about the succession to the throne of Scotland. The Maid of Norway's body was returned to Norway, to Bergen, to lie beside that of her mother, and the battle for power in Scotland began in earnest again.

Thirteen nobles put forward a claim to the throne. With no agreement on who should be Scotland's next monarch, Edward I, King of England, was invited to decide the so-called Great Cause.

Up to now, Edward had been keeping pretty busy in Wales. He had invaded Wales in 1277 and defeated Llywelyn ap Gruffudd, and built lots of castles to make the point that he was in charge in Wales. Now he wanted to add Scotland to his collection.

Edward had lost out on marrying his son to the Queen of Scotland; he did not intend to lose out on controlling Scotland again. He chose John Balliol as king, and he expected Balliol to obey him. In 1294, Edward told the Scots to send troops for his war with France. Instead the Scots made an alliance with France, often regarded as the start of the Auld Alliance, and in 1296 Edward invaded Scotland, capturing Balliol and seizing, and removing, the Stone of Scone.

Soon after, William Wallace (yep, Braveheart) rebelled against Edward, beginning a period of Scottish history including Robert Bruce, Bannockburn, etc., which will be far more familiar to most than will the poor little Maid of Norway. Things might have happened very, very differently, and even been different today, if little Margaret had lived longer.

The Vanishing of England's Sixth-Richest Town

Invaders were one of England's exports during the Middle Ages, but it was also known for a much less heavily armed and, generally, much more cuddly export: wool.

The story of Dunwich is a story of just how rich wool made parts of medieval England, but it's also a story of how big wealth can disappear so suddenly.

The recent storms which battered the east coast during the winter and washed away sea walls were a reminder of the power of nature, but they were not the first time that life on the east coast of England has had to adapt to the weather. Two storms at the turn of the fourteenth century destroyed the economy of one of the richest towns in England. This once thriving community, which had elected two MPs to Westminster, now lies mainly in ruins a few hundred yards off the east coast of England and feet below the North sea – which, as you can imagine, hasn't improved trading conditions. This is the story of the town of Dunwich which some have nicknamed a British 'Atlantis'. However, there's currently little sign of it being this year's major new Disney movie.

Dunwich is situated on the Suffolk east coast, north of Aldeburgh and just south of Southwold, where the Dunwich River once flowed into the North Sea. The original town may have been named Dumnoc, a combination of the Celtic *dubno*, meaning deep or dark, as in a port with deep water, and *wic*, or town. It appears in the *Anglo-Saxon Chronicle* for 636. St Felix was made Bishop of Domnoc by Archbishop Honorius in 631 and charged with converting the eastern Angles to Christianity. St Felix was buried in Dumnoc until his body was removed to Soham at a later date. St Felix's link with Dunwich has been questioned by some who would prefer to locate Dumnoc nearer to Felixstowe and claim it was the priory at Walton which was given to St Felix. However, what is clear (in this slightly unclear situation) is that, even before the Norman Conquest, there was an important Anglo-Saxon settlement at Dunwich. This is evidenced by the Saxon names such as Snotyng the Rich, Alwyn Blunt and Walter Leadenpenny, all of whom were recorded as benefactors of Blythborough Abbey. Ah, Snotyng the Rich, Alwyn Blunt and Walter Leadenpenny. We don't have enough fun names like that anymore.

The Norman Conquest provided a boost to the economy of Dunwich as trade with the Continent increased. According to Domesday Book, between 1066 and 1086 the number of taxpaying households had increased from 120 to 236. Dunwich gave an income to the landowner of £50 and 60,000 herrings (though, obviously, the value of herring against the pound has dropped rather massively since then) compared with £10 before the Conquest. The manor was taken away from the Saxon Edric of Laxfield and given to Duke William's friend Robert Mallet. The number of churches had also increased from a single church to three. The reason may be the arrival of twenty-four 'Franci', who made their living through trade with Europe.

Dunwich thrived economically under the Normans, and by the end of the twelfth century it was about the sixth-largest town in the country; only London, York, Norwich, Lincoln and Northampton could really claim to be much richer. If things had gone differently, today you might have had big, posh shops boasting branches in Paris, Tokyo, New York and Dunwich.

Way out on the east coast, Dunwich escaped the fighting

and violence of the early Middle Ages unscathed. An attempt by Hugh Bigod and the Earl of Leicester to besiege the town in 1173 ended in victory for the burghers of the town. Even wives and maids were brought in to help 'the valiant knights' with the defence, according to Jordan Fantasome, a local monk. The Earl of Leicester 'retired completely mocked', unsurprisingly.

While King John may have been a disaster for the barons (and for himself), he was a hero for the good citizens of Dunwich. In 1199, John granted the town its first charter. Its seal shows a boat with castles at either end sailing across a sea full of fish while a sailor tugs at a rope to unfurl the sails. The charter granted the town self-governance and exemption from feudal dues in return for a payment of 200 marks. John reduced the amount which had to be paid in fees as the town was hit by economic depression. The town remained loyal to the king until the end of his reign. In 1215, when King John was forced by Magna Carta to recognise the rights of the barons and the local lords, the royal charter ensured he had no control over Dunwich, which was free to govern itself. Any of Bigod's villeins who made it as far as Dunwich and stayed for a year and a day were free men. Hooray!

At its peak in the thirteenth century, Dunwich had over 5,000 citizens and measured about a mile north to south and about half a mile from west to east. Its main asset was the deep-water haven which lay to the north of the town, where the River Dunwich flowed into the North Sea. The northern shore of the anchorage was provided by Kingsholme spit, which unfortunately was ultimately to grow southwards and block the sea lanes into the harbour. Down by the harbour were shipyards, workshops, alehouses and fish smokeries (all those herrings again), which would have added a distinctive odour to the sea air. The poorer housing was down on the low-lying ground by the harbour, which had a tendency to flood as the growth of Kingsholme spit backed up water in the haven. Those who had made their money built their houses higher up and closer to the centre of the town.

The hub of the town was its market square, where there was a market seven days per week. Twenty-one regular stallholders paid an annual rent. Those vendors who wanted to avoid tax sold their wares direct from their boats, moored in the harbour. Occasionally stall holders would attack these rivals selling direct from their boats, and the justices would be left to resolve the issues. Surprisingly, in view of the deeply religious nature of society, Sunday trading was allowed and may even, on some level, have been encouraged as merchants had to pay the Church a special tax for the privilege.

There were three great annual fairs. The first was St Leonard's, which was held from 5 to 7 November and dated back to 1075. It continued until the mid-fourteenth century, when its site was washed away by the sea (a sign of things to come). It was replaced by St James' Fair, which was held at the end of July. This fair continued (despite the loss of much of the town) into the nineteenth century, by which time it had earned a reputation for vandalism and drunkenness. Finally, there was the Herring Fair (hooray for herrings) between Michaelmas and Martinmas (end of September to November).

Dunwich had its own mint and there are examples of coins minted at Dunwich during the reign of King Stephen in the British Museum. The coins bear the names of the men who minted them: Hinri, Rogier, Turstein and Walter.

There were nine churches in Dunwich, along with some smaller chapels, a base for the Knights Templar, a leper hospital and an almshouse. These buildings were built of stone, while the commercial and residential buildings were made of wood or half-timbered. This proved something of an advantage for the churches after they went into the sea, in the sense that divers have been able to identify some of their remains. The churches were All Saints, St Bartholomew's, St James', St John the Baptist, St Leonard's, St Martin's, St Michael's, St Nicholas' and St Peter's. Only St James', which was founded before 1086 and whose remains stand beside today's parish church, has survived.

Dunwich was a Crusader port, from which knights left to

journey to the Holy Land. The Templars, the military order established in 1118 to guard the road to Jerusalem, had a base in the south-west of the town. The physical strength of the Knights Templar made it the religious house of choice for those criminals seeking to escape the law by claiming sanctuary. In 1287, they sheltered a self-confessed thief by the name of Adam le Trompere of Chelmondiston.

Once the Crusades were over, the Templars served the town as bankers and had amassed considerable wealth when they were closed down by Edward II in 1308. By this time there were only seven Templars in Dunwich, but their fortune included £111 14s 6 ¼d plus 35 gold florins, gold and silver cups and seven gold rings. It is less clear about the value of the 1,000 herrings, nineteen lambs and twenty cheeses that are also listed as their belongings, though presumably even by that stage the herring-to-pound exchange rate was substantially different to what it had been at the time of the Norman invasion. And we're not entirely sure about all the fluctuations in the herring-to-cheese exchange rate in Dunwich.

As well as their wealth, Crusaders returning from Jerusalem had brought a rather less welcome import: leprosy. St James' Hospital for Lepers was established to the west of the town outside the defensive walls and with its own Lepers' Gate. The lepers also had their own chapel and the softest water in the town, drawn from a 'Holy Well'. The hospital was established by either Richard I or possibly King John. The hospital was also allowed to look after the poor and the old, who contemporaries thought would not be frightened of lepers. The hospital was generously supported by Walter de Riboff, who gave it 40 acres of land at Brandeston and a daily supply of two loaves from his own oven and one and a half pints of ale from his brewhouse. There was a bonus of eight bushels of wheat as a gift at Michaelmas.

The real wealth of Dunwich, however, was generated from trade. By 1279, Dunwich is recorded as having 'eighty Great Ships', one of which was a giant vessel of over 125 tons, used on the Gascon wine run. That's a *lot* of Gascon wine. Ships from Dunwich exported wool and woollen cloth to France, Germany and the Low Countries, as well as making the longer trip to Iceland. The strongest links were with Holland, where Suffolk wool was taken to be turned into woollen cloth by Dutch weavers before being taken back to England for sale. By the end of the Middle Ages, Dutch weavers had set up shop in Dunwich and other ports in East Anglia, so there was no longer a need to export the wool to Holland to be turned into cloth.

Not all of the goods flowing out through Dunwich, however, were legitimate trade. When Edward I put a curb on the export of wool to protect English weavers, wool still left Dunwich under cover of darkness bound for the Low Countries. Bans on exports of gold and silver introduced during Edward I's war with Scotland and Edward III's campaigns in France were also ignored as the profits on offer were huge.

Travellers also used Dunwich as a point of departure. Shell badges found in the ruins suggest that, as well as Crusaders, some travellers were pilgrims bound for Santiago de Compostela in Spain. Along with Ipswich, Dunwich was the only Suffolk port licensed to deal with pilgrim voyages, the package tours of their day.

The port of Dunwich also made a contribution to the medieval navy. It was understood that cogs built by merchantmen could potentially be commissioned by the Crown in times of war. There were also specific war galleys built in the shipyards at Dunwich. King John had five galleys based in Dunwich in 1205. In 1257, Dunwich built a fifty-six-oar royal galley and a barge of twenty-eight oars for a cost of £132 11s 8d. The naval influence of Dunwich continued after the port's commercial activities began to fall. Unfortunately, it wasn't just the commercial activities that were falling; so was the town.

Dunwich fought a long battle against the environment and coastal erosion. As early as 1086, Domesday Book recorded that Dunwich was 'then 2 carucates of land now one: the sea carried away the other'. During the thirteenth century, storms brought flooding to low-lying areas and the expansion of Kingsholme spit gradually closed off the harbour, forcing locals to dig to keep the channel open.

However, this was no preparation for the great storms of 1287 and 1328, which effectively destroyed the prosperity of Dunwich and made it a shadow of its former self. On New Year's Eve 1287, a violent storm took away between 100 and 400 yards of the coastline and destroyed about 10 per cent of the town. It also helped to divert the River Dunwich out into the sea by Blythborough and Walberswick, which now made better ports than Dunwich.

Although the people of Dunwich attempted to revive their fortunes and rebuild their town, a further storm struck in 1328, suggesting that lightning could indeed strike twice. The second storm sealed off the harbour for good and swept away about 170 of the 200 houses in the town's richest parish, St Nicholas. The town never fully recovered from this storm and, unsurprisingly, businesses moved away, looking for safer ports.

Today, Dunwich is a tiny village with less than 200 inhabitants. The only remnant of the great medieval town is the dyke which protected its far western flank. All the churches have gone, and local legend has it that fishermen can hear their bells on the seabed. Coastal erosion destroyed Dunwich, but England's political system was slower to respond to the disaster than its businessmen. Despite its dwindling population, it continued to elect two MPs to represent it right up until the Great Reform Bill in 1832. It was one of the rottenest of rotten boroughs.

18

Gallic Terror on the South Coast

We've all heard of the Hundred Years War, of great English victories like **Crécy** and Agincourt. A lot of us, however, tend to be a lot hazier on how and why we actually ended up losing the war and very few are aware that, right at the beginning of the war and just a few years before **Crécy**, it was Frenchmen who were on the rampage across English soil, not the other way round.

The reasons behind the outbreak of war in 1337 were, as causes of war so often are, multiple and varied.

The English throne had had possessions in France ever since William the Conqueror had done his conquering in England, and the marriage of Eleanor of Aquitaine to Henry II in 1152 brought in a whole lot more. It had reached the stage at one point where the King of England actually had real control over more territory in France than the King of France. Perhaps not surprisingly, the French royals weren't hugely keen on this situation and had set about nibbling away at assorted areas of English control south of the Channel. They did this so successfully that, after the so-called War of Saint-Sardos in 1324, pretty much all England had left was a chunk of territory in Gascony in south-west France, and the French wanted that too.

However, both the English and French thrones were about to see a change of occupants and that would change everything. In 1327 the young Edward III came to the throne in England,

and in 1328 Charles IV of France died. This caused something of a succession crisis, since Charles IV had no male heir. He did have daughters (one not yet born when he died), and in Edward III he had a potential male heir, as he happened to be Charles's nephew. However, succession through the female line was controversial in France, so Charles's cousin Philip ended up becoming Philip VI of France.

Added to this was a cocktail of other elements, including Scotland, Flanders, Robert III of Artois and a Crusade. France had a military alliance with Scotland against England. and Philip gave refuge to David II of Scotland (Robert the Bruce's son) in 1334 after the English victory at Halidon Hill. Our key trading partner, Flanders, had links to both England and France and both the countries had political and financial ambitions there. Edward was giving shelter to Robert III of Artois, with whom Philip had fallen out and whom Edward made Earl of Richmond. And there was the Crusade, to which we will return. All in all it was an explosive combination, and in 1337 it led to war.

Edward held his land in Gascony as Duke of Aquitaine, and, though he was King of England, in Gascony he was theoretically subject to Philip. Philip announced in May 1337 that he was confiscating the lands, but confiscating lands from a king isn't always that easy. Edward predictably refused to have his lands confiscated, and in return would bring up the old dynastic question by announcing that he claimed the French throne as his right by descent. The war was on.

Fortunately for Philip, but very unfortunately for Edward and even more unfortunately for the inhabitants of assorted parts of the English coast, Philip had a fleet ready and waiting for a war. It had been waiting for that Crusade which we mentioned earlier, a Crusade in which Edward had also intended to take part. When plans for the Crusade fell apart, Philip had sent the fleet north to the Channel. Soon it was ready to attack, not in the Holy Land but on England's coast and the Channel Islands.

Edward's war strategy was to gather an army in Flanders

and strike into France from there. While he was concentrating on that (and desperately trying to find the money to pay for it all – war was devastatingly expensive even then), he was paying less attention than he should have been to what was happening elsewhere in the Channel region.

Already, in March 1338, a French fleet had sailed cheerfully into Portsmouth and wrecked the place before heading off to Jersey and doing pretty much the same there. This then encouraged assorted entrepreneurial types along the French Channel coast to join in by organising little cross-channel raiding parties of their own.

And worse was to come.

In August a bunch of Italian galleys that the French had hired finally arrived from the Mediterranean, and in September a French fleet struck at the Channel Islands again. The defenders had concentrated their forces in Jersey to prevent another attack there, so, rather unsportingly, the French struck at Guernsey and Sark instead. On 8 September the French assaulted Castle Cornet, which was held by just sixty-five men. The castle fell and all the men died. Jerbourg Castle on Guernsey was held by only twelve archers. It didn't last long either. A bit of a battle took place at sea in which two Italian galleys were lost, but basically it was all a bit of a disaster from our point of view.

And things weren't about to get any better. On 11 September, the French surprised five English ships off Walcheren, and these weren't just any English ships. Two of them were *Cog Edward* and *Christopher*, some of Edward's best ships. The English ships were totally unprepared for battle, some of the crew still ashore. Despite defending their ships desperately, it was another disastrous defeat for Edward (and even worse for those opposing the French that day, many of whom were executed).

And then, on 5 October, the French fleet arrived in the Solent and a few thousand attackers came ashore. Once again, little went right for the English defenders. Ships and local militia who should have turned up to defend Southampton failed to arrive. The panicked ringing of church bells warning of the invasion left some confused and thinking a church service was on. A few men, including the castle garrison, put up something of a fight, but plenty of the townspeople just fled, leaving the French, Italians and others in control overnight to loot at their ease. They stole anything obvious and easily carried and even things that weren't obvious, like the weighing scales from the Custom House. In the morning, when the locals began to rally and start to threaten an advance into Southampton, the attackers withdrew. In the process, as well as all the looting, plenty of fires had been lit as well. Some suggest that up to half of Southampton's houses were burnt during the raid.

By now, the activities of the French fleet were starting to cause panic along the south coast and among merchants, damaging morale and trade. Fortunately for England, not for the first time, the combination of Channel and weather came to its rescue. Winter had arrived and it was going to be a hard one, particularly for the French fleet with its galleys. By the time the French campaign restarted in earnest in 1339, the defenders were much better prepared.

Hastings did get burnt, but attacks by the French on assorted towns, including another attempted attack on Southampton, were driven off. Edward had assembled ships to defend England as well. An embarrassing diplomatic incident did occur when some of the ships' captains decided to loot Flemish vessels instead, but they showed their worth when an attempted attack on the Cinque Ports ended in a somewhat humiliating rebuff for the French. Worse still for King Philip, when his Italian mercenaries demanded a pay rise and he refused, the Italians resigned and departed, depriving him of some of his most effective crews.

Soon it was English ships and their allies that were raiding the French coast instead. The year after, in 1340, came the great English naval victory at the Battle of Sluys, when Edward's fleet devastated the French fleet. England's great crisis of 1338 was finished, but the Hundred Years War had only just started. Six years later, in 1346, came Edward III's great land victory at **Crécy**.

19

HMS Middle Ages

It's worth taking a quick break at this point to review the rise of English sea power.

Most Brits are very accustomed to the idea of the Royal Navy ruling the waves. Admittedly we don't have anything like as many ships as in the past, but we still associate the idea of sea power very much with the history of this island and its defence, particularly with the history of England.

However, the reality is that for much of the period between 1066 and 1588 there wasn't anything that most people in Britain today would really recognise as a royal navy, and the sea was very much seen as a threat as well as an opportunity.

The first English king known to have had a navy was Alfred the Great. In 896, he ordered the building of longships that he had designed himself. Alfred's longships were supposed to be larger than those of his Viking enemies, and some had more than sixty oars. His new ships secured a victory over the Vikings in 896, when nine of his new ships overcame six Viking ships. But, as they say, 'size isn't everything'. The larger size of Alfred's longships does not always seem to have been an advantage, because some Vikings were able to escape as their lighter ships floated off the sandbanks of the river estuary more rapidly than did Alfred's. Nevertheless, a start had been made at an English ruler building a navy to help protect the country from foreign invaders.

Alfred tried to maintain a navy by funding it through taxation. Areas close to the coast were divided into 'ship sokes' of about 3,000 hides, and each 'ship soke' was to provide a manned longship. (A hide was the amount of land required to support a family. It didn't have an exact physical dimension.) The longships had a crew of about seventy-five, making them much larger than the typical Danish *drakkar* which had about thirty-six oars. However, this didn't prevent England becoming part of the Norse Empire of Sweyn Forkbeard, King of Denmark, by 1013.

The limitations of the Saxon navy as a defensive mechanism for England were also somewhat highlighted by the events of 1066. Harold assembled both the fyrd and its naval equivalent at Sandwich in the summer of 1066 and headed to the Isle of Wight. However, by September the fleet had run out of food and it sailed for London before dispersing. There was therefore no fleet to oppose Duke William when his army left Saint-Valery-sur-Somme on 28 September. Even if the fleet had still been on station at the Isle of Wight, it is unlikely that they would have been able to prevent the invasion. Battles between longships were mostly fought in river estuaries rather than in the open sea, and intercepting the invasion force would have been, frankly, completely a matter of luck.

The success of William's invasion did, however, add a new dimension to naval strategy for the English king as he now had territories on both sides of the English Channel. It was therefore a naval priority to ferry men and supplies between England and the Continent as rapidly as possible.

Then the Crusades came along. Richard the Lionheart gathered a fleet to support the Third Crusade in 1190. The king gathered more than 1,000 ships at Dartmouth and ordered them to sail south across the Bay of Biscay, around Spain, through the Straits of Gibraltar to rendezvous with the king in Marseille. This was an epic expedition for the time and 106 ships were reported as having made it to Marseille. By the time the ships arrived, however, in a slight anti-climax for the fleet, Richard I had already hired a further thirty ships and departed.

Richard I is recorded as having clashed with a Saracen vessel off Beirut. Chroniclers made Richard the 'hero of a naval battle'. The Saracen ship captured was apparently second only to Noah's Ark and it was disabled by a sailor diving in and throwing a rope around the rudder. For good measure, it is mentioned that the ship was armed with 200 serpents that drowned. The chronicler clearly enjoyed his story and the details should not be taken too seriously, though at least it would look great in CGI. The Muslim records suggesting the Saracen captain scuttled his own ship may be closer to the truth. However, to be fair to him, Richard was the first English king to have fought at sea since Alfred the Great.

The strategic dynamic changed again in the thirteenth century as the Capetian kings of France sought to increase their control of their country. This, of course, brought them into conflict with the kings of England, who had a duty to defend their lands in France. While most of this conflict was fought on land, there were a number of important naval encounters.

The opening encounter between King John and Philip Augustus was fought off Flanders near Damme. You can find more about the fascinating politics of all this in the Swoftsword *vs* Lion chapter above, so we'll just deal with the naval bit of it here. In 1212, Philip had gathered a fleet at Boulogne to invade England but had changed his mind when John decided to submit to the Pope. Philip decided to use the forces he had assembled to deal with Flanders, whose rulers in turn appealed to John for help.

A fleet of 500 ships led by the Earl of Salisbury, which also included 700 knights, sailed to the low countries. The English found the French fleet beached near Damme, where the French knights had – rather unwisely, as it turned out – disembarked to pillage the surrounding countryside. The French ships were set on fire after their valuable cargoes had been loaded into the English ships to be sent back to England. The encounter was as much land battle as sea battle, and as such was similar to the Viking battles fought by Alfred the Great. However, it also showed that England saw Flanders as an area of strategic importance.

Philip Augustus was to seek revenge, and in 1216 a small group of French knights led by Louis the Dauphin landed in Kent. The following year, Philip sent reinforcements. Had they landed, these extra troops may have made all the difference and allowed Louis to keep the English crown. However, Hubert de Burgh led the English ships to a decisive victory over the French, led by Eustace the Monk, off Dover.

Sir Hubert's cog was able to board the *Bayonne* of Eustace the Monk because it was higher in the water and had a higher freeboard, while the *Bayonne* was weighed down by siege equipment. The battle followed a pattern which was to be typical of the next 300 years. The first stage was to get close enough to the enemy to engage it with arrows fired from either crossbows or longbows. These were supplemented by almost anything else that could be thrown. For Sir Hubert this included pots of lime. The next and decisive manoeuvre was to come alongside and board the opposing ship. English sailors cut the stays on the mast of the *Bayonne*, capturing the French 'like birds in a net'.

The victory saved England from invasion in much the same way as the defeat of the Spanish Armada, even though it doesn't have anything like the name recognition these days. It was a decisive moment when England was saved by its sailors. The ships involved were provided by the Cinque Ports (Dover, Sandwich, Hythe, Romney and Hastings). The Cinque Ports had been granted a royal charter giving them certain trade and legal privileges. In return for these breaks, they had to provide fifty-seven manned ships for a fortnight a year without pay. This obligation was one of the origins of the later Royal Navy.

Edward I was spurred into action to commission new ships by the French king, Philip IV. Philip IV set up the Clos des Galées at Rouen as a royal shipyard to increase the size of his navy. This sparked off a medieval arms race, with Edward I vying to complete even more ships. Edward ordered twenty-six towns to build twenty galleys of 120 oars each. The galley built at Newcastle cost £205 2s 4¾d and was about 120 feet long and the longest oars were 23 feet. The galley had a castle at both front and stern. It was brightly decorated in red, blue, yellow and green; not so much battleship grey for these lads. The galley, however, was not one of the toughest ships built in Newcastle. After her voyage to Winchelsea in 1296 she needed extensive repairs, and five years later she was sold back to Newcastle for a mere £40 because she was 'almost rotten'. This shows the cost not just of building but also maintaining ships. This is why, in the medieval period, it often made more sense for kings to hire ships from local ports rather than maintain a standing navy.

The decisive campaigns of Edward I were, of course, not against the French but against our Celtic neighbours. In his campaigns in both Wales and Scotland, Edward I made extensive use of ships to provide logistical support to his campaigns. In Wales, Edward I's castles at Caernarvon and Conway included harbours so that they could be resupplied by sea. In Scotland in 1301, Edward used fifty-four ships to support his invasion. Three of these came from Flanders, but the rest were brought in from around England, particularly from the east coast. At the siege of Caerlaverock Castle on the Solway Firth, it was siege engines and food supplied from the sea which proved decisive. Edward I's strategic priorities were control of Scotland and Wales, rather than fighting the French. The role of his ships was to support these operations.

By the fourteenth century, the strategic priority for English kings had returned to the south and events in France. Philip VI and Edward III were competing to be King of France in the first stages of the Hundred Years War. French raids on Portsmouth and Southampton in 1338 (see previous chapter) demanded a response from Edward III. Edward III, ignoring the advice of his chancellor Archbishop Stratford, raised a fleet of over 120 ships in Ipswich and set off for Flanders. He was intending to destroy the much larger fleet of 250 ships that Philip VI had gathered to invade England. The battle took place in the estuary of the River Scheldt at Sluys.

The English fleet came across the French fleet and their Genoese allies chained together in three lines. In the shallow waters of the estuary, this gave the French little room for manoeuvre. The battle was a series of fierce boarding actions, where the English took advantage of their archers and experienced men-at-arms to capture 160 enemy ships. The chronicles suggest that this was a bloody and decisive action, in which the French suffered 30,000 casualties. These figures, which suggest the scale and brutality of the battle, are probably closer to the truth than the story that one of the English ships carried a party of English ladies who were determined to use the expedition as an opportunity to visit Queen Philippa at Ghent after the birth of her son. The victory put an end to the French raids and ensured that the Hundred Years War would be fought on French soil rather than English. Lucky for us, not so lucky for them.

The next naval encounter of the Hundred Years War took place mid-Channel in August 1350. A truce had been signed in the war after the English victory at Crécy and the incapacitating effects of the Black Death. However, by 1350 Edward III was ready to take action against the Castilian allies of the French. The Castilians had upset Edward by attacking English wine ships bringing fine French claret from Bordeaux to England. Edward ordered his ships to attack a convoy of Castilian ships taking valuable cargo from Flanders back to Spain.

Edward's fleet captured twenty-four of the Castilian ships and their cargo. While the chronicler Froissart describes the naval encounters as a series of jousts, the reality is that this was a series of vicious boarding actions. The writer Geoffrey le Baker describes 'torn out teeth, split noses and plucked out eyes'. The key differentials in boarding actions were the relative height of the vessels above the water and the ability of the sailors to lay alongside the enemy ship. This encounter, known as Les Espagnols sur Mer or the Battle of Winchelsea, was of little strategic importance but it does show that boarding an enemy vessel was still the key to victory. In allowing this to happen, the skills of the sailors and ship designers were as important as those of the soldiers on board.

The medieval story of the king's navy is, inevitably, not one of totally unblemished success. Embarrassing failures happened as well, such as the Battle of La Rochelle in 1372. The Earl of Pembroke set off with 224 knights, eighty archers and £12,000 to secure royal power in Aquitaine. The English met a fleet of Castilian galleys off La Rochelle. The English ended up running aground, their ships set on fire by flaming arrows from the Castilian galleys, and the Earl of Pembroke was captured. This defeat was a setback to the royal navy and the response was to build more oared vessels, known as balingers, rather than the purely sail-powered hulks and cogs.

In the fifteenth century, Henry V chose to renew the Hundred Years War. Alongside his victory at Agincourt was a naval victory at Harfleur and a significant increase in the scale of spending and the type of vessels available to the king.

At Harfleur in 1416, Henry V's brother the Duke of Bedford defeated a combined fleet of French and Genoese ships to relieve the siege of Harfleur. Three Genoese carracks were taken into royal service and renamed *George*, *Marie Hampton* and *Marie Sandwich*. It was the threat of these larger and more powerful carracks that caused Henry V to set about enlarging the size of his own ships.

Henry V's largest ship was the *Grace Dieu*, the remains of which have been discovered on the River Hamble near Bursledon. She was a ship of 1400 tuns. (A tun was a barrel containing 210 gallons of wine; medieval ships were categorised according to the number of such barrels they could carry.) The *Grace Dieu* was 177 feet long and the fore stage was about 45 feet above the waterline.

Eventually, of course, we lost the Hundred Years War and Englishmen turned to slaughtering each other in the Wars of the Roses. In 1485, no royal navy as we would recognise it existed. No paid standing fleet with a permanent base existed. The officials in charge, the clerks of the ships, were closer to accountants than naval commanders. Their expertise was in providing logistics and keeping costs under control rather than strategic thinking.

Under Henry VII and then Henry VIII, a more organised standing navy would begin to take shape. The ships themselves would change as cannons and naval gunnery became more important than archers and boarding vessels. Specialist mariners would be required to sail and fight these new ships. Their rates of pay would be laid down by the Crown, from 3s 4d per week for the master down to 1s 3d for the cook. The first permanent naval base at Portsmouth would also be developed. These were the foundations of the navy that was to triumph against the odds in defeating the Spanish Armada.

Making a Killing in Medieval Italy

The Hundred Years War wasn't just some theoretical clash of competing forces. It was very real, very long and very bloody, and it had a deep impact on many of those who served in it and on their lives.

John Hawkwood was born around 1320 at Sible Hedingham in Essex. He was one of the three sons and four daughters of Gilbert Hawkwood, a tanner in the village. The family also farmed lands held from the de Vere family, earls of Oxford and owners of Hedingham Castle, which overlooked the village. The family were yeomen of some status, and on his father's death in 1340 John was left £20 in cash (£20 was a lot more fun then than it is today). He was also given five bushels of wheat and five of barley, as well as a bed. All useful. However, sadly for John, the house went to his elder brother. You can only do so much with a bed and some barley, so John would have to use his inheritance to make a living for himself.

There are suggestions that he left Sible Hedingham for London and made a living as a tailor (possibly as an apprentice to a hosier), but there is no written or legal document to support this. The only supporting evidence seems to be that his nickname in Italy and his Italianised name, 'Acutus', may have been based on his alleged former profession.

It seems more likely that he left Sible Hedingham sometime after 1344 to join Edward III and his army in the Hundred Years War. By this time, his elder brother had married and had

a son and therefore there was less room in the family house. John de Vere, Earl of Oxford, was gathering a retinue to fight in support of the king and it is likely that John Hawkwood joined it either as a vassal or as a volunteer.

In 1340, Edward III declared himself King of France and then launched a series of campaigns to make the idea more of a reality, leading to his victory at Crécy and the victory of his son the Black Prince at Poitiers.

There is no proof that John Hawkwood was present at either battle, but we do know that he was in France. It also seems safe to assume that he served with distinction as he was promoted to captain and then knighted. When the fighting in France temporarily finished with the Treaty of Brétigny in 1360, John had to make a crucial decision about what to do next. His military prowess had made him a knight, but he had not turned his inheritance into a fortune. He was forty years old, which was well into middle age in the fourteenth century, and, in the words of the French chronicler Froissart, John was 'the poorest knight in the army'.

He decided to sell the only skills he really had (presumably any attraction to hosiery as a profession had long since gone). John joined a band of English, French and German soldiers heading south through Burgundy looking to see if they could make money from Pope Innocent VI in Avignon. Pope Innocent decided – perhaps understandably, given the arrival of some rather ruthless-looking types on his doorstep – that it was a safer bet to buy off the 'Great Company' rather than risk the sack of Avignon. He also suggested that the Marquis of Montferrat in northern Italy was in need of an army and that some of the 'Great Company' might find employment there, safely and conveniently (from the Pope's point of view) far, far distant.

To be fair to the Pope, it was a pretty good destination from Hawkwood's point of view as well. By the mid-fourteenth century, the wealthy rival cities of Milan, Florence, and Siena had developed a system of fighting that relied on mercenaries rather than feudal obligations. So much more convenient for

the wealthy townspeople. And it was all ordered in a very businesslike fashion.

These mercenary soldiers took the Italian name *condottieri* from the contracts that they signed with their employers, and they were accompanied by their own lawyers and accountants as well.

Sir John Hawkwood joined the German knight Albert Sterz and 5,000 others in heading east into Italy to help the Marquis of Montferrat defend himself against the Visconti of Milan. This group was to eventually become known as the 'White Company' and to be the private army of Sir John Hawkwood. Sir John was to spend the rest of his life in Italy, carving out (sometimes rather literally) a remarkable career as a mercenary.

Every good business needs something that picks it out from the competition. The White Company brought with it exciting new tactics and weapons to tempt the locals. The English victories against the French knights at **Crécy** and Poitiers had been based on the use of the longbow. Sir John Hawkwood brought with him experienced archers, who were able to show off their deadly talent. The longbowmen were supported by lightly armoured men-at-arms, who fought on foot. Both longbowmen and men-at-arms travelled on horseback, so the White Company was very mobile. The Company also showed an outstanding commitment to its customers. They didn't knock off at five or in September. They were prepared to fight in winter and to undertake night attacks as well. Pope Pius II saw this as a violation of 'the rules of war'; others (customers) rather appreciated it.

In 1363, the City of Pisa offered the White Company 40,000 florins for six months' service against their Florentine neighbours. They were so successful in plundering the area around Florence that the Pisans were quick to offer an extension to the contract. This time the price had risen to 150,000 florins, so business was booming. An attack on Florence in 1364, however, was a military failure as the White Company didn't have the necessary siege equipment to storm well-protected towns.

But it wasn't bad news for all of the White Company, some of whom went over to the Florentines instead. Sir John Hawkwood stayed loyal to his employer, the City of Pisa, but he was left with less than 1,000 soldiers.

Finding himself short of an employer for the next three years, Sir John and his men learnt to survive and even thrive by getting money from towns belonging to Perugia and Siena. The technique was fairly simple and the sales patter persuasive: those towns that failed to pay were sacked. St Catherine of Siena became so incensed by Sir John's behaviour that she wrote to him, accusing him of being a 'soldier of the devil' and suggesting that he should find employment on a Crusade. Sir John somehow found it in himself to decline the saint's offer.

While St Catherine had little regard for Sir John Hawkwood and his profession, elsewhere in Italy his stock was rising. In 1368, he attended a royal wedding in Milan. Lionel, Duke of Clarence, the third son of Edward III, married Violante, daughter of Galeazzo, the joint ruler of the duchy. Sir John was given the role of captain of a 400-strong bodyguard that the Duke of Clarence had brought with him. It was a celebrity wedding, attended by Petrarch, Jean Froissart and Geoffrey Chaucer, and would no doubt have featured in the pages of celebrity magazines if they'd been invented by then. Sir John does, in fact, crop up in Froissart's chronicles, and he may be the role model for Chaucer's knight in the *Canterbury Tales*.

In the next few years, after a slightly unfortunate incident involving being taken prisoner by two German mercenaries (occupational hazard), Sir John ended up doing a spot of work for the Visconti dukes. He ambushed Florentine forces near Mirandola and took their commanders prisoner, and in June 1372 he defeated Lutz von Landau's much larger army.

Sir John's next employer was Pope Gregory XI, who, although still based in Avignon, was trying to reassert some control in Rome. The papacy at that time could be a rather poor employer and somewhat tardy in making payments in cash. However, fortunately the papacy had plenty of land and

Gregory solved his financial crisis by paying Sir John with land in the Romagna. The Englishman now began to build up a property portfolio in northern Italy. He made his headquarters at Cotignola. To add to the fun (from Hawkwood's point of view), feeling threatened by the presence of his soldiers, the Florentines decided to give Hawkwood an annuity of 1,200 florins in return for a pledge not to attack their property.

Despite the slaughter and extortion, it would be very wrong to see Hawkwood as a man with no morals. His morals were not those of St Catherine, but they did exist. While serving Pope Gregory, he was instructed to help a troop of Bretons subdue Cesena, where the inhabitants were not respecting Cardinal Robert of Geneva's authority. The Bretons began to murder the people of Cesena, including women and children. Hawkwood himself was so appalled by what was happening that he launched a rescue mission and escorted 1,000 women and children away from the city. He then resigned his command in disgust. Even as loyal an employee as Hawkwood could only take so much.

In May 1377, by which time Sir John would have been getting on for sixty, he married Donnina, the illegitimate daughter of Bernabo Visconti and a local Milanese noblewoman. Hawkwood's reputation within Italy was such that the marriage was thought worth a mention from the Mantuan ambassador. Yet another celebrity wedding.

However, it was in the service of Florence, fighting against the Milanese, that he was to spend most of the rest of his life. In the 1370s, the Florentines did not trust Hawkwood. He had, after all, attacked the city in 1364. In 1379, though, he supplied the Florentines with inside information about a plot against them. The information proved to be accurate and Hawkwood became Captain General of the Florentine Guard.

By 1390, the City of Florence was becoming increasingly concerned about attempts by Gian Galeazzo Visconti of Milan to take control of all northern Italy. The Florentines recruited Hawkwood to take action on their behalf. Although nearly seventy years old by now, he marched towards Bologna and

in June 1390 defeated the Milanese army of Jacopo dal Verne. The following year he continued his campaign and reached the gates of Milan itself. However, once there he found himself hugely outnumbered. His subsequent retreat was well organised and well disciplined. He was able to bring most of his 7,500 soldiers safely home. The Florentines were very impressed by his service and he was richly rewarded. He was granted a new, tax-free annuity of 2,000 florins in addition to the 1,200 florins he was already being paid. His old age was reflected in the fact that his wife, Donnina, received a pension of 1,000 florins per year, to be paid when Hawkwood died, and each of his three daughters was given a dowry of 2,000 florins. Although the campaign did not deliver a decisive victory, it did produce substantial rewards and showed once again that he was as much concerned with business and profit as honour and fighting.

Hawkwood lived long enough to see the dowries of his two eldest daughters spent. His eldest, Gianetta, married Count Brezaglia of Porciglia. His second daughter, Caterina, married the German *condottiere* Conrad Prospergh, who had fought for Hawkwood. Although he had his daughters married in Italy, Hawkwood wanted to settle up in Italy and return to England. However, he died before he was able to leave, in March 1394.

Florence gave Sir John Hawkwood a grand funeral at the taxpayers' expense. His body was covered in cloth of gold and the city also covered the cost of new clothes for his wife and children. In total, the city paid 410 florins for its departed captain. All in all, quite a send-off for a man who had started life as the second son of a tanner and had inherited a bed and some barley.

Brits on Crusade

And, of course, Brits weren't just fighting abroad as mercenaries. In the Middle Ages, Brits had the opportunity – well, many opportunities actually – to go abroad and fight as Crusaders.

When it comes to the Crusades, people in Britain particularly tend to think of Richard I and his involvement in the Third Crusade. But quite a lot of people also know a bit about the First Crusade, which captured Jerusalem and established Crusader states in the Middle East, and about the Fourth Crusade, which was originally aimed at Jerusalem again but instead diverted to attack and sack the Christian city of Constantinople. Whoops.

However, many people know a lot less about all the other crusading activity going on and British involvement with that.

Not surprisingly, considering that a First and a Third Crusade took place, so did a Second. The Second Crusade was a bit of a disaster – actually, quite a lot of a disaster – from the Crusaders' point of view, and included a rather disastrous decision to attack Damascus. It did include some success for English Crusaders, though, because a bunch of them diverted and helped the Portuguese capture Lisbon from the Moors. Of course, it wasn't just Englishmen going from these islands to the Crusades. In 1188, for instance, Gerald of Wales toured Wales with the Archbishop of Canterbury recruiting for the Third Crusade, and Alan FitzWalter, High Steward of Scotland, also went on that Crusade.

The Fifth Crusade was basically a bit of disaster from the Crusaders' point of view. They managed to take the port of Damietta in Egypt and then advanced on Cairo but didn't reach it, instead suffering a rather nasty defeat and having to hand over Damietta again. Crusaders from the British Isles did play some role in this affair. For instance, the earls of Hereford, Chester, Winchester and Arundel were all there, though the Earl of Chester, perhaps rather wisely, departed soon after the original capture of Damietta in November 1219.

The next Crusade involved rather less fighting for the Crusaders and rather more success, and again some English participation. As preachers were drumming up support for the Crusade in spring and summer of 1227, a travelling fishmonger from Uxbridge had a vision of Christ which may have contributed to religious fervour. One source claimed 40,000 English recruits, though that seems a massive exaggeration. However, delays by Emperor Frederick II caused chaos with the Crusade and even more confusion occurred when he managed to get himself excommunicated, it hardly being conventional to have a Crusade led by somebody who'd been excommunicated. The result was that, when he got to the Holy Land, Frederick didn't actually have much of an army, which forced him to negotiate rather than fight. And thus, in the end, he actually managed to take control of Jerusalem peacefully, rather than with the usual mass slaughter.

In 1240–41 Richard of Cornwall briefly got in on the act on the crusading front (see Chapter 15). With the Crusade after that it was a return to Damietta in Egypt, a return to mass slaughter (from everybody's point of view) and a return to disaster (from the Crusaders' point of view). Again the Crusade included participants from the British Isles. For example, William Longsword led an English contingent that was all but wiped out along with most of the rest of the Crusader army at the Battle of Mansourah in 1250. Louis IX of France had led the Crusade and had the good fortune to be taken prisoner alive rather than slaughtered like so many of

his followers. Undeterred, in 1270 Louis thought that it would be a good idea to launch yet another Crusade. It wasn't a good idea. It fact, it was a very bad idea, as some people at the time had already worked out. Jean de Joinville, for instance, a chronicler who had gone on the Seventh Crusade with Louis, decided that this time he had pressing engagements somewhere else, almost anywhere else. Louis decided that he was going to attack the Holy Land by first attacking Egypt, and that he was going to attack Egypt by first attacking Tunis. Soon after arriving in Africa, a big chunk of the army came down with sickness and Louis himself died as well, and the siege of Tunis had to be abandoned. However, into this mess had wandered a certain Prince Edward of England. Yep, the future Edward I had arrived on the scene. He rapidly saw that sticking around in Tunis wasn't going to achieve much, so in 1271 he arrived in Acre, in the Holy Land. He had, however, arrived with only thirteen ships and perhaps about a thousand men. Ultimately he wasn't really going to make a big difference to the balance of power in the region, and in 1272 he set off for Sicily, and by 1274 he had returned to England for his coronation.

Crusades aimed at securing Christian power in the Holy Land had, apart from the first one, mostly been either partial failures or total disasters. However, the idea of charging around slaughtering people AND getting thanked by the Church for doing it (plus assorted other crusading benefits) had so captured the imagination of many of Christendom's knights that loads of other 'Crusades' aimed at loads of other targets would follow.

Some of these, like the Crusade against the Albigensians, with Simon de Montfort slaughtering Cathars and assorted others, are already famous, or indeed infamous. Some, such as Despenser's Crusade and John of Gaunt's Crusade, now seem ludicrous – though the people who died in them weren't laughing. In 1378, Urban VI was encouraging a Crusade against the supporters of his rival for the papacy, Clement VII. English supporters of such a Crusade had two options. One turned into Despenser's Crusade, in which Despenser, Bishop of Norwich, rampaged somewhat aimlessly around Flanders a bit before returning to England and getting impeached. The other turned into John of Gaunt's attempt to seize the throne of Castile. John's army, along with its Portuguese allies, wandered around Castile failing to achieve much apart from losing loads of men to disease and assorted other causes.

One area of serious crusading effort, though, which today comparatively few people in the UK know about, is the Baltic region. And this became of particular interest to a certain Henry Bolingbroke, the future Henry IV of England.

Crusading in the region of Prussia and the Baltic states lying beyond it had become an increasingly attractive option for many Western knights as the fourteenth century progressed. The Teutonic Knights had originally been based in the Holy Land but had lost their bases there in 1291. So they relocated to Prussia and started crusading against pagans further east. Signing up for a spot of fighting alongside the Teutonic Knights didn't have quite the prestige of actually campaigning in or somewhere near the Holy Land, but it did have other advantages for British knights. Increasing levels of trade with the Hanseatic League meant that getting to the battlefront was a lot easier, and, frankly, once they got there things were usually a lot easier too. The fighting had settled down largely into a sort of stalemate where Crusaders could launch little raids without the danger of getting involved in the sort of battlefield mass defeat that had been the fate of so many Crusaders in the Middle East. The Teutonic Knights ran what was, in a sense, an almost package tour operation where knights could drop in for a few weeks of hunting, feasting and the occasional raid before returning home. It wasn't, however, cheap to take a bunch of men with you crusading and to be fair it wasn't without danger, either. John Loudeham, for instance, borrowed £50 for his crusading 'package tour' when £50 was a lot of money, and ended up killed on a raid, dead at the age of twenty-five and buried in Konigsberg (now Kaliningrad, a Russian enclave).

Bolingbroke had considered crusading in Tunis but in the

end, probably wisely, in 1390 he headed for the Teutonic Knights instead. He liked it so much he made a second crusading expedition in 1392.

He didn't go alone. It is unclear quite how big his retinues were. A contemporary estimate at one point went as high as 300, but evidence from other sources suggests a figure more around the 100 mark, including less obvious members such as minstrels. Bolingbroke wanted music on his Crusade. And all of it didn't come cheap; in 1390–91 he spent almost £4,500.

For all the money spent, in the end he didn't achieve anything huge (apart, of course, from acquiring the prestige of crusading). After his experience in the north, however, Henry did go on pilgrimage to the Holy Land and said that he would return there on Crusade. But he never did.

Instead, in 1399 Henry kicked out Richard II and installed himself as Henry IV, King of England.

22

Dead Almost-Kings, Arthur and Henry

Pretty much all Brits know about Agincourt and the archers, with Henry V beating the French. However, this was, of course, followed by the bit where Henry V died and the French finally won the Hundred Years War. And then came bitter civil war, with the Wars of the Roses leading to the arrival of, you guessed it, the Tudors.

Henry VIII with his wives and Charles I with the English Civil War are two of the most widely known of English kings. One of the less well-known things about both these controversial kings, each with fairly obvious character flaws, is that neither was supposed to be king. Both spent the early years of their lives with elder bothers, and at that stage it was the elder brothers who were both Prince of Wales and supposed to be king instead. How different might British history have been if they had become king instead of their younger brothers?

On 22 August 1485, Henry Tudor defeated Richard III at the Battle of Bosworth and installed the Tudor dynasty on the English throne. On 18 January 1486, he strengthened his claim to the throne by marrying Elizabeth of York, eldest daughter of Edward IV and Richard's niece, thus uniting the houses of Lancaster and York. It didn't take long at all for the couple to produce a son and heir who would be the embodiment of that union. On 19 September 1486, their eldest son was born at St Swithun's Priory in Winchester. They named him

Arthur, after King Arthur himself, a figure known and loved in both Wales and England from works such as Geoffrey of Monmouth's *History of the Kings of Britain* and, of course, *Le Morte d'Arthur* by Sir Thomas Malory, which had first been published by Caxton in 1485. It was hoped the young prince would eventually be a new King Arthur, introducing a new golden Arthurian age to Britain.

The year 1489 saw his investiture as Prince of Wales, and in 1492, at the age of just six, he was appointed as keeper of England and king's lieutenant while Henry was in France. It was a big job for a six-year-old, but obviously he had helpers. Gradually he acquired more power and authority, particularly in Wales.

Meanwhile, plans had long been afoot for his marriage to someone who would boost the new dynasty's international profile and authority. In 1490, Henry agreed that his son and heir should marry Catherine, the daughter of the rulers of Spain, Queen Isabella I of Castile and King Ferdinand II of Aragon. That future bride is in fact much better known in Britain than her husband; better known, that is, as Catherine of Aragon.

Catherine arrived in Plymouth in October 1501, and in November they were married in St Paul's Cathedral. Shortly after they left for Ludlow, where they established their residence. It could have been the start of a bright future for the royal couple, but it wasn't. Arthur fell ill and, on 2 April 1502, at the age of just fifteen, he died. His parents were stricken with grief.

The young prince was buried in Worcester Cathedral and then eventually the question came up of what to do with Catherine of Aragon. In the end, of course, she married Arthur's younger brother, Henry, who would become Henry VIII. Eventually, despite Catherine's assertion that her marriage with Arthur had never been consummated, Henry would abandon Catherine in favour of Anne Boleyn, and he would abandon the Pope in favour of the Church of England.

The parallels with our next almost-king are interesting. Just as Henry Tudor had come from Wales to install a new dynasty in London, so King James came from Scotland, after the death of Elizabeth, to install the Stuart dynasty in London. Things hadn't always been friendly over the previous century between Scotland and England. James IV of Scotland had married Margaret Tudor, daughter of Henry VII of England and Prince Arthur's sister, but had then ended up being killed in battle against an English army at Flodden in 1513. That had left his son, James V, as king at less than a year and a half old. And James V died in 1542 after another defeat by an English army, this time at the Battle of Solway Moss. This left his infant daughter Mary, Queen of Scots, on the throne. She'd had a tough time of it and had been forced to abdicate in favour of James VI when he was only an infant too (plus she ended up being executed in England). But with King James, England now had a Scottish king.

And just as the new Tudor dynasty had once focused its hopes for stability and acceptance by its new people on Prince Arthur, so in the period after 1603 the new Stuart dynasty would focus its hopes for stability and acceptance on Prince Henry Frederick. And just as Tudor hopes would be crushed, with the next reign bringing conflict, the same would happen after James.

Henry had been born on 19 February 1594 at Sterling Castle as the eldest son of James VI of Scotland and his queen, Anne of Denmark. James and Anne would to some extent compete for control of the young prince, but soon he would have other things to think about.

In March 1603, Elizabeth died and James VI of Scotland took the English throne as James I of England. Henry became Duke of Cornwall. On 30 June 1603, he arrived at Windsor Castle and was made a Knight of the Garter at the age of just nine. Ahead lay years of education, training him to be the next King of England and the next King of Scotland. He seems to have spent some time on intellectual studies, but his particular passions appear to have been sport and military training. He hunted, jousted, hawked and fenced. He also seems to have liked dancing and enjoyed theatrical productions. He was also something of a fan of Sir Walter Raleigh, even though James was keeping him locked up in the Tower of London. In terms of religion, he seems to have been very unenthusiastic about Catholicism and seems to have firmly rejected the idea of taking a Catholic bride himself (unlike his brother, who would eventually marry the Catholic Henrietta Maria of France in a move that was widely unpopular in England and Scotland).

On 4 June 1610, soon after his sixteenth birthday, and amid massive and expensive pomp and ceremony, Henry was declared Prince of Wales. And on 5 June, he was jousting again. But the young prince was also starting to show an intriguing interest in culture. He planned architectural projects and collected paintings and sculptures.

But just as Arthur had died when people were getting accustomed to the idea of the reign of a new King Arthur, so the life of the intended King Henry IX was about to be cut short as well. In October 1612 Henry was struck by a fever, and on 6 November he died. His funeral took place at Westminster Abbey amid widespread mourning on 7 December.

Instead of Henry IX, England would eventually get Charles I, who would fall out irreconcilably with Parliament and would see civil war rip his country apart, eventually losing his head.

23

The Che Guevara of Norwich

Apart from the turmoil over things like the Reformation, Tudor England could be a turbulent place in other senses, too.

We've all heard of the Peasants' Revolt of 1381, but how many have heard of Kett's Rebellion? Rebels putting their lives on the line for their vision of a better, fairer England, rebels who captured England's second city and defended it against foreign mercenaries?

This is, on some level, a story of whether people or profit should be put first, so considering the concerns of our own time it is in some sense surprising that it's not better known.

By 1549 the population was growing, and this was putting pressure on resources. Landowners were keen to exploit common land for their own use by enclosing it and using it for sheep farming. The woollen industry was one of the richest industries in Tudor England and big money could be made from exports. At the same time, though, peasants were becoming increasingly dependent on the common land to farm their livestock and maintain their subsistence lifestyle. Landowners and peasants were on a collision course.

As always tends to happen with these things, in the end it was a toxic cocktail of greed, grievance and competing ambitions that caused the final explosion.

Lord Somerset, who had control of the country while Henry VIII's heir, Edward VI, was still a minor, had organised enclosure commissions in both 1548 and 1549 to root out illegal enclosure. His motive may have been political, aiming to strengthen his popularity and show his belief in a 'commonwealth' of men, or it may have been religious, providing proof of his piety through his good works. Whatever his motive, the rebels of 1549 appealed to Lord Somerset for aid and believed that they had a friend at the top.

The religious turbulence set off by Henry VIII's break with Rome over his marriage would also play its part. The rebels were upset by the pace of religious change following on from the Reformation and they complained about the standard of the local clergy. Seven of their demands could be seen as requesting a more protestant religious settlement.

In Norfolk, one of the areas affected by the clash over enclosure and control of land, the grip of the authorities had seriously slipped. Recruitment for the war with Scotland, the most important priority for Somerset, meant that East Anglia was short of military leaders, who may have been able to contain the rebellion in its early stages. And the power of the Howards, traditional figures of central authority in the region, was severely diminished. Catherine Howard, Henry VIII's fifth wife, had been executed and Thomas Howard, Duke of Norfolk, had been in the Tower since 1547 while his son was executed in 1546.

The uprising started in Wymondham on 7 July 1549. Crowds had gathered at Wymondham to commemorate the death of Thomas Becket. Discontent about enclosure was aired. Perhaps spurred on by a pardon given by the king on 14 June to those who had torn down enclosure fences, a mob descended on the village of Morley and removed the enclosure fences there. Then, when they attempted to do the same at the neighbouring village of Hethersett, the local landowner, John Flowerdew, offered them a bribe and pointed them in the direction of Robert Kett's land. Bad blood had existed between Robert Kett and John Flowerdew dating back to attempts to destroy the Abbey of Wymondham during the Reformation. John Flowerdew had sought to make money out of the destruction of the abbey, while Robert Kett wished to see it preserved as a place of worship for local people.

Robert Kett was not an obvious leader of a revolution. He was fifty-seven and one of the richest landowners in Wymondham. He had much in common with John Flowerdew as part of a growing middle class who had invested their money in property and saw enclosure as an ideal opportunity to cash in on the growing profitability of wool.

We will never know Kett's full motives but, for whatever reason, faced with the choice of defending his profits or championing people who had suffered because of them, he chose the latter course.

He declared, 'You shall have me if you will, not only as a companion, but as a captain, and in the doing of so great a work before us, not only as a fellow, but for a general standard bearer.' And from this time he became the leader of the rebellion.

It grew rapidly. Soon after the rebels had torn down Kett's fences. he addressed them at an oak tree outside Wymondham, which still bears a plaque remembering the rebellion. He decided to lead the rebels to Norwich, England's second-largest city and the centre of royal power in the region.

Kett had by now gathered something like 12,000 rebels, a formidable force, and the local authorities were scared. Edmund Pynchyn was sent to London to ask for help and the Sheriff of Norwich tried in vain to disperse them. By 21 July the rebels had set up camp outside Norwich at Mousehold Heath, overlooking the city. Soon their numbers grew even more, as they were joined by thousands of the poor and disaffected from within the city.

For a time it was stalemate. The rebels needed food from the city in order to continue their action, but they were also anxious to prove that they stood for good government and justice. The city of Norwich, by contrast, was powerless against the rebels and was hoping for help from central government.

The truce ended on 24 July when Somerset offered the rebels a pardon if they dispersed peacefully. Whether he was genuinely trying to help or just buying time, it made no difference. The rebels rejected the offer. It was a decisive point in the uprising. By doing so, and continuing their actions, the rebels made it plain that they were acting against the authority of the king and were prepared to accept the consequences. Things were about to get bloody.

Mayor Codd of Norwich closed the gates of the city to the rebels and thus cut off their food supplies. With no more access to food, Kett was faced with a choice: either try to send his followers home or seize Norwich. He decided to take the city. After a brief fight, the second-largest and richest city in England lay in rebel hands.

The Duke of Somerset responded to this threat to his authority by dispatching the Marquess of Northampton to raise an army and retake the city. Meanwhile, in Norwich, Kett set out to show what he believed good government looked like. He established a form of local government where more than 80 per cent of the hundreds in Norfolk had representatives. He set up a local court, which operated in the open, underneath the Oak of Reformation on Mousehold Heath. Local landowners were summoned to the court and punished for enclosure and rack renting. Those found guilty were imprisoned.

Kett also drew up a list of twenty-nine assorted grievances which he addressed to Protector Somerset. As well as an end to illegal enclosure and a desire to return rents to the levels of the early years of Henry VIII, the rebels demanded that all bondsmen may be made free, 'for God made all free with his precious blood shedding'. However, rather less stirring to the modern mind is the demand that 'no man under the degree of a knight keep a dove house'. The twenty-nine grievances also included religious demands, a concern at a lack of education among the clergy and anger at how they managed and made money from their estates.

As Northampton's army approached Norwich, Kett decided to pull his men back to Mousehold Heath. Northampton had an army of about 1,500 men, including Italian mercenaries. Lord Somerset's main concern at this stage was fighting the Scots, and there were few troops available to suppress insurrection. Kett was able to use the rebel's local knowledge to launch night attacks. The street fighting that followed was vicious and the casualties included Lord Sheffield. He is alleged to have been thrown from his horse and, expecting to be captured and ransomed, he had taken off his helmet. If so, it was a major mistake. Instead of being taken prisoner he was promptly killed by a blow to his head. Finally, having sustained heavy losses, Northampton was forced to withdraw to Cambridge, leaving the victorious Kett and the rebels in control of the city.

In the end, though, Lord Somerset decided he could not afford to leave England's second city in rebel hands and he gathered a stronger army. This time John Dudley, Earl of Warwick, was put in command of close to 12,000 men who had been recruited in Essex, Suffolk and London. The forces also included 1,500 German landsknechts, mercenaries who were armed with pikes and handguns. Kett's rebels now faced an army which matched it in terms of numbers and had the advantage of better training and equipment.

As Warwick approached Norwich, Kett was once again offered a pardon. The pardon was once again rejected and the rebels chose to fight. On 24 August, Warwick forced his way into the city and the rebels withdrew to Mousehold Heath once again. Although the rebels attempted to raid the city at night and burn it, they were outnumbered. As more troops arrived, Warwick was able not only to secure the city but also to move against the rebels outside the walls.

The final battle was fought at Dussindale on 27 August, and Kett and his men were, in the end, no match for Warwick and his German mercenaries. Kett lost between 2,000 and 3,000 men while Warwick lost only about 300. The morning after the battle, between 30 and 300 rebels were hanged outside Magdalen Gate, Norwich.

Robert Kett and his brother William were eventually captured at Swannington and taken to London. If Lord Somerset had ever had any sympathy for the rebels previously,

Above: 1. Milecastle on Hadrian's Wall, the line that, despite repeated Roman invasions of Caledonia, marked for lengthy periods the northern limits of firm Roman control in Britain.

Below right: 2. In Rome, the Arch of Septimius Severus, the emperor from Africa who defeated Clodius Albinus and later invaded Caledonia.

Below left: 3. The Abbey of St Gildas de Rhuys in Brittany, founded, according to tradition, by Gildas, the man who chronicled the end of Roman Britain and the arrival of the Saxons.

Left: 4. Close to Hexham and Hadrian's Wall, the site of the Battle of Heavenfield, in which Oswald defeated and killed Cadwallon of Gwynedd, ending the Welsh invasion of northern England.

Below left: 5. Cross at Heavenfield commemorating the one raised by Oswald before his victory there.

Below right: 6. The Gates of Rome. The end of the road, or pretty much the end of the road, for seventh-century warlord and king Cædwalla, who abdicated and travelled here but died soon after.

Right: 7. St Boniface, the man from England who set off to convert Germany (and pretty much succeeded), commemorated outside Southampton at Nursling, site of a monastery where he trained when young.

Below left: 8. King Alfred, from G. F. Watts' *Alfred Inciting the Saxons to Resist the Landing of the Danes.* (Courtesy of Jonathan Reeve, JRb60p136 800900)

Below right: 9. Memorial in Swanage to a disaster for the Danes in Alfred's time (complete with delightfully anachronistic cannonballs!).

Above: 10. Corfe Castle, Dorset, scene of Edward the Martyr's death (see Chapter 8) and home for a while to the young Richard of Cornwall (see Chapter 15).

Below left: 11. It became commonly believed that Ælfthryth herself was responsible for Edward's death, as demonstrated in this later portrait. (Courtesy of Elizabeth Norton)

Below right: 12. Some people are in no doubt as to who killed Edward 'the Martyr' at Corfe Castle.

Right top: 13. Nicholas Breakspear, Adrian IV, the only English pope ever (so far). Not exactly the best-known figure in British history, but at least he does have his own commemorative plaque.

Right middle: 14. Looking from Roman Verulamium up to the saint's shrine in St Albans Abbey. St Germanus visited here just after the end of Roman Britain and the young Nicholas Breakspear had connections with the town and abbey.

Right bottom: 15. Rochester Castle. King John improved its defences, but then found himself having to attack it in 1215.

Below left: 16. A later portrait of King John. (Courtesy of Stephen Porter)

Above: 17. Berkhamsted Castle. Berkhamsted has handy commuter access to London, but a long time before that its castle was the scene of both the English witan submitting to William the Conqueror and the death of the English King of Germany.

Below left: 18. Memorial commemorating the Battle of Lewes in 1264. After defeat there, Richard of Cornwall, King of the Romans (King of Germany really), ended up being rather ingloriously captured in a windmill.

Below right: 19. A bit of unassuming masonry that sums up the vanishing of mighty Dunwich; this was the last buttress of All Saints Church. The church itself closed in the eighteenth century and fell over a cliff between 1904 and 1919. The buttress was rebuilt in its current location soon after.

Above: 20. An impressive stretch of medieval defences in Southampton. Unfortunately, it was only properly defended *after* the French sacked the port in 1338.

Below left: 21. The Hawkwood Memorial in St Peter's church, Sible Hedingham (see Chapter 20).

Below right: 22. Detail of the Hawkwood Memorial.

Top: 23. *An Allegory of the Tudor Succession*, after an original by Lucas de Heere, depicting Henry VIII, Elizabeth I, Mary I and Edward VI. Were it not for Prince Arthur's early death, perhaps none of these future monarchs would have reigned. (Courtesy of the Yale Center for British Art, Paul Mellon Collection)

Above left: 24. Ketts Oak outside Wymondham, scene of Kett's address to the rebels in 1546 before he led them forward to seize Norwich.

Below left: 25. The end of the rebel. A memorial to the executed Kett.

Above left: 26. The Reformation in England had its victims, and so did Mary's (eventually unsuccessful) attempt to undo it. Monument in Smithfield, London.

Above right: 27. Mary I. (Courtesy of Ripon Cathedral)

Below: 28. Abbey Gate, Colchester, at the site of the home of the Lucas family. During vicious fighting it fell to Parliamentary forces, but an explosion in a Royalist gunpowder store blew the roof off.

Above: 29. Oliver Cromwell in front of Westminster Hall, where Charles I was tried and condemned to death. Pretty much everybody in Britain has heard of Oliver Cromwell, but what about his son and successor, Richard? (Courtesy of Son of Groucho under Creative Commons 2.0)

Below left: 30. The lesser-known Richard Cromwell. (Courtesy of the Internet Archive under Creative Commons ShareAlike 2.0)

Below right: 31. Jordans in Buckinghamshire was a key centre of early Quakerism, and contains one of the earliest Friends' Meeting Houses.

Mrs BEALE, & her Son CHARLES.

Above left: 32. St Mary's church, Putney, where the Putney Debates began in 1647 (long before the first Oxford/Cambridge boat race) with the participation of radical Levellers, discussing ideas for a new constitution.

Above right: 33. Pioneering female artist Mary Beale, as depicted by Thomas Chambars, with her son Charles, who was also a painter. (Courtesy of the Yale Center for British Art, Paul Mellon Collection)

Below: 34. Petersham churchyard. After living in Petersham, groundbreaking female painter Joan Carlile was buried there.

Above: 35. View of Edinburgh old town. Alexander III rode to his death from the castle in 1286, bringing the Maid of Norway to prominence. In 1777, Edinburgh had twelve legal whisky producers but allegedly hundreds of illegal stills. (Courtesy of Douglas O'Brien under Creative Commons ShareAlike 2.0)

Below left: 36. John Paul Jones bringing the American Revolution to the shores of Britain, and spiking a cannon in Whitehaven.

Below right: 37. Portrait of John Paul Jones. (Courtesy of the Library of Congress, Harris & Ewing Collection)

Above left: 38. A commemorative plaque marking former slave Olaudah Equanio's stay at what is now 73 Riding House Street, Paddington. (Courtesy of zimpenfish under Creative Commons ShareAlike 2.0)

Above right: 39. St Andrew's church, Soham, where Olaudah Equiano married local woman Susannah Cullen.

Below: 40. Woolwich Arsenal, where Congreve's work on rockets really took off.

41. Bexhill still contains signs of the presence of the King's German Legion during the Napoleonic Wars, including these Memorial Gardens where hundreds of Germans who served the British king lie buried.

42. The nineteenth century saw new ideas on education and new schools in Britain.

43. The end of a dream. Memorial to pioneer British pilot Percy Pilcher, commemorating his death on 30 September 1899 in a crash at Stanford Hall, near Market Harborough.

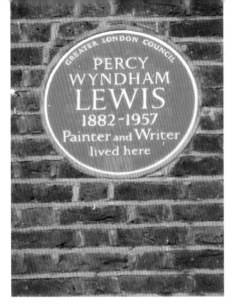

Above left: 44. A plaque marking the former home of Wyndham Lewis in Kensington.

Above right: 45. The Sportsman pub. In 1940, a German Junkers 88 crashed near the pub in sight of British troops billeted there, thus starting the Battle of Graveney Marsh.

Below: 46. The First World War didn't just take place overseas. This contemporary photograph shows damage to Whitby Abbey near Scarborough sustained in a raid in 1914. (Courtesy of the Internet Archive under Creative Commons ShareAlike 2.0)

47. Blue Streak. Not exactly Saturn V, but still quite an achievement. Here on loan from National Museums Liverpool. (Courtesy of World Museum Liverpool)

he showed none now. Robert Kett was found guilty of treason and returned to Norwich. His body was hauled up from the ground and left hanging from the walls until it disintegrated – a warning to anyone who dared to challenge the state. His brother William was also found guilty of treason and was hanged from the west tower of Wymondham Abbey. The authorities had been badly shocked and were determined that such an uprising should never happen again. The date 27 August became a local holiday in Norwich. Church bells were rung and lectures were given on the sins of rebellion. This tradition continued for over a century.

In more recent times, though, things have changed. In 1949, a plaque appeared celebrating Kett as part of Norwich's 'dissenting tradition'.

24

Mary's Revenge, Undoing the Reformation

Most people in Britain know something about the Reformation in England, about Henry VIII and closing down the monasteries and all that, and they probably know that Bloody Mary isn't just a vodka and tomato juice drink, but the full extent of Mary's determined effort to counter the religious trends of her father's and brother's reigns can come as something of a surprise.

Mary proclaimed herself Queen of England in the summer of 1553 on the death of Edward VI. She did, however, face a Protestant rival in the form of Lady Jane Grey. John Dudley, the Duke of Northumberland and Leader of the Privy Council, knew that once Edward VI had died, both his position and the position of all Protestants within the country was under threat. Therefore, he had tried to arrange for the succession to pass to the Suffolk family. As Frances, Duchess of Suffolk, was too old, the crown was to pass to her eldest daughter, Lady Jane Grey.

Dudley hoped that he had secured his own future by marrying his son Guildford Dudley to Lady Jane Grey in May 1553, and he had attempted to legitimise taking the succession away from the Tudors by a letters patent that Edward had signed in June 1553. However, Dudley did not send troops to arrest Mary Tudor at Framlingham, and when he did many of them deserted.

Dudley's support faded away as the Privy Council

acknowledged Mary as queen. Dudley senior, Dudley junior and Lady Jane Grey herself would all be on trial fairly soon, before being executed. In September 1533 Mary was crowned, and there was popular support for her within London. Some supported her legitimacy; some, like Mary herself, saw her triumph as a sign of God's own support.

Mary, as the daughter of Henry VIII and Catherine of Aragon, had a clear plan: she would return England to the papacy. She had not forgotten how Henry had dealt with her mother in divorcing her to establish the Church of England and she had scores to settle, particularly with Archbishop Thomas Cranmer.

The job she faced was enormous. It is hard to estimate how many Protestants there were in England in 1553. There were certainly powerful and close-knit groups in London and in other towns in the south-east.

A larger and more expensive problem was that the monasteries had been destroyed, and Church property and materials needed for a Catholic service had been sold. Rood screens and altar pieces had been torn down and destroyed. The ceremonial vestments of the clergy had been burnt and many of the clergy had married. Church services were carried out in English using Cranmer's prayer book, and the literate laity could read the Bible from William Tyndale's translation. The physical task of restoring churches, creating the ornaments and vestments required and finding an unmarried priest for every parish was as demanding as wiping out the idea of Protestantism.

To advise her, Mary turned to Cardinal Pole, who returned to England and became Archbishop of Canterbury. He had delivered the opening address of the Council of Trent and had almost secured enough votes to become pope himself in 1549. (Yes, we almost had a second English pope to add to Adrian.) Therefore, it is likely that he was well informed about the Counter-Reformation being launched by the Catholic Church. Mary married Philip, son of Emperor Charles V, who brought with him Spanish Catholic advisors like Bartholome

Carranza. Carranza would have known about the way the Spanish Inquisition had functioned in Spain under Tomas Torquemada. Philip was more concerned with the fight against Protestant beliefs in the Spanish Netherlands and knew how the papal inquisition worked there. Mary had the support of the political power of the emperor and the spiritual power of the papacy.

The earliest encounters of the reign were inconclusive. Mary had scored a propaganda triumph when Dudley confessed his sins and confirmed his belief in the Catholic faith before his execution in 1553. However, a riot broke out in London at St Paul's Cross in October 1553, sparked off by Bourne, who chose to preach in defence of the queen and in defence of Bishop Bonner of London but against the Protestant Bishop Ridley. Not all sermons are rapturously received, but this one got a particularly boisterous reception. It came to an abrupt end when one of the congregation threw a dagger at Bourne, which struck the side post of the pulpit. Bourne escaped into a school, allegedly helped by Mr Bradford, a famous Protestant reformer. This incident frightened some of Mary's Spanish and Imperial advisors, who advocated caution at this stage and tried to dissuade the queen from executing heretics.

The most high-profile Protestants were Thomas Cranmer, Archbishop of Canterbury; Hugh Latimer, Bishop of Worcester and chaplain to Edward VI; and Nicholas Ridley, Bishop of London. All three were burnt at the stake, Ridley and Latimer in the autumn of 1555 and Cranmer in the spring of 1556. The burnings were preceded by a show trial in Oxford, where leading Catholic lights slugged it out with their Protestant rivals over the nature of faith. By dying at the stake they became martyrs, still remembered in Anglican services and with Church of England schools named after them. One of the major factors in Cranmer's death may have been Mary's anger about how he had dealt with her mother.

The ultimate aim of Mary's policy was to convert as many Protestants to Catholicism as was possible and to frighten the remainder into political and religious subservience. She was in line with much political thinking throughout Europe in seeing no possibility that any country might allow freedom of worship and religious tolerance. Protestant belief was seen as treachery and a threat to her political power as well as heresy and damnation for the believer. As such, it was as much up to the lay authority to enforce conformity as it was up to the bishops. In fact, some of the most zealous heresy hunters were the laity. In Kent there was Justice Draynor, or 'Justice nine holes' as he was nicknamed in *Foxe's Book of Martyrs* for his habit of spying on the congregation through holes in the rood screen to see who was paying attention in church. At St Osyth in Essex, Edmund Tyrell organised midnight raids on the houses of suspects and pressured local constables to name and pursue those who were absent from church.

At times apprehending the suspects could be difficult, but the authorities were determined to root out heresy. In Ipswich, Dr Richard Argentine noticed that one fugitive on his list, Agnes Wardell, had secretly returned to her house. He organised a posse to arrest Agnes, who escaped by hiding in a cupboard, where she almost suffocated, before escaping to a ditch full of nettles from which she was rescued by a friendly member of the town watch who coughed and distracted the guards while poor Agnes made her escape.

Not paying attention at Mass, failing to attend services at Easter or making fun of the Church were sufficient grounds for the authorities to investigate. More outspoken Protestants were hunted from parish to parish. The authorities in London, Essex and Kent were particularly zealous in hunting out heresy.

Once they had apprehended the accused, the Church authorities took time to try and persuade them of the error of their beliefs. Some bishops were more energetic than others. One was recorded as having fallen asleep during his attempt to extract a confession. However, Cardinal Pole and Bishop Bonner spent many hours arguing their cases.

If the accused was prepared to recant, this was usually taken in good faith. Many priests were ready to recant and continued to serve under Mary, as they had done under Edward VI and Henry VIII. Some were allowed to go to confession and settle the issue privately, while the more recalcitrant faced public humiliation.

It was only those who refused to recant and the hard-line opponents of the new regime who faced being burnt at the stake. Mary burnt 286 protestant heretics during her reign, which has earned her that 'Bloody Mary' epithet.

The idea of executing heretics was not, sadly, that unusual in sixteenth-century England. Edward VI and his Protestant revolutionaries had burnt Anabaptists who refused to conform. While Elizabeth did not burn any Catholics, she did have more than 200 executed through a process of being strangled, dismembered and disembowelled. But the numbers executed by Mary were large by European standards. In the late 1560,s only forty-six Protestants were burnt in Italy, thirty-eight in Spain and twenty-six in France.

The first burnings took place in 1555, when seventy-five victims were burnt. Eighty-five died in 1556, eighty-one in 1557 and less than forty in 1558. The decrease in numbers for 1558 may be an indication that the policy was working, or a sign that epidemic disease and disruption had affected the policy or that Mary had had a change of heart. The nature of burnings had certainly changed. In the early years, heretics tended to be burnt one at a time in the area where they were found. By 1557, this had turned into group burnings carried out in places that were seen as the centre of Protestant enthusiasm, like London and Colchester.

While Catholics hoped that the show of the burnings would inspire fear and prevent insurrection, they also gave the Protestants the opportunity for a show of defiance. A routine for the martyrs was quickly established. They appeared dressed in white, flowing robes, an allusion to the white-robed army of martyrs who lay under the altar in the Book of Revelation. The robes were made of thin material so that they burnt more quickly and death came sooner. Victims often kissed the stake and the faggots before prostrating themselves in prayer. The authorities made agreements with the victims not to engage in lengthy preaching before entering the flames. Somewhat surprisingly, considering that they really didn't have much to lose by that stage ('What are you going to do about it? Burn me at the stake?'), the victims seem to have honoured these agreements. John Denley, however, did manage to sing a psalm while in the midst of the flames. This annoyed one of the executioners sufficiently for him to throw a faggot at Denley's head. Supporters of the victims, however, did also use the opportunity to gather and make their views heard.

It should also be pointed out that Mary's campaign also included a determined attempt to win back hearts and minds. A Catholic message was delivered from the pulpit every Sunday, and in 1555 alone Mary had 132 Catholic books printed. These were often passed around by the bishops, with instructions to be read aloud once a week. While the scale of publication did not match the effort of the Protestants in the reign of Edward VI, it was significant.

By the time she died in 1558, after a reign of just over five years, Mary had succeeded in clearing out the older Protestant clergy in the Church, those who had been responsible for the Protestant Reformation of Henry VIII and Edward VI. She had replaced them with a younger breed of leaders who were in tune with their Counter-Reformation counterparts on the Continent. The majority of the laity had either been frightened into submission or welcomed the new certainties. Those who didn't had either fled abroad or were being hunted by zealous JPs, supported by the bishops.

How the religious future of England and Britain might have changed if she had lived longer and had children is one of those great questions to which we will never have an answer.

25

Lady Grace and a Dose of Elizabethan Medicine

Life could be tough for Tudor women, and having two women on the throne during the period made little difference. As well as the challenges of life that everyone faced in Tudor times, women had an extra burden of discrimination to suffer. The law allowed a man to beat his wife providing the stick was no thicker than his thumb, and across the border in Scotland John Knox wrote that 'woman in her greatest perfection was made to serve and obey man'.

However, some women did still exist who were able to live the lives they wanted to lead, almost in the sense that we would expect today. Lady Grace Mildmay was such a lady.

As now (but even more so then) having money helped give you more choice in life. Grace was the second daughter of Sir Henry Sharington and was born at Lacock Abbey in 1552. Sir Henry himself had been knighted by Queen Elizabeth I and became the Sheriff of Wiltshire. When Grace's eldest sister, Ursula, died, Grace became co-heir of the Sharington estate. Lucky girl.

As a child, Grace was educated by a governess, Miss Hamblyn, who was a niece of her father. Miss Hamblyn kept Grace busy and taught her writing and arithmetic, as well as needlework, drawing and music. Grace was acquiring the skills she would need to run a household but also the cultural skills regarded as desirable in a high-status female. This repertoire of skills was supplemented by a basic knowledge of Tudor medicine, which she learned from William Turnbull's *New Herbal*. She would, after all, be expected to take responsibility for the medical care of her household and provide charitable health care for the local community as well.

It would not be long before she would put her learning to use. Grace married young. She was only fifteen when she married Anthony Mildmay. Then again, he himself was only eighteen. He was the eldest son of Sir Walter Mildmay, who had been Chancellor of the Exchequer to Queen Elizabeth and founder of Emmanuel College, Cambridge. In the marriage settlement, he gave Grace an annual allowance of £1,200 and the promise that she would be well provided for on his death.

For much of their early married life, however, the couple lived apart. While Anthony carved out a career as a diplomat and soldier, Grace lived with her in-laws in Northamptonshire. He was to earn a knighthood in 1596 from Queen Elizabeth. She was able to develop a largely independent life of her own.

She was able to get on with the Mildmays and devoted her time to her music, prayer, the Bible and her medical work caring for the sick. Perhaps influenced by her Puritan upbringing, she seems to have largely avoided plays and feasts, preferring instead to spend her time in quiet contemplation, developing her skills in running a household or developing her knowledge of medicine. We are lucky that she recorded much of her thinking both on the Bible and also on medicine.

Grace kept four notebooks devoted to medicine and her meditations. One book was devoted to anatomy, one to herbs and drugs, one to recipes for medicines, and the final book contained her thoughts on medical treatment.

By Tudor times, medicine was beginning to change. Most physicians still relied on the work of Hippocrates and Galen, as they had done since Ancient Rome and Greece. Hippocrates had stated that the body was made up of four humours: blood, phlegm, black bile and yellow bile. Disease was thought to be caused by an imbalance of these humours. It was diagnosed by physicians studying their patients' urine and treatments like bleeding were recommended to restore the balance. Physicians were expected to supplement this classical explanation of disease by reference to astrology and the stars.

New ideas had, however, been generated by the Swiss doctor Paracelsus, who linked different parts of the body to different minerals. Thus the heart was linked to gold and the lungs to mercury. Diseases in these particular organs were thought to be due to an imbalance in minerals in that particular organ and the remedy was to prescribe a mineral which would restore the balance in the organ. Medical knowledge was about to be further increased by the anatomical discoveries of Vesalius and the physiological work of William Harvey on the heart. However, most physicians' knowledge was still based on ideas that had been around for over 1,000 years. This was what they paid good money to go to university to learn.

Then as now, a clear financial and social pecking order existed in medicine. Physicians were at the top of the medical tree, charging high prices for their specialist knowledge. Those who were less well off often sought help from barber-surgeons. Surgeons did not go to university and trained as apprentices to master surgeons. They were happy to drum up trade bleeding patients or using their clysters to give them enemas as well as dealing with amputations. On the next rung down were midwives. Their role was about to be taken over by men. The invention of forceps led many wealthy women to choose a male physician to deliver their baby rather than a midwife. Forceps were deemed too technical for women. At the bottom of the pile in terms of charges and Tudor social respectability were wise women and quacks. These were regarded as suitable for the poor but were regarded with disdain by the physicians at the top of the medical pecking order.

Grace and similar ladies of the gentry were, however, lucky enough not to be part of this somewhat rigid system. They were not scorned or seen as a threat by physicians as they provided their services largely free of charge. Grace's role was philanthropic. She was expected to act as a mother and carer to her household and to provide charity for the wider community.

In terms of her knowledge of anatomy, it has to be said that Grace was inevitably at a major disadvantage as only men could go to university. Without access to university she was unable to attend dissections, so she'd have to have learned anatomy from whatever books were available.

Grace's notebooks show that she used a wide range of diverse ingredients when concocting what she hoped would be remedies. Alongside a wide range of herbs, flowers and spices were animal parts such as elk hooves, crab claws and even a human skull. Following the new ideas of Paracelsus, Grace also used many minerals, including gold, lead and amber.

She even had bezoar stone, a stone-like mass which forms in the stomach or intestine of goats and other animals. This was thought to be a cure-all, but by 1575 the French Surgeon Ambroise Paré had proved that it did not work. He carried out an experiment on the royal cook, who was accused of theft. The cook was poisoned with arsenic and then given the bezoar stone, only to die in agony. Despite the painful results of this French experiment, Grace added a bezoar stone to her armoury anyway.

Whatever she was doing it all for, it wasn't for the money. Given the cost of ingredients, and the fact that she could not charge for most of her services, it is hardly surprising that even the Mildmay finances were stretched and Grace often found herself short of funds. Grace may have recouped some of the costs by selling some of her medicines, as she was known to provide medicines for other healers.

Any budding master chef would be impressed by the detailed instruction Grace gave on how to prepare her medicines. Fortunately, she kept her recipes separate from her medicine notes; this was unlike most other noblewomen providing medicines, who kept their cooking recipes and medicine recipes in the same notebook. Lady Mildmay's 'precious balm' contained 160 herbal ingredients and required ten distillations. Another balm needed to be left untouched for between six and nine months.

Though she drew the line at surgery or being a midwife,

Grace was happy to attempt to tackle a wide range of medical conditions. 'Falling sickness' or epilepsy, jaundice, gout, digestive problems, scabs, sores and ringworm are all in her records. She was also prepared to try to tackle syphilis, which was more often left to surgeons, and 'penile afflictions'. Alongside diseases which are still recognised are some others which say more about Tudor times and ideas. She was called upon to try to tackle lethargy, madness and melancholy (a disease then thought to be caused by an excess of black bile). Lady Mildmay's definition of success in dealing with these aliments was not that the patient was cured, but rather that the symptoms were alleviated. She provided a bespoke medical service and was prepared to change her approach depending on things like the age and gender of the patient.

One of the things which separated Grace from other ladies of the manor was the scale of her medical production line. She made ten-gallon batches of her 'agua vitae'. Her oil of cinnamon required five pounds of cinnamon and five gallons of wine. Her salt of pearls needed to be stored in either silver or ivory. The Mildmays were no doubt relieved when their inheritances were finally resolved and Grace could attend to her medicine without worrying about where the money was coming from.

Grace died in 1620 at the age of sixty-eight. This was a reasonable innings for a woman in Tudor times. Sadly, we will never know whether her medical skills did anything to prolong her own life, because she was too modest to record how she dealt with her own health.

26

Siege Suffering in Essex

By the time Grace died, the dramatic reign of Elizabeth I was also finished. The Tudor dynasty had ended and King James had arrived from Scotland to start the Stuart dynasty. In March 1625, James died and his son Charles took the throne. Trouble lay ahead, as king and Parliament increasingly irritated each other.

They say bad things come in threes, and the English Civil War actually comprised three separate civil wars.

The first started in January 1642, when King Charles left London after his failure to arrest his political enemies in Parliament, and ended in spring 1646 when he surrendered to the Scots. A second civil war began in 1648 as Royalist supporters in Kent, south Wales and Yorkshire, supported by the Scots, took up arms against the New Model Army; this one ended with Cromwell's victory at Preston, Sir Thomas Fairfax's victory in Colchester and the execution of Charles I in January 1649. Game over for Charles I, but this was followed by a third civil war as Charles II attempted to use the Scots to help him get Cromwell out and return the Stuarts to the throne.

We tend these days to think of the English Civil War as a series of pitched battles fought amid open fields, with cavalry streaming across them in the sunshine. Sometimes we forget quite how bitter and horrifying the war was both for combatants and civilians, and sometimes we forget that it wasn't all sunlit battlefields either. Sometimes it was brutal and cruel warfare around towns, in vicious sieges that few now remember. One such was the Siege of Colchester, which marked the end of Royalist resistance in the Second Civil War.

At the start of the Second Civil War there was a rebellion in Maidstone, Kent, where the Royalists were led by Lord Goring, Earl of Norwich. However, things quickly took a turn for the worse for the rebels as Maidstone was captured by Parliamentary general Sir Thomas Fairfax in May 1648. Lord Goring, accompanied by about 500 Royalist troops, accordingly took a turn for Essex, desperately hoping to link up with Royalist supporters in Suffolk and Norfolk. In Chelmsford they did at least manage to join up with Sir Charles Lucas, who had put himself in charge of the Essex regiment, which had also rebelled in support of the king. In total, therefore, Goring and Lucas had between them about 4,000 men. But they had little idea what to do with them. Having totally failed to capture weapons from the Parliamentary arsenal in Braintree, their next plan was to take shelter in Colchester on 12 June 1648; not a great plan as it turned out, because Sir Thomas Fairfax and about 4,000 Parliamentarians arrived outside Colchester the following day.

The attraction of Colchester to Lord Goring was obviously the Roman walls, which made it a safe haven. To the citizens of Colchester, who had supported and helped fund Parliament since 1642 and had avoided being dragged into the First Civil War, the arrival of Royalist troops held no attraction whatsoever. In fact, it was a disaster. Their houses were taken to billet the Royalist army, their food was requisitioned to feed the Royalists and their leading gentlemen were taken prisoner to ensure the good behaviour of the remainder.

Fairfax wasted no time, and his forces clashed with the Royalists outside Head Gate on 13 June. It didn't go too badly for the Parliamentary forces, who captured almost 1,000 prisoners, but, no doubt to the massive disappointment of the pro-Parliament citizens of Colchester, Fairfax's forces weren't able to force their way into the town and liberate it.

A Royalist diary, perhaps trying to make the best of a bad situation, reports a Royalist cannon as doing 'great execution'.

Fairfax didn't really have enough troops to storm the town or to mount an effective siege. Instead, he sent troops to the north of the town to stop the Royalists trying to escape in that direction and link up with Royalist forces in Suffolk and Norfolk. He sent more forces to Mersea island to stop supplies arriving by boat. Meanwhile he positioned himself firmly on the road to London and called for reinforcements. No opportunity for a bit of summer sunbathing, though; disappointing British summers aren't just a feature of modern life, and this was to be one of the worst summers recorded. Both sides settled in for a protracted, and very wet, siege. As the rain poured down, Fairfax began building a set of forts around Colchester to seal off the town and starve it into submission while Lord Goring's forces, slightly less damp because they were in the town, put their faith in a Royalist army from the north relieving the town. They should probably have put it elsewhere.

By July, Fairfax had received reinforcements and cannon from London and decided to use these to attack the home of the Lucas family, St John's Abbey. After a day-long bombardment, the house was seized in hand-to-hand fighting. The survivors withdrew to St John's Abbey gateway. A Parliamentary grenade then landed in the Royalist gunpowder store, blowing the roof off the building. Not content with that, and frustrated that there was little left to loot in St John's Abbey, Parliamentary soldiers set about exhuming the body of Sir Charles Lucas's mother, Elizabeth, and putting locks of her hair on their hats. Respecting the dead clearly wasn't high on their list of priorities.

The capture of St John's Abbey was, however, about more than a search for loot. It allowed Fairfax to set up heavy cannon on St John's Green, and he used these to destroy the cannon at St Mary-at-the-Walls that had done such damage a month earlier. Some claim that this incident is the basis of the Humpty Dumpty rhyme. The claim is that 'humpty dumpty' was a phrase of the time for overweight people and in this case was applied to the cannon placed on the walls of St Mary's. Once Fairfax's cannon had destroyed the tower of St Mary's, the cannon came tumbling down and all the king's horses and all the king's men couldn't ... etc. Whatever, the truth of the link with the nursery rhyme (and there are a number of other suggestions for its origins), the capture of St John's Abbey and the destruction of the tower of St Mary's do seem to indicate that events had turned in favour of Fairfax.

They certainly hadn't turned in favour of the Royalist troops trapped inside Colchester and their reluctant citizen hostages. For them, the situation was looking very bad. They were cut off from outside supplies, and the Royalist soldiers were dependent on eating dogs; they would save part of their bread ration in order to use it to attract dogs, which they could beat to death. A side of a small dog could be sold for 6 shillings. Civilians were even worse off, reduced to eating candles, which were made from mutton fat, and rats and mice. In their desperation, Royalist soldiers were accused of poisoning bullets by chewing the soft lead and rolling it in sand to cause horrific injuries.

By August, starving civilians gathered every night outside Lord Goring's headquarters in Colchester. The men were beaten away by the Royalist troops, but at least they refused to beat the women and children who remained on the street howling and crying for bread. Having received no help from Lord Goring or Sir Charles Lucas, the women were finally desperate enough to try to cross the frontlines and try their luck with the Parliamentary army. After all, they had sided with Parliament throughout the war. However, if they expected sympathy and food they were in for a shock. Parliamentary Colonel Rainsborough threatened to strip the women naked if they did not return to the town. The callousness and lack of compassion of Rainsborough is bad enough, but he wasn't alone. Some of his troops laughed at the humiliation of the tragic starving women, and it has been suggested that Fairfax himself much preferred to leave to the Royalists the problem of dealing with starving women and children rather than to waste his own resources helping them. The Civil War had become this cruel.

Just when the Royalists in the town were thinking that their situation couldn't get any worse, it suddenly did. On 22 August, news reached Colchester that Oliver Cromwell had defeated the Duke of Hamilton at the Battle of Preston and that consequently there was no hope of anyone relieving the siege. Fairfax, not a man to keep bad news from his enemies, rammed home the message by firing arrows into the town carrying news of Cromwell's victory at Preston.

Some Royalists had had enough by now and did desert, but some Royalists still had enough defiance, or just sheer despair, to return an arrow with a turd attached to it, bearing the message 'an answer from Colchester as you may smell'. Nevertheless, the long, bitter and brutal Siege of Colchester was almost finished. Three days later, Royalist leaders summoned their men for what was planned to be a last desperate attempt to break out and escape. But it was not to be. Ordinary soldiers and lower-ranking officers had already decided that they had suffered enough and were not going to die for a lost cause. They mutinied as they thought their senior officers were only after saving themselves and Lord Fairfax had offered the ordinary soldiers 'fair quarter'. On 28 August, after almost three months of siege, the Royalists surrendered and Fairfax entered the town.

The brutality of the siege, however, did not end there. On the very day that Fairfax entered the town, he had the two Royalist leaders, Sir Charles Lucas and George Lisle, executed outside the walls of the castle. Both had been captured in the First Civil War, Sir Charles Lucas at the Battle of Stow-on-the-Wold and George Lisle at the Siege of Farringden. Both had been released on condition that they did not fight again. The pair desperately argued that this was an entirely different civil war, bearing no similarity whatsoever to the other civil war, and therefore the promise did not count. Fairfax had little hesitation in rejecting their argument.

Lucas and Lisle were soon seen as martyrs for the Royalist cause and Lisle soon had attributed to him the dramatic last words, 'Shoot, rebels; your shot, your shame; our fall, our fame.' He is also supposed to have joked with his executioners, asking them to come closer as they had missed him from a much closer range during the siege itself.

Lord Goring was a bit luckier. In fact, a lot luckier. He was put on trial for treason and sentenced to death, but his life was spared on appeal by the Speaker's deciding vote. Another Royalist leader, Lord Capel, however, despite being granted quarter by Fairfax, was also put on trial and there was to be no reprieve for him. Lord Capel was executed, his heart was cut out and put in a silver casket and it was eventually presented to Charles II. Not the jolliest of presents.

And for the innocent citizens of Colchester who'd suffered from both sides, there was still a little more suffering to come. If they thought they were going to get compensation for being starved, shot at, humiliated and having their town turned into a battleground, they were in for a nasty surprise. Fairfax ordered them to pay a massive £14,000 (a few million in today's terms) and have the ancient walls demolished. Sir Thomas Honywood, a local man, was given this job, but, fortunately for today's lovers of Roman archaeology, he never finished it.

Some signs of the bitter eleven-week siege can still be seen in Colchester today. Sir Charles Lucas and Sir Thomas Honywood both have secondary schools named after them, and a monument in Castle Park marks the spot where Lucas and Lisle were executed. Fairfax, by contrast, has only managed to have a road named after him. The tower of St Mary's, where some claim Humpty Dumpty once stood, is made from a different material to the rest of the tower, and musket-ball holes can still be seen in places like the Siege House.

27

The Fifth Monarchy
Men Are Coming

Many people today tend to think that radical new ideas on how society should be run first became a feature of politics in the nineteenth century, or, at the very earliest, with the French and American revolutions in the late eighteenth century. What this view ignores, among other things, is that the period of the English Civil War wasn't just a period of a violent struggle for power on the battlefield. It was also a period of intense and dramatic experimentation with radical political, social and religious ideas in the middle of the seventeenth century, leading some to consider it an English revolution.

As the Parliamentary armies of Fairfax and Oliver Cromwell closed in on victory against the Royalist army of Prince Rupert in 1647, they were forced to focus on how England was to be governed after the fighting had ended.

The first group among a wide variety to challenge the established order was the Levellers. They weren't an organised political party as we would recognise today, but they were an organised group, meeting in inns around London and drawing much of their support from the New Model Army. The Levellers included Edward Sexby, 'Major' John Wildman, Colonel Thomas Rainsborough, Richard Overton, William Walwyn and John Lilburne.

Each regiment in the New Model Army elected agitators to represent them in the General Army Council. By the summer of 1647, these official agitators had been augmented by unofficial agitators from six cavalry regiments who had a more radical agenda. 'Major' John Wildman expressed their grievances in *The Case of the Army Truly Stated*. Wildman wanted MPs to understand that power lay with the people. He suggested Parliamentary elections every two years and a wider franchise. He also expected that everyone should have certain political rights and freedoms, including religious toleration. Wildman argued that everyone had these rights because God had given them reason and therefore they could make reasoned decisions about their own lives. *The Case of the Army Truly Stated* was redrafted later to become *An Agreement of the People*.

Sir Thomas Fairfax summoned the unofficial agitators and John Wildman to explain their case to the Army Council. The debates commenced at St Mary's church, Putney, and have become known as the Putney Debates. Colonel Rainsborough summed up the Levellers case thus:

> I think that the poorest he that is in England hath a life to live as the greatest he; and therefore truly, sir, I think it's clear, that every man that is to live under a government ought first, by his own consent, to put himself under that government.

Not all of these, though, were exactly peasant revolutionaries. Wildman was a lawyer by trade, and by the time he died he had become a knight with a large estate in Berkshire. Lilburne, or 'Freeborn John' as he liked to be known, was the son of a gentleman with an estate of more than 500 acres in Northumberland. They were both ambitious, made money in London from financial speculation and urged the abolition of monopolies, free trade, and the ending of all sinecures. *The Case of the Army Truly Stated* did include a demand for suffrage for all freeborn men over the age of twenty-one, but this demand was dropped from the subsequent *An Agreement of the People*. When asked during the Putney Debates whether servants, apprentices and those that 'receive alms door to door' should be included in the franchise, the Levellers said they should be excluded.

Things were not, however, to turn out great for the Levellers. Sir Thomas Fairfax and Oliver Cromwell were rather more concerned at this stage with discipline within their army than common rights. Although they listened to Rainsborough and the agitators, Cromwell took advantage of the escape of King Charles I on 11 November 1647 to reassert control. A mutiny in the army at Corkbush Field near Ware was suppressed and one soldier was shot. The Second Civil War forced the army to focus on fighting the Royalists once again. The Levellers presented *An Agreement of the People* to Parliament, where it was sidelined. In 1649, Leveller influence in the army was finally dealt with at Burford, where Cromwell hunted down 300 Levellers who were refusing to disband and shot three of their leaders.

Something of the spirit of the Levellers, however, lived on with Gerrard Winstanley and the Diggers, who called themselves the 'true Levellers'.

Gerrard Winstanley was born in Wigan in 1609 and his father worked in the wool trade. Gerrard considered himself 'unlearned', and he moved to London to become an apprentice. By 1637 he had become successful enough to be admitted to the Company of Merchant Taylors as a freeman. However, his business suffered due to the economic depression brought on by the Civil War and he moved to Walton on Thames to work as a herdsman for his in-laws. He turned against what he called 'the thieving art of buying and selling' and, while working on the land Winstanley, had a vision of how life really should be.

In January 1649 at the time that King Charles was executed, Winstanley set out his vision in a pamphlet, 'The New Law of Righteousness'. His main idea was equality. He wrote that 'in the beginning of time God made the earth. Not one word was spoken at the beginning that one branch of mankind should rule over another, but selfish imaginations did set up one man to teach and rule over another.' Elsewhere he referred to the land as a 'common treasury' for all to share. His view that private ownership had exhausted the 'common treasury' has allowed some to see the Diggers as the first Green Party.

In April 1649, helped by William Everard, he set out to make his vision reality. He took over some common land on St George's Hill in Surrey and planted it with parsnips, carrots and beans. The principle was that the community would coexist on a principle of equality and sharing. The Diggers on St George's Hill probably numbered about thirty, but they were copied by other Digger groups at Cox Hill in Kent, and Wellingborough in Northamptonshire. Local landowners were outraged. They tried to starve the Diggers out by refusing to trade with them and called on Thomas Fairfax to evict them.

Thomas Fairfax sent Captain Thomas Gladman to investigate. Gladman quickly concluded that Everard was a lunatic and the remaining Diggers were simpletons. However, he did not recognise them as Royalists or a serious threat to law and order. Everard and Winstanley were ordered to appear before Fairfax. The general was outraged that neither Digger was prepared to take off his cap to a gentleman, but was satisfied that as long as the Diggers only cultivated common land which had not been farmed, rather than private property, they were no serious threat to social order.

Local landlords were no so easily appeased, and they took the Diggers to court on a charge of trespass. The Diggers defended themselves as they were unable to pay a lawyer and the jury found against them. Unable to pay the £10 penalty or the legal costs of 29 shillings and a penny, the Diggers had their goods and equipment seized by bailiffs.

By the summer of 1650, the Digger community on St George's Hill had been dispersed. Winstanley moved to Hertfordshire, where he ended up working as a rent collector and overseer for Lady Eleanor Douglas. By the time of the Restoration in 1660, Winstanley's visions had moved on once again and he joined the Quakers.

And now we come to the Ranters. The Ranters took the opportunity of the execution of the king to pursue the issues of religious freedom and individual liberty. Abiezer Coppe claimed that he was free to 'kiss and hug ladies, and love my neighbour's wife as myself, without sin'. He also preached in the nude. His justification for his behaviour was that man was not in a position to judge what was sinful and what was not. He claimed that God was in all things and it was up to individuals rather than the established Church to decide how to behave.

The seventeenth-century press loved the Ranters as tales of their behaviour sold plenty of pamphlets. As a result, it is difficult to establish exactly what they got up to as the vast majority of the evidence comes from their press opponents. However, the fact that the Rump Parliament passed the Blasphemy Act in 1650, along with John Bunyan and Gerrard Winstanley both mentioning the Ranters, suggests that they did, in fact, have something of a significant impact on society. The Blasphemy Act made it an offence to encourage drunkenness, adultery or swearing. It became an offence to claim that Heaven and Hell were the same, to claim that there was no difference between morality and immorality or to deny the existence of God, Heaven and Hell.

Abiezer Coppe was put on trial and forced to sign a recantation before serving a short spell in prison. His fellow Ranter Jacob Bauthumley had his tongue bored for writing a blasphemous book. Ranter activity faded during the 1650s as many former Ranters became Quakers and joined the Society of Friends. However, those who upset the authorities in the 1650s might still find themselves labelled as Ranters. In 1652, the unfortunate Mary Adams of Tillingham, Essex, found herself called a Ranter. She claimed she was the Virgin Mary and had conceived a child by the Holy Spirit. The child was born severely disfigured and, in an age before social services, Mary was locked up.

Another religious group to seek inspiration from the events of 1649 were the Fifth Monarchists. They regarded 1666 as the biblical number of the beast, indicating the end of earthly rule by carnal human beings, and they wanted to be prepared. Their beliefs were drawn from the Old Testament and the book of Daniel. Nebuchadnezzar dreamt that there would be four empires, followed by the return of Jesus as king of kings. Babylonian, Persian, Greek and Roman empires had already passed, so 1666 was to be the year of the return of Jesus to rule on earth, supported by his saints.

There were, in fact, some influential leaders who held this view. Thomas Harrison and John Carew both sat as judges at the trial of Charles I and signed his death warrant. Robert Blackborne was to become Secretary of the Admiralty and later of the British East India Company. Fifth Monarchists were leading critics of the Rump Parliament, and it was Thomas Harrison's idea to introduce the Nominated Assembly (Barebones Parliament). He thought that the rule of the saints would usher in the reign of Christ on Earth. He was to be sadly disappointed.

Letters in the name of the Lord-General and the Army Council were sent to Congregational churches in every county in England to nominate those they considered fit to take part in the new government. Free elections might have produced a parliament which was more threatening to the elite, and Cromwell was keen to compromise. This assembly was known as the Barebones Parliament and ruled between the demise of the Rump Parliament and the rise of the Protectorate in 1653. It marked the high point of the Fifth Monarchy movement.

In the end, the Fifth Monarchists turned against the Protectorate of Cromwell and plotted to topple him. Plots in 1657 and 1659 were discovered and broken up. But the influence of the Fifth Monarchists continued to some extent even after the Restoration of 1660. True, Thomas Harrison was hanged, drawn and quartered for his role in signing the death warrant of Charles I, but in January 1661 Thomas Veneer and fifty followers tried to seize London in the name of 'King Jesus'. Most were killed or taken prisoner, and Veneer himself was hanged, drawn and quartered for high treason.

The only radical group from this period to survive and still exist are, of course, the Quakers. This is where some of the Diggers, who wanted equality; some of the Ranters, who felt no need for an organised Church to see the light; and some of the Levellers found succour in the 1650s as the Protectorate of Oliver Cromwell established itself.

The Quakers drew their inspiration from George Fox. Like many others in this period of civil war and evolution, Fox felt dissatisfied with the spiritual guidance of the established Church. As he searched for the inner truth, the clergy suggested both tobacco and bloodletting as possible cures for his soul. Fox thought that he needed a more personal link with his God, and in 1652 he had a vision on Pendle Hill in Lancashire. Inspired by this message from God, Fox set off to preach his message across the country.

His message was that man should live a simple life like the early disciples and that much of what the Church had developed to help worship was not necessary. He saw no need for Church services to have hymns, for the Church to collect tithes or for baptism. Indeed, he saw no need for churches, or 'steeple houses' as he called them. What was essential was for the individual to be open to the Lord's message. Inevitably, these views brought him into conflict with the authorities.

Brought before magistrate Gervase Bennet on a charge of blasphemy, Fox warned the court that they should quake and fear God's judgement. Bennet may have been responsible for naming the group Quakers. Others saw the name as coming from the habit of worshippers quaking in services when filled with the Holy Spirit.

George Fox's message was popular, and by 1660 he had attracted about 60,000 followers. While most radical groups had been born in London and spread northwards, the Quakers were a movement started in the north, spreading south. Many of the converts were women, as Fox could see no distinction between men and women in the eyes of God. As the Quaker message spread to the New World, it was particularly influential in the setting up of the states of Pennsylvania and Rhode Island. A little less than half of the Quaker preachers who left for the New World were women.

However, as membership of the movement grew, the authorities became more suspicious of Quakers. General Monck was alarmed to find evidence of Quakers in his regiment in Scotland. Quakers found themselves falsely accused of everything from witchcraft to human sacrifice. Many were attacked by mobs as they travelled and preached. The authorities could use Elizabethan vagrancy laws or the Blasphemy Act to control them. George Fox was considered such a potential threat that he was taken to London to meet Cromwell. The Lord Protector found Fox's views misguided, but he enjoyed his meeting with the Quaker leader.

Persecution of the Quakers continued after the Restoration of Charles II with the Quaker Act of 1662 and the Conventicle Act of 1664. It was not until the 1689 Act of Toleration that they were finally allowed to worship in peace.

28

The Other Commonwealth Cromwell

Oliver Cromwell, though, isn't the only Cromwell to have ruled in this island. What about Richard Cromwell? Yep, it's Oliver's successor and son.

Richard was born at Huntingdon on 4 October 1626. He was the third son of Oliver and Elizabeth Cromwell. The eldest brother, Robert, died in 1639 and Oliver junior was killed in 1644, fighting in the Civil War. By the time Oliver Cromwell became Lord Protector, he had only two surviving sons: Richard and his younger brother Henry.

Richard was educated at Felsted School in Essex, which was close to his mother's family home. No record exists of him attending university, but in 1647 he did become a member of Lincoln's Inn. He appears, however, not to have fought in any of the battles of the Civil War, although he may have served at some stage as a captain in Thomas Fairfax's lifeguards.

Oliver was a man who worried about his son, as fathers often do, and thought a good woman would steady him, as fathers sometimes do. In 1649, the year of Charles I's execution, Oliver Cromwell was involved in the blood-soaked Siege of Drogheda during his campaigning in Ireland. But for Richard, 1649 was the year that he married Dorothy Mayor, daughter of Richard Mayor, a leading member of the Hampshire gentry. Richard moved to the Mayors' estate at Hursley, where he seems to have enjoyed riding and hunting – and apparently some strenuous indoor leisure pursuits as well, because in the 1650s he had nine children. Richard also ran up large debts, which were to trouble him for the rest of his life.

At this point he was not, in his father's eyes, a huge success with a burningly bright future. Old Oliver wrote to Richard Mayor that he wanted his son to 'understand business, read a little History and study Mathematics'. Considering the influence Cromwell senior held in the country, this doesn't sound too ambitious. In this situation, it was therefore no huge surprise that it was Richard's younger brother, Henry, who was appointed to the Nominated Assembly in July 1653. However, things were about to change.

The Instrument of Government of 1653 made Oliver Cromwell Lord Protector for life. Richard Cromwell now found himself referred to as 'Lord Richard' or, as a joke, 'Prince Richard'. Joke or not, father finally began to prepare Richard for a serious role in public life, and the positions he encouraged Richard to take were modelled on the steps Oliver had taken in his own career. It had not served Cromwell senior so badly, after all.

Richard moved up from sitting as an occasional magistrate in Hampshire to being elected MP for Hampshire in the First Protectorate Parliament. He was appointed to the Committee of Trade and Navigation in November 1655. In the Second Protectorate Parliament in 1656 he became the MP for Cambridge University, and in the following year he succeeded his father as Chancellor of Oxford University. Thus both universities were represented by someone whose own university career is unrecorded. Interesting.

And Richard Cromwell's status as heir apparent to the Protectorate was strengthened by the so-called Humble Petition and Advice of 1657. This was an attempt to provide some form of written constitution and it gave Oliver Cromwell the right to name his successor. Richard accompanied his father in the state coach when Oliver was installed as Lord Protector for a second time. Richard was appointed to the Council of State in December 1657 and also sat in the newly reconstituted Upper Chamber – a pretty rapid promotion for a man who had only first become an MP in 1654.

Oliver Cromwell also started to fill in the gaps in his son's military curriculum vitae. In January 1658 he became honorary colonel of a cavalry regiment and in May 1658 a new warship was named the *Richard* in his honour. Always fun to have a warship named after you. Although not exactly the sexiest warship name ever for anybody serving on board.

Things were looking bright for Richard on the career front, and when Oliver Cromwell finally died, on 3 September 1658, Richard was immediately appointed as his successor. There is no written record of Oliver Cromwell formally nominating his son as his successor. John Thurloe suggests that the nomination was done orally, shortly before his father's death. Some unkind sources even suggest that Cromwell senior preferred his son-in-law Charles Fleetwood to his own son. Whatever the truth of these rumours, it was Richard who did actually emerge as the new Lord Protector.

The initial transfer went smoothly. Very smoothly. It was commented that 'there is not a dog that wags his tongue, so great a calm are we in'. The calm was, however, not to last long. And dogs' tongues probably started wagging again pretty fast, as well.

The trouble was that, along with his job, Richard had inherited some serious problems from his father. The government, for instance, was deeply in debt. It owed £2 million (when £2 million was a big, massive, huge amount of money) and army pay was in arrears (never a good situation). In order to clear the debt he would have to call Parliament, but in Parliament he would find that the country was still deeply divided. There were Republicans and there were also Royalists. There was no agreement on how the country should be governed. And the Protectorate itself was unpopular. It had not exactly helped itself on this front when, in 1655 under the major-generals, it had banned horse racing, stage plays, cockfighting and bear-baiting in an attempt to maintain the moral order.

Big problems, and Richard didn't have much in the way of big solutions. He hadn't even, for instance, managed to deal with his own private debts, which didn't inspire huge confidence in his ability to deal with the national debt. What's more, the New Model Army didn't trust him because he hadn't served in the Civil War and had no military experience. They wanted their pay and did not feel like waiting any longer. The godly, too, looked at Richard's private life, and many were disappointed that he did not match up to his father. And, of course, in dealing with politics and Parliament he ultimately had little experience. It looked like things could only improve. Unfortunately, they didn't.

The Council of State was divided between military and civilian factions. The military faction was headed by Charles Fleetwood and John Disbrowe, while John Thurloe was the most prominent civilian.

Charles Fleetwood, unlike Richard, actually had had a distinguished military career. He had fought at Naseby and at the Siege of Oxford. He had served as commander-in-chief in Ireland and he had also served as one of Cromwell's major-generals. He had also married Oliver Cromwell's daughter Bridget after the death of her first husband, Henry Ireton. Although he offered his support to Richard Cromwell, he was disappointed when Richard passed him over for Commander-in-Chief of the Army and took the role himself. He accepted the rank of lieutenant-general, but his house became a base for plots against Richard. It's tough when even people in your brother-in-law's house are out to get you.

And it's also pretty bad when your uncle hates you. Because John Disbrowe also disliked Richard, and he had been married to Oliver Cromwell's sister Jane (although she had died in 1656). Disbrowe, too, had fought with honour at Naseby and Langport, as well as joining Cromwell in the Siege of Oxford and Fairfax at the Siege of Colchester. He was the major-general given control of the West Country and was seen by many as a role model.

However, for support against the army grandees, Richard

could at least look for support from John Thurloe, his father's spymaster.

Richard met with the army grandees and tried to win them over. Although he kept the role of commander-in-chief for himself, he did promise to sort out pay arrears as soon as he could. On the surface, it began to look as though the army might be prepared to accept their new commander.

However, to raise the money needed to settle the arrears, Richard had to call the Third Protectorate Parliament. His opening speech went down well and the Parliament confirmed him in his post as Lord Protector. However, behind the scenes, the army grandees were worried that Parliament might choose to balance the books by cutting army pay rather than by increasing taxes to settle the arrears. Austerity, eh?

The mood was also somewhat affected by the impeachment of Major-General William Boteler. Boteler had been major-general for Northamptonshire under the rule of the major-generals and he had been zealous in dealing with both suspected Catholics and Quakers. He suggested there was biblical authority for stoning to death the Quaker preacher James Nayler and he had imprisoned the Earl of Northampton for failing to pay his taxes (considering what Boteler was contemplating for Nayler, the earl might have thought he'd got off somewhat lightly).

And the tension was about to get a whole lot worse. Parliament chose to debate the reorganisation of the New Model Army and the formation of a new militia. On 18 April 1659 they went further and suggested that the army could not meet without the explicit permission of the Lord Protector and Parliament.

Oops. A victorious army that had just gone through a brutal civil war wasn't about to take that lying down. Lieutenant-General Fleetwood and Disbrowe demanded that the Lord Protector dissolve Parliament. Richard refused.

The standoff was not, however, to last long. Fleetwood and the army grandees ordered the army to assemble at St James's. The army's commander-in-chief, the Lord Protector, ordered the army to meet in Whitehall instead. It was a simple choice for the soldiers. They gathered at St James's with their officers.

Richard Cromwell did not have the stomach for a fight. When John Disbrowe visited him on 21 April and asked him to dissolve Parliament and put himself under the protection of the army, Richard agreed. The following day, Parliament was dissolved and the army's Council of Officers was left in control of the government.

Fleetwood and Disbrowe intended to keep the Protectorate under army control, but pressure from junior officers and republicans forced them to recall the Rump Parliament. Richard did little to maintain his position. Although under army control at Whitehall, he could have given a lead to army regiments in Scotland or to his brother in Ireland. When the Rump Parliament met in May 1659 and voted to end the Protectorate, Richard wrote his resignation.

He stayed in Whitehall until the summer of 1659, before the Rump insisted that he return to his estates in Hursley. As part of the deal for going quietly, the Rump offered to settle Richard's debts and provide him with a pension. They then reneged on their promises.

In 1660, as the country prepared for the return of King Charles II, orchestrated by the army in Scotland under General Monck, Richard Cromwell left his wife and went into exile abroad. Some Royalists regarded him as a threat and enjoyed referring to him as 'Tumbledown Dick' or Queen Dick. He in fact seems to have had no interest in a political return and to have lived under an assumed name instead. He appears to have returned to the country in 1680 and lived quietly at Cheshunt in Hertfordshire until his death in 1712. Somehow, you sense it didn't quite turn out how old Oliver Cromwell envisaged it. Not at all.

29

Women Take Control of the Canvas

The seventeenth century wasn't just a time of intense political change in the country, though. The period saw dramatic cultural experimentation, too, and it wasn't just men who were making the running in the big picture. And the same is true of smaller pictures, as well.

In the early seventeenth century, painting in Britain was regarded as a male occupation. There had been women painters, in particular Levina Teerlinc, a Flemish miniaturist active in the courts of Henry VIII and his children, and Esther Inglis or Kello, a Scottish miniaturist and calligrapher. However, in the space of a few decades in the mid-seventeenth century, three remarkable women were to be active on the English art scene. They would not end the practice of painting being an overwhelmingly male profession, but they would signal changes to come, both in painting and in other spheres, and one of them in particular has left a legacy for British art that is still very much alive today.

Around 1606, during the reign of James I, one William Palmer, an official of the royal parks, and his wife, Mary, had a little baby girl named Joan. In 1626, she married a certain Lodowick Carlile or Carlell, of Scottish descent. For some reason he tends to be now known as Carlell and she tends to be known as Carlile, though one imagines that they bore the same surname in life. Lodowick would also become a keeper of Richmond Park, but perhaps more significantly he was also Gentleman of the Bows to Charles I and a poet and court dramatist. His plays apparently include some notable forest scenes (perhaps due to all that time spent in the park). However, it turned out that he was not the only one in the marriage with major artistic talent for Joan soon acquired for herself a reputation as a painter, gaining the attention of King Charles I himself. The king is said to have at one stage given Joan and Sir Anthony Van Dyck ultramarine costing more than £500. Impressive. No wonder the Stuarts ran out of money.

She copied Italian paintings and painted individual and group portraits. One of the portraits attributed to her, that of Thomas and Lady Browne, can now be seen in the National Portrait Gallery. Some rather intriguing titles are also mentioned in her will, like 'the Princesse in white sattin' and 'the little St Katherine and the Mercury'.

For a long time, the couple lived at Petersham, Richmond (handy for Richmond Park), but in 1654 they moved to Covent Garden in London, which already had a reputation as a place of the arts, and where Joan no doubt hoped her talents would flourish. If so, things don't quite seem to have gone to plan, because two years later they returned to Petersham. Lodowick finally died in 1675, and Joan died in 1679. They are buried next to each other in Petersham churchyard.

While Joan was growing up in England, far away in Italy another woman was developing spectacular painting skills of her own. Artemisia Gentileschi was the daughter of established artist Orazio Gentileschi. She is by far the best known of these three women. Her sometimes tragic life – including her ordeal during the trial of Agostino Tassi for raping her – and her dramatic, spectacular, sometimes violent paintings have made her famous. Less well known, though, is her connection to Britain. Her father, Orazio, was made court painter by Charles I and in 1638 Artemisia joined him in London. Sadly, Orazio died in 1639 and it is not thought that Artemisia stayed long in England after that. However, still in the Royal Collection today is a superb painting by Artemisia that may have been painted during her stay here. It is the so-called *Self-Portrait as the Allegory of Painting*. It seems a powerful statement of the right of women artists of the seventeenth century to be what they wanted, to paint what they wanted.

Mary Beale was born Mary Craddock at Barrow rectory in Suffolk in 1633, when Artemisia Gentileschi was already a painting star. Her father was the Revd John Cradock. He was a puritan but he was also a painter himself, and it is thought that he introduced his little daughter to the art.

In 1652, at the age of just eighteen, she married a young man from another puritan family, one Charles Beale, whose family came from Walton Manor in Buckinghamshire. But while their families might come from the countryside, Mary and Charles were definitely intent on the bright lights of central London. They settled in Covent Garden like Joan Carlile, but, unlike Joan, who soon returned to Petersham, Mary Beale was to have a much longer and intimate association with central London. In about 1660, the couple moved Hind Court, Fleet Street.

Mary rapidly acquired for herself quite a reputation as a painter and she seems to have taken influences from other well-known painters of the time, such as Robert Walker and Thomas Flatman. By 1664, however, Charles had run into problems on the employment front and he and Mary and their children retreated to Albrook, Otterbourne, Hampshire, for a few years. As it turns out, it was not a bad choice to be absent from London for a few years. Not a bad choice at all. The Great Plague hit in 1665, and that was followed up in 1666, of course, by the Great Fire of London. Not only did they miss being in London during these catastrophes, but Mary took the opportunity to do some writing as well. Mary would never have the flamboyance of someone like Artemisia Gentileschi, but she was clearly a woman capable of creating her own vision of the future and then implementing it. Her 'Essay on Friendship' stresses the advantages of equality between women and men. She painted many self-portraits, including one now in the National Portrait Gallery, a self-portrait from about 1665. She shows herself looking firmly at the viewer, one hand resting on an unfinished painting, her palette hanging on the wall behind her. While it cannot match the power and drama of Gentileschi's self-portrait, it does show a firm self-confidence and sense of who she is and what she has achieved.

When Mary and Charles returned to London, she set up her own studio in their house in Pall Mall and soon became a successful professional artist, with a wide range of clients keen to have her paint their portraits. Charles spent time preparing colours for her and dealing with commissions and payments and bookkeeping and she also took on and trained female studio assistants. At her height she was earning hundreds of pounds a year, when hundreds was big money.

Court painter Peter Lely visited her and became a big fan of her painting, as she became of his. She eventually died in 1699, and is buried at St James's Piccadilly. Charles outlived her, scraping into the eighteenth century and dying in 1705. One her sons, another Charles Beale, himself became a painter.

Mary Beale wasn't the first English woman artist and she wasn't the only one painting at the time, but both in her art and in her life she was something of a trailblazer and she has left an inspiring legacy and fascinating collection of work, one that is still relevant and can still be enjoyed today.

30

Companies Take Over the World

Big, bold moves had also been taking place on the economic front in the Britain of the sixteenth and seventeenth centuries, moves that would help expand English influence around the globe and lay the foundations for the British Empire itself.

These days we take companies for granted. We take it for granted that legally regulated commercial bodies carry out a vast range of activities which make the societies we live in possible. A lot of small businesses are, of course, still owned by individual people, often the people who run them. However, we take it for granted that large companies capable of dealing with the commercial demands of a complex, global society are in a position to attract financial resources. These can represent vast amounts of money from large numbers of outsiders who often have little to do with the day-to-day running of the company. We take the financial and commercial advantages that the system offers so much for granted that it is easy to forget that the world was once very different.

Britain can't claim to have invented the basic idea of a number of people sharing the risks of commercial ventures and the subsequent profits. Teamwork has, of course, been around pretty much as long as human beings themselves, and along with complex civilisations, commercial demands and money came commercial teamwork. Under the Roman Empire, for instance, groups of *publicani* would pay the taxes for a particular area and then seek to recoup their expense (often at a vast profit, and with rather unscrupulous methods) from the locals. This system of tax farming became widely used across Europe. The Middle Ages saw the development of a number of forms of shared commercial activity. For instance, guilds, cities and the Church all produced different forms of shared commercial activity. The cost of building a ship might be shared out among different individuals, and a range of ventures rather more similar to what we might call companies were also operating.

Perhaps one of the earliest examples of what we might recognise as something like a modern joint-stock company was the Société des Moulins du Bazacle, the Society of Bazacle Mills. A structure was built in and along the River Garonne to take advantage of the power of the water for watermills. The society was formed sometime around 1250, starting with ninety-three shares, in order to finance the mills. Shares in this society could be traded on the open market in Toulouse and their value fluctuated along with the value of the mills and their output. In Sweden, as early as 1288, it is recorded that the Bishop of Västerås had a 12.5 per cent share in the Swedish mining company of Stora Kopparberg.

However, it was the sixteenth and seventeenth centuries in England that were to see a transformation in commercial companies that would help change not just Britain but much of the world as well.

Some of these early English companies were, like Stora Kopparberg, involved with mining. In 1568, Queen Elizabeth I incorporated by royal charter two companies linked with mines: the Company of Mineral and Battery Works and the Company of Mines Royal. Both companies were allotted monopolies in assorted mining and metalwork areas. It is interesting to see that Sir William Cecil, Elizabeth's chief political advisor, happened to be a shareholder in both companies.

However, it was in the area of foreign trade and exploration that English companies of the period were perhaps to have the most long-lasting impact.

In 1551, the Mystery, Company and Fellowship of Merchant Adventurers for the Discovery of Regions, Dominions, Islands, and Places Unknown was formed. It's not the briefest of company names, but at least it's pretty descriptive of the aims of the new company. One of the founders was the famous explorer Sebastian Cabot, and 240 'adventurers' or shareholders chipped in £25 each, a lot of money in those days. The company, however, didn't get off to a great start. Three ships set off to find a new route to China by travelling north to Scandinavia, then around the North Cape and heading east. We, with our knowledge of what exactly is up there, can now see that this could be a problem. And indeed, the crews of two of the ships sadly perished without achieving anything much.

However, one of the ships was a lot more fortunate. Richard Chancellor's crew put into shore and Chancellor travelled overland to Moscow, where he met Czar Ivan the Terrible. Now, obviously Ivan the Terrible is something of a controversial character, but Chancellor emerged from the encounter with a letter to the King of England inviting trade between the two nations. Very sensibly, the Mystery, Company, and Fellowship of Merchant Adventurers for the Discovery of Regions, Dominions, Islands, and Places Unknown decided to focus a lot of its efforts on this Region, Dominion and Place Known, and this led to the creation of the Muscovy or Russia Company.

The Levant or Turkey Company, founded in 1581, was also aimed at Regions, Dominions and Places Known. It set up factories (trading centres) in a variety of locations, including Aleppo, Istanbul, Alexandria and Smyrna/Izmir. The Venice Company of 1583 was also very much in known territory.

However, other companies were also being formed that would send English explorers and traders around the world to areas little known to England at that stage – areas that, by the middle of the eighteenth century, would form the core of the emerging British Empire.

The East India Company was established in 1600, with

an initial fifteen-year monopoly on trade east of the Cape of Good Hope and west of the Straits of Magellan. Elizabeth I was herself a shareholder and the East India Company was in the vanguard of adopting limited liability. In 1601, Sir James Lancaster set off on the first East India Company mission. The company soon set up a number of trading posts, including Surat (1613), Fort St George at Madras (1639) and Bombay/ Mumbai (1668). It wasn't just India itself that the company was interested in; one of its earliest trading posts was at Banten in Java. Pretty much from the start, the East India Company showed that it was capable of the kind of mix of commercial and military action that was to become such a characteristic of building the British Empire. For instance, at the Battle of Swally in 1612, company forces defeated Portuguese competitors.

While the East India Company was developing its operations in the east, on the other side of the Atlantic, in the west, other English companies had been hard at work as well. They wouldn't all find the commercial success of the East India Company, but they did lay jointly the foundations of British rule in that part of North America.

In the early seventeenth century, the Virginia Company of London and the Virginia Company of Plymouth set off to colonise the New World. The Plymouth Company was allotted land further north and had a tough time of it. For instance, its Popham Colony only lasted about a year. The Virginia Company of London was given territory further south. It, too, had a tough time, but despite a range of problems and an often financially precarious situation it did manage to establish a permanent English presence in America, and when the company reached a final crisis point in 1624, James I stepped in and made Virginia a royal colony instead.

The Hudson's Bay Company was formed in 1670 and, far to the north, it would spread English and British influence across vast territories and go on to be a major commercial success. Many more English and British companies would eventually become key components in spreading British influence and Western commercial models around the world.

31

An Elephant on the Thames

We're all used to worrying about global warming these days, but for big chunks of Britain's history its inhabitants had a very different problem to worry about.

The historical record for London and the River Thames seems to suggest that there was a mini Ice Age here between 1150 and 1460 and a further very cold spell between 1560 and 1850. Average temperatures were certainly much colder than they are today. It was during this period that the Thames regularly froze. It gave rise to the so-called frost fairs and strange phenomena such as elephants walking across the ice in the middle of London. Impressive.

The Thames had frozen before this. For instance, some record survives of a big freeze in 695 and suggestions of a market being held on the ice. Again, in 1092, during the reign of William the Conqueror's son William Rufus, the chroniclers recorded that 'the great streams [of England] were congealed in such a manner that they could draw two hundred horsemen and carriages over them'. In 1282, the frosts were so harsh and there was so much ice that parts of London Bridge were destroyed and had to be rebuilt.

Henry VIII and his third wife, Jane Seymour, are supposed to have crossed the river on horseback at Greenwich. It must have been very cold, and the ice very thick, to support the king and his retinue. A further freeze took place in 1564, and here the first reports of football being played on the river appear. Queen Elizabeth instructed archery butts to be set up on the river and she is supposed to have used them for her own archery practice. She was apparently a mean shot with the crossbow.

So, a spectacular sight; but how did you record it in the days before cameras and mobile phones? In 1677, a Dutchman, Abraham Hondius, produced a large painting of the scene. The river was sufficiently frozen to have icebergs, which appear to be at least six feet high, floating on the frozen river downstream from London Bridge. The frosts of 1677 must have been spectacularly severe, freezing the Thames several feet deep, for the ebb and flow of tides below London Bridge to create the icebergs. There may be an element of artistic licence in painting the icebergs higher than the figures on the river, but it's very jolly nevertheless.

The watermen, the boat owners who provided a water taxi service across the Thames, were obviously having a rather more difficult time than usual on that front, but instead they made money by charging those who ventured down onto the ice sixpence to use the steps to get down to the river level. Their compatriots on the opposite bank then charged a further sixpence to enable the adventurous to exit the ice. Londoners took to the ice for the excitement of exploring this strange phenomenon and they were often accompanied by their dogs.

The Dutch seem to have played a key part in this early exploration of the river. Early skaters on the ice had Dutch skates of bone to help them and the spectators wore Dutch hats. The Dutch knew about ice, and, judging by the number of medals they get in Winter Olympics speed skating, they still do.

In 1677, we have no evidence of tents or inns actually on the river. Alcoholic refreshment was instead provided by inns overlooking the Thames, the drinks delivered by serving girls who carried them on serving trays on their heads.

Eight years later, however, the Thames froze over again. It froze from mid-December 1683 to mid-February 1684. This time the action was focused on the area upriver from London

Bridge. The old London Bridge was a huge wooden structure that had nineteen arches and rested on twenty small islands, known as 'Starlings', built upon the riverbed. This reduced the flow of water down the river and acted as a large weir. The slow-moving water froze more easily and handily produced a smoother surface that was more suitable for organising fairs. Not so many problems with massive icebergs this time.

In 1684, the watermen set up a series of tents on the river stretching from Temple Stairs on the North Bank to the South Bank. Some of them still managed to use their boats to ferry passengers along the ice; this time the boats were either dragged by willing watermen or by horses.

The frozen river provided the setting for assorted fun and games. Some played football, although it is not clear how they kept on their feet; no doubt plenty of sliding tackles took place. Crowds gathered to watch the Dutchmen perform tricks on their skates (those Dutch again). Others went nine-pin bowling or gathered to watch bull-baiting. Some, including King Charles II, took to the ice on horseback to hunt foxes. A few even tried to brave the ice on stilts. In the winter of 1683/84, the river had become a giant playground for Londoners. Almost like the Winter Olympics, but sadly with no Torvill and Dean.

To sustain all this activity Londoners could partake of a wide variety of meat and drink, including roast ox. To wash it down, revellers were offered 'beer, or ale or brandy'. Refreshments were clearly an important element of all frost fairs.

The city must have had confidence in the strength of the ice. The 1684 frost fair saw an early form of roundabout known as 'a whirling sledge'. Another hi-tech exhibit was a primitive form of clockwork car. It relied on the slipperiness of the ice to make progress. Even the royal army took to the ice either to train or to fire a ceremonial salute from several cannon.

The most famous visitor to the fair was, of course, the king, Charles II. He was accompanied by his queen, Katherine, and their son James, Duke of York (later James II), and their daughter Princess Anne (later Queen Anne). Their visit is recorded on a souvenir card printed by G. Groom. Many of the tents constructed by the watermen were given over to printers, who used them to produce either engravings or souvenirs which were literally printed in presses set up on the ice.

In 1715, the Thames froze again between December 1715 and January 1716 and it became the centre for an even larger frost fair. The live entertainment was provided by 'Will Ellis the Poet and his wife Bess', who were 'Rhiming on the Hard Frost'. Elsewhere, a stage had been set up and the performance attracted a large crowd of men and women. The ox was roasted by a Mr Atkins and Mr Hodgson, who claimed to be the descendant of the gentleman who had roasted the ox in 1684 – a proud boast indeed. The same family was to go on to serve ox on the frozen river in the following frost fair of 1739. The meat was washed down with goodly quantities of ale and gin.

Among the celebrity visitors to the fair this time was the Prince of Wales (later to become George II). The engravings of the fair suggest that visitors wore standard Georgian fashion (no anoraks or salopettes) and there seem to have been few concessions to the practicalities of getting about on the ice. Once again, printing presses, both simple flatbed ones and the more complex rolling press, were on hand to provide souvenirs of the experience.

By 1739, work had begun on a new bridge at Westminster. The piers for the bridge had been completed and these provided good viewpoints for seeing all the action on the ice. The piers were sufficiently high that ladders and ropes were required to scale them. At this end of the river the primary attractions appeared to be drinking in the many taverns established on the ice, while watching others slide, fall and crawl around en route to the taverns and presumably even more so on the return journey.

However, further downriver and close to London Bridge the river had taken on the look of a shopping centre. Goldsmiths, milliners, wood turners and toy shops could all be found flogging their wares on the river. Even gambling tables were set up for those who fancied a flutter on the ice. The novelty attraction for children and adventurous adults was a primitive carousel ride. This was a development of the simple roundabout first seen in 1684.

One VIP visitor on this occasion was the artist William Hogarth, who had a souvenir card printed in honour of his pet dog, Trump. It was made on the ice at Whitehall on 16 February 1740.

In the winter of 1788/89, the river eventually froze from Putney down to Rotherhithe. This was the only time that it was sufficiently cold to freeze the river downstream of London Bridge. The river remained frozen through both December and January. Some will argue that there was an obvious causal link between this extremely harsh winter and the revolution which was to begin a few months later in Paris as the starving peasants rose to support rebellion. In France the weather may have caused a revolution, but here it caused another fair.

The final frost fair took place in 1814, when the river froze for a single week between 29 January and 5 February. By this time London Bridge had been standing for 600 years and was in danger of collapsing. As a precautionary measure, the government had taken down all the houses and shops on the bridge and widened it a little. It provided a good vantage point for spectators.

The young artist George Cruikshank provided an illustration of the fun and games to be enjoyed on the river that week. He pictured a disabled man with a peg leg discovering that the ice was not sufficiently thick to support his weight. Cruikshank showed a rather rotund lady falling flat on her backside while grabbing the wig of a nearby gentleman in an attempt to save herself. In a nearby tavern he drew one young couple courting, while behind them another couple are squaring up for a fight. The woman is threatening to beat her partner over the head with a bottle, while he has grabbed a set of bellows to retaliate. Once again, for the week of the frost fair it seems that the river became a centre for drunken revelry.

The fair took place at the height of the Napoleonic Wars and some of the taverns on the ice had very appropriate names. One tavern advertised 'Good Ale' and was called the 'Wellington for ever', while another, which claimed to serve 'Fine Furl, Good Gin and Rum', was named 'the City of Moscow', evoking Napoleon's retreat from Moscow in 1812. Another stall was called the 'Orange Boven' or the 'the Orange are on top'. This was a reference to the French retreat from the Orange forces of the Dutch in Holland.

In terms of fairground attractions, there were two swing boats. However, the highlight of the fair must have been the elephant that was brought down to walk on the ice.

The longest queues on the ice were not for refreshments but for printed souvenirs. Three presses were moved on to the ice: the 'Frost Fair Printing Office', the 'Letter Printing Press' and 'Copper Plate Printing'. Well, if you couldn't take a selfie on your mobile phone you had to make the best of what you had.

Scotch Whisky, Distillation of a Nation

In 1688, James II, Charles II's brother, was forced from power and replaced by William of Orange and his wife, James II's daughter Mary. Yes, daughter and son-in-law replaced the father. James did not, however, give up immediately on the dream of power. The defeat of his army at the Battle of the Boyne in Ireland in 1690 was a crushing blow to those hopes. Nevertheless, some retained the idea of placing James or one of his line on the throne. Thus was born the Jacobite cause.

Soon the Hanoverians would arrive on the scene. And soon battle would be joined in Scotland, not just over the Jacobite cause but also over an element of Scottish culture and history that has lasted rather more strongly – whisky.

The first written record of whisky in Scotland is not until 1494. The first written record in Ireland is slightly earlier, in 1405. There seem to be two possibilities for the origin of whisky. One is that it was brought to Scotland through monks and the Christian Church. This would provide a link with the earliest records of distillation, which started in the Middle East. The second is that whisky distilling was an independent discovery made by 'Celts and Gaels' at some point before 1494.

The word itself is an abbreviation of the Gaelic *Uisge beatha*, meaning lively water or water of life. This is a Gaelic translation of the Latin aqua vitae, which is used to describe a variety of spirits distilled by Christian monks for medicinal purposes. Those favouring a purely Gaelic origin for the spirit see it as having been produced by Gaelic farmers looking to find a use for excess barley.

While the name is Gaelic, it seems likely that the process of distillation originated from the Middle East. Distillation is first recorded in the second millennium BC by the Babylonians. By the third century AD, it had spread to the Greeks at Alexandria. From Alexandria the practice was adopted by the medieval Arab world in the ninth century, before being transferred from the Arabs to the medieval Christians in the twelfth century. All this early work was based on the development of perfumes rather than alcohol. It was in thirteenth-century Italy that the first records appear of wine being distilled. It was through the monasteries that the process of distillation to produce alcohol was spread throughout Europe. Medieval monks took their medical duties seriously, and distilled liquors known as aqua vitae were, perhaps not surprisingly, popular with patients.

After 1494, the development of whisky production and drinking reaches more secure historical ground. The Royal Exchequer Roll for 1494 recorded the sale of 'eight bolls of malt to a Friar John Corr wherewith to make aqua vitae'. This is the proof of the monastic link with alcohol production in Scotland. The scale of production, with eight bolls amounting to over 1,000 kilograms of malt and being sufficient to make about 1,500 bottles of aqua vitae, suggests that Friar Corr's aqua vitae may have been for social as well as medicinal purposes. Either that, or he had a *lot* of patients.

The medicinal reputation of aqua vitae remained strong. When James IV required aqua vitae in 1494, it was supplied by barber-surgeons. This is the first of several references in the accounts of James IV that suggest he had a penchant for aqua vitae. In 1505, the Guild of Barber-Surgeons in Edinburgh was granted a monopoly on the production of aqua vitae within the city.

The production of aqua vitae also became an important part of the farming economy in the Highlands. The summers could be used to grow the barley and the winters to distil the liquor. It provided a cash crop for farmers and could be used to pay the rent or settle debts. The scale of production must have been substantial, as in 1555 the Scottish Parliament responded to a poor harvest by forbidding farmers to use barley to brew aqua vitae rather than using it to make bread.

By the seventeenth century, it is clear that aqua vitae had moved beyond being considered just a medicine. In 1618, it is recorded as being consumed at the funeral of the Highland chief John Taylor. In 1644, too, the Scottish Parliament realised the moneymaking potential of aqua vitae and placed a duty on the spirit in order to raise funds. Obviously, this was not quite the last time governments in this land sought to make money from drinkers.

The Act of Union of 1707 produced much closer links between England and Scotland. As the Hanoverians sought to extend their political control to all areas of Scotland and wipe out the Stuart legacy, they also sought to turn the whisky industry into a profitable, taxpaying legal business. There was a certain common purpose between the Hanoverian campaigns against the Jacobites and those against illegal distillers. This was not least because they both shared a common base in the Highlands of Scotland.

In 1690, the first commercial distilleries had been established in Scotland. This was an important landmark as the eighteenth and first part of the nineteenth century were to be dominated by fierce competition between those distillers who wished to do legal business and were prepared to pay the excise duty demanded by the Revenue and illegal distillers who saw there was more money to be made from ignoring the Revenue and trading illegally.

In 1713, the government tried to introduce a new tax on malt into Scotland. To the government it was a simple act of standardising taxes and dealing with the Scots the same as the English. However, not everybody saw it in quite that light. In fact, the move resulted in a riot in Glasgow which destroyed the home of Daniel Campbell and killed eleven people living with him. However, the compensation he received, £9,000, was sufficient to buy the Isle of Islay. Handy.

In 1715, a Jacobite rebellion in favour of James II's son James Francis Edward Stuart (or the 'Old Pretender') erupted in Scotland. It even received some support from English Jacobites as well. A combined force of Scottish and English Jacobites was, however, defeated at the Battle of Preston, and the rebellion finally collapsed early in 1716. In 1745, of course, the Jacobites tried again, this time with James's son Charles Edward Stuart (the 'Young Pretender'). Again, despite some early successes and some sympathy from English Jacobites, the rebellion eventually collapsed after defeat at the Battle of Culloden.

As the century wore on, the government increased excise duty. As the government raised the duties, distillers who were prepared to pay the duty struggled while there was a larger market share for those prepared to flout the law. Legal distillers like Gilcomstan in Aberdeen were forced to close. By 1777, Edinburgh had twelve legal whisky producers but an alleged 400 illegal stills. It is estimated that more than half the whisky consumed at this time was produced illegally. Government attempts to control the whisky trade through excise duty had descended into chaos by the beginning of the nineteenth century.

Other government action also had unintended consequences. The Gin Act of 1736, which was intended to reduce alcoholism and dependence on gin south of the border, increased the production of whisky north of the border. Between 1708 and 1736, whisky production rose from 100,000 gallons per year to 250,000 gallons. While the extra production was intended for sale south of the border, it was in fact consumed in Scotland.

The military roads built by General Wade to campaign against the Jacobites and keep the Highlands under control proved essential to smugglers producing whisky in the Highlands and wishing to take it to markets in the lowlands.

To encourage illegal distillers to give up their stills, the government introduced a reward of £5 for anyone prepared to hand over their equipment. Enterprising entrepreneurs, however, then proceeded to hand over worn-out stills to the government and used the £5 reward to invest in newer and better equipment.

Throughout the eighteenth century and into the nineteenth century, illegal producers of whisky fought a battle with excise officers. To farmers in the Highlands, whisky was a route to making their meagre crops of barley more profitable. This was the time of the clearances, when many farmers faced being driven off their land in order to give it over to sheep farming. The Highland farmers needed all the help they could get, and in the battle with the excisemen they got plenty of help.

Some ministers of the Church saw no sin in hiding illegal whisky in their pulpits or allowing coffins to be used to hide the contraband. Women filled pigs' bladders with whisky and hid them under their skirts. Wives warned their husbands that the excisemen were approaching by hanging out the washing. Local JPs were reluctant to punish the lawbreakers. As landowners, they realised that, if they wanted their tenants to pay their rents, the illegal trade needed to continue.

The excise officers were known as 'gaugers'. One Malcolm Gillespie of Skene impounded thousands of gallons of whisky and seized hundreds of stills. Gillespie trained his dogs to attack the ponies carrying the whisky by biting their noses. He suffered forty-two wounds while serving as an excise officer, and was left close to death on several occasions.

Emergencies abroad, such as the revolutions in America and France, saw the raising of excise duty rates. War, as always, was a major governmental expense. One of its weapons was to increase excise duty. In 1793, duty stood at £9 per gallon. By 1803, it was £162 per gallon. Ouch.

Ultimately, though, the government was engaged in an unwinnable battle against the illegal producers of whisky. In 1823 the Duke of Gordon, on whose estates some of the finest illegal whisky was produced, suggested that the government change tack and make it easier to make a profit from the legal production of whisky. The 1823 Excise Act suggested an annual licence fee of £163 and a small levy per gallon of proof spirit produced.

This solved the log jam, and within ten years many illegal whisky producers had decided that the future lay in legal production. Many new and legal distilleries were built on the site of old illegal stills. Some illegal stills continued up to the start of the twentieth century, but the new rules had created the basis of a profitable industry. Cheers.

33

A Pre-Twentieth-Century Communications Revolution

And it wasn't just in the whisky industry that the period saw the foundations of the Britain we know today. Across a wide range of areas, exciting developments were on the move.

These days we're very used to the idea that we live in a world of communications. So much of this, of course, is electronic communication of one sort or another, but almost all of us at least still occasionally trek off to the nearest red post box with a stamped envelope in our hands and still look to see what the post has delivered through our letter box. Many of us will also be aware of the penny black, basically the first modern pre-paid adhesive postage stamp, which appeared in 1840 and revolutionised postal systems the world over. In fact, the story of the penny black is such a familiar landmark in British history that many people might think Britain had no postal service before it. But, of course, it did.

Henry VIII (when he wasn't divorcing wives or chopping their heads off) had a hand in it. As early as 1516, he created the job of Master of the Posts. But, as in so many other respects, Henry here wasn't thinking of the good of his people or helping them out. It was more, at this stage, about official government mail. The post got another right royal boost when Henry's daughter Elizabeth I died in 1603 and James VI of Scotland became James I of England as well. James was faced with the prospect of running two countries with capitals far apart, so, not unreasonably, he ordered an upgrade to the royal postal service between London and Edinburgh. The internet it wasn't, but it was better than nothing. Then, in 1635, things really began to take off. Looking at the reign of Charles I, it's very easy to see just the bad side of it. However, he did at least open up the post to the general public in 1635.

We've become increasingly aware in recent years of the possibility of assorted official bodies snooping on communications. Well, it's not a new thing. A merchant called Thomas Witherings, who had already had experience with international mail to Europe, wanted to open up a public operation in England and Scotland as well. One of the arguments he used in order to persuade Charles what a good idea this would be was by pointing out all the juicy intelligence that could be gathered from people's letters. Accordingly, on 31 July 1635, a proclamation went out announcing the 'Letter Office of England and Scotland' and assigning a monopoly to Witherings and Witherings' men started paying the postmasters to use their horses. Tens of thousands of letters were being transported out of London each week with the recipients paying postage.

Whatever intelligence Charles managed to get out of the post, it wasn't, of course, sufficient to prevent him getting involved in a civil war and losing it to Cromwell (and others). A prominent supporter of the Parliamentarian side, Edmund Prideaux, became Master of the Posts, Messengers and Couriers and expanded the post to new destinations throughout Britain and across the sea in Ireland. He seems to have found the whole experience rather profitable.

While Cromwell obviously had plenty of complaints about Charles, he was very happy to take up the practice of spying on people's mail. In 1655, Secretary of State John Thurloe (see the Richard Cromwell chapter) was put in charge of the Post Office. He also basically became Cromwell's head spy and seems to have rather improved and expanded whatever spying efforts were going on previously. He had a room next to the Foreign Office and went in there every night at about eleven o'clock when post was being processed and stayed there opening, reading and closing again any mail he thought suspicious until three or four o'clock in the morning, when it was time for the mail to go. In fact, Thurloe proved so useful and knew so much that, when the monarchy was restored under Charles II, the new regime, instead of executing Thurloe for treason, allowed him to go free on condition that he assist the new government when asked to do so.

In 1657 a monopoly Post Office was instituted across the country, and in 1660, after the monarchy was restored, Charles II established the General Post Office; yes, the good old GPO. What's more, in 1661, the first Postmaster General was appointed and the first dated postage stamp was used. Not quite the penny black yet, but still a big advance.

Another major innovation was about to arrive. The mail-runs across the country from London served one function, but what if you wanted to send mail *within* London, quickly and easily? In 1680, William Dockwra launched the London Penny Post. Hundreds of 'receiving houses' were established around London in locations like pubs and coffee houses and mail was carried between them. Eventually the government stepped in and took over, closing Dockwra's service and starting a new and very similar one under the control of the Postmaster General.

Just as the arrival of new electronic communication systems has changed how we communicate, do business and live our lives, so increasingly in the eighteenth century did the post as people began to rely on it.

Just as in recent years we have come to enjoy (and expect) increases in speed of communication, so did Britons in the late eighteenth and early nineteenth centuries as the Industrial Revolution erupted. In 1784, businessman and theatre owner John Palmer demonstrated that he could slash the time it took for post to arrive by using a mail coach. It was the start of yet another communications revolution, which saw mail coaches running across the country, making the post faster, easier and more reliable. The mail coaches would soon sport smart Post Office livery, and so too, starting in 1793, would the delivery staff.

But mail coaches were only the start of it. Britain was in the grips of a world-leading Industrial Revolution powered by steam, and in 1830 the first mail to be carried by train travelled between Liverpool and Manchester. By 1838, mail was already being sorted on a moving train in a converted horsebox.

Then, in January 1840, Uniform Penny Post was introduced and in May of that year the penny black finally turned up. Obviously the penny black was a big step forward, but the foundations for our modern reliance on fast, reliable, long-distance communication were laid well before it.

34

Lady Mary and Her Inoculation Innovation

The late eighteenth century was a period of intense experimentation and progress in fields like science and medicine, and you didn't necessarily have to be a professional scientist to take part.

Lady Mary Montagu isn't exactly among the best-known characters in British history, and yet she helped transform Western medicine and ultimately save millions upon millions of lives, which has got to be pretty good. Oh, and she was pretty handy with Latin and Classical Greek as well.

Lady Mary Montagu was born in May 1689, shortly after Parliament had chosen to invite William and Mary to be rulers of Britain. She was the eldest of the three daughters of Evelyn Pierrepont, Earl of Kingston-upon-Hull, and Lady Mary Fielding.

Her mother tragically died in 1693, when Mary still tiny. Despite her youth, she was soon trained to take on many of her mother's social duties. She was, for instance, expected to preside over her father's dinner table and carve meats for his guests.

Evelyn Pierrepont was a proud father, and he took great pride in his young daughter's prettiness and precocious talents. By the age of eight she was, according to her granddaughter's memoirs, the toast of the political and literary Kit-Kat Club, and she was 'passed from the lap of one poet, or patriot, or statesman, to the arms of another' and 'feasted with sweetmeats'.

Her education was put in the hands of a governess for whom the determined and intelligent Mary had little time. Instead, she used the extensive library at Thoresby Hall to teach herself. She must have been both very determined and a gifted linguist. By the age of twenty-one she had produced her own translation of the work of Epictetus and sent it to Bishop Gilbert Brunet, accompanied by a long letter supporting women's right to a formal education.

In this early period of her life, before she married, she was great friends with the early feminist writer Mary Astell and supported Astell's idea of a retreat for young women where they could be educated in religious and intellectual matters without the economic pressure of looking for an early marriage. Mary Montagu felt that such a retreat would have suited her down to the ground.

She also wrote to Anne Wortley Montagu, granddaughter of the 1st Earl of Sandwich, and it was these letters that were to lead to her marriage. It seems that Anne did not always write her own letters and many were copied from drafts written by her brother Edward. When Anne died in 1709, Edward Wortley Montagu was able to continue the correspondence without an intermediary. However, Evelyn Pierrepoint, by now Marquess of Dorchester, did not trust Edward and did not want to see Edward inherit his estates. Instead, he proposed the improbably named Clotworthy Skeffington as a suitable husband for Mary. Mary was having none of it (perhaps the name didn't help), and so in 1712 eloped with Edward Wortley Montagu, marrying him in Salisbury.

For a short time Lady Mary kept a low profile, giving birth to a son named Edward. However, in 1715 her husband became MP for Westminster and she moved to London. Here she set about making a name for herself, and she became a prominent member of the court. She could count as friends George I and the Prince of Wales, as well as Lady Walpole and Sarah Churchill. She also built up a circle of literary friends such as Alexander Pope and Jonathan Swift. All in all, she could hold quite a dinner party.

Her time in London, however, came to a dramatic end in 1716. In December 1715, she caught smallpox. The illness left her face scarred and she also lost her eyebrows. While recovering from this assault on her physical beauty, her reputation at court was also rather ruined by the publication of her satirical 'Court Eclogues', which were interpreted as an attack on Caroline, Princess of Wales. While she had intended her writing to remain private, she had clearly made enemies, who were only too happy to publicise her views. She may have been delighted that her husband was appointed to be ambassador at Istanbul, which gave her an opportunity to leave the country.

She arrived in Istanbul in 1716 and was to leave two years later. This brief sojourn was to shape the rest of her life and help save so many others. It was here that she was to learn about inoculation, and it was from Istanbul that she was to write so many letters which are the basis for her reputation as a feminist and Orientalist.

Lady Mary's life in London had been shaped by smallpox, and she had only to look in the mirror to be reminded of this. Therefore, she was intrigued to find that in Istanbul smallpox was not considered much of a problem. In her letters she described how women gathered up the children and took them to be inoculated as part of a group. The recipient would then catch a mild dose of smallpox, being confined to bed for three or four days, but would then recover without scars or lasting marks – providing the patient did not suffer from blood poisoning or a particularly bad batch of smallpox. The patient would then be immune to smallpox and had nothing more to fear. Lady Mary was so convinced by this that she had her son inoculated in 1717, and the French ambassador wrote about these shared inoculations almost as if they were some sort of spa visit.

When she returned to England in 1718, Lady Mary made no immediate use of this newfound knowledge. However, when an epidemic of smallpox in 1721 threatened her young daughter, Lady Mary was quick to ensure that her daughter was inoculated as she had seen done in Istanbul. Her chosen doctor was Charles Maitland, who had been in Istanbul and knew something of how it was done there. Lady Mary's daughter became a bit of a celebrity as influential friends flocked to see the miracle cure. Dr Maitland was given permission to carry out further trials at Newgate Prison. Seven prisoners who were due to be hanged were offered the chance of freedom in return for taking part in the trial. All survived, and this encouraged the Princess of Wales to have her daughters inoculated in the same year. Presumably the animosity between the pair, which had led to Lady Mary leaving London in 1716, had now been forgotten.

There was an enormous amount of interest in inoculation both in Britain and in Europe. In the eighteenth century, Voltaire estimated that 60 per cent of France would catch smallpox, of which 20 per cent would die and a further 20 per cent could expect to be scarred for life. Inoculation offered a solution to this threat, and royalty led the way in making inoculation popular. It rapidly became big business for many doctors, who charged heavily for their services. There were also those, like some in the Church, who criticised the practice, regarding it as doctors trying to do God's work. Many minsters recommended relying on prayer rather than inoculation.

Those doctors making a good living from such inoculation were challenged seventy years later by Edward Jenner and the discovery of vaccination in 1796, which, by using cowpox to develop the antibodies rather than relying on weakened but live smallpox germs, was significantly safer. However, many living in the eighteenth century owed their health and good looks to Lady Mary Montagu.

Lady Mary's short time in Istanbul also gave her the opportunity to consider the relative experiences of women in Islamic Istanbul compared with Christian London. She was writing at a time when there was a renewed interest in the Orient due to the translation of the *Arabian Nights*. She considered it a duty to learn Arabic so that she could communicate with the local women, and this provided a direct link with their ideas.

She was surprised by what she found out about their lives. It is no surprise to find that she was frustrated by the lack of formal education available for English girls in London or that she felt the marriage laws were unfair. In eighteenth-century England, women who married passed all their possessions to their husband and divorce was thus impossible for many as they would be penniless. She found Islamic women to be a model of freedom. For Lady Mary, the veil provided women with privacy and an independence to live their own lives. She marvelled at their financial independence and their ability to run their own businesses. As she stripped off to share a Turkish bath with women and to chat about the news, she compared the liberation of the veil to the forceful shaping of the European bodice, which Islamic women saw as a controlling mechanism. She expressed these ideas in her letters, which were mostly addressed to Mary Astell. However, the letters are also addressed to a wider audience and it is likely that she always intended them to be published, as they were, shortly after her death. However, being an aristocrat, she did not want to be bothered with dealing with publishers directly.

Following her return to England and the success of inoculation, Lady Mary continued to lead a colourful and independent life. She struggled with her two children. Edward, being a boy, had the advantage of a formal education, though it was not an advantage he appreciated as he kept running away from school. Her daughter Mary followed in her mother's footsteps and eloped with a man that Mary senior did not like. However, he turned out all right; Lord Bute went on to become Prime Minister. Lady Mary put her energy into writing. She engaged in a poetic war of words with Alexander Pope, who appeared to blame her for the money he had lost in the South Sea Bubble. She also wrote a periodical with the wonderful title the 'Nonsense of Common Sense' and espoused women's rights.

Lady Mary Montagu and Edward Wartley Montagu went

on to live separate lives. He inherited Wortley Hall in 1727, spent the rest of his life parsimoniously and died a millionaire. Lady Mary didn't. Instead, she divorced him and left England to travel around southern France and northern Italy. While she entertained many men, she did not remarry.

In many ways, Lady Mary Montagu was a typical noble. However, she felt strongly that she should have the same opportunities as any male aristocrat. She left a significant medical advance by encouraging inoculation, and she was a role model for future women travellers. She helped to create the idea that women travellers, by being able to talk to ordinary women, are more accurate recorders of society than men.

35

From Slave to Freedman and Bestselling Author

Of course, many people in the Georgian period both here in Britain and around the world in Britain's expanding empire had few of the advantages of someone like Lady Mary Montagu. In fact, many did not even have freedom. This is the extraordinary story of one man: Olaudah Equiano.

Equiano describes his childhood in his autobiography, *The Interesting Narrative*, where he claims to come from the Eboe region of Benin in West Africa. However, there are church records which suggest he was born in Virginia and the naval records of his arctic expedition list Carolina as his place of origin. It may be that the official records contain careless errors from clerks in a hurry, or it may be that Equiano fabricated his early life to make his book a more powerful anti-slavery text.

Whatever the truth about his place of birth and early life, he ended up being bought as a slave by the English Naval officer Michael Henry Pascal. Equiano had a very different life from those slaves working on the plantations. Pascal was a lieutenant in the Royal Navy and he took Equiano with him back to England. It was Pascal who gave Equiano his slave name of Gustavus Vassa, threatening to beat Equiano if he did not respond to his new name. England was a very alien world to the young Equiano. When he first saw snow, he thought it was salt and tasted it.

When Pascal and Equiano went to London, Equiano

was suffering from chilblains. He was taken to St George's Hospital, where the doctors wanted to amputate his legs. Fortunately, Equiano was able to persuade them to leave him alone and he recovered. The sisters of one of Pascal's friends, a Mr Guerin, took it upon themselves to teach Equiano to read and write. Miss Guerin went on to be Equiano's godmother when he was baptised. Equiano was very loyal to his master and accompanied him on many naval missions.

In 1758, as a young teenager, Equiano joined his master on the *Namur* as part of Admiral Cornish's fleet to attack the French in Canada. This is where he met General Wolfe, who was on board, en route to Quebec. Equiano remarked that the general was 'good and gallant'. He also had cause to thank Wolfe, as he saved Equiano from a beating for fighting with another lad. Equiano was in the thick of the action off Nova Scotia. He recorded seeing one sailor shot by a musket ball which went in through his mouth and exited through his cheek. He held aloft the scalp of a native American king, which had been cut off by the Scots.

After his success in Canada, Pascal was stationed in the Mediterranean at Gibraltar and Equiano went with him. In a vicious fight with the eighty-four-gun French ship *L'Ocean*, Equiano operated as a 'powder monkey', bringing the gunpowder up to the British cannons. His reward for his bravery and loyalty was that he was promoted to captain's steward.

Equiano used his service in the Navy to extend his education. On the *Aetna*, the captain's clerk improved his reading and writing and also taught him some arithmetic. An older sailor named Daniel Queen helped Equiano to read the Bible and explained what it meant. He gave Equiano the title 'Black Christian'. Equiano also learnt the basics of riding a horse, as the Spanish in Barcelona had made fun of him by sitting him on a donkey and then kicking it to make it gallop off, laughing as Equiano tried to stay in control.

Life in the eighteenth-century Navy was brutal and dangerous. Many of the crew had been press-ganged into service and punishments were harsh. At Gibraltar, Equiano witnessed a sailor being hanged by his heels after trying to desert. He saw the captain of a frigate dragged behind his boat and dismissed for cowardice.

Faced with all the dangers of a life at sea, Equiano became a firm believer in the power of providence and he began to believe that the Almighty had mapped out his future. This was confirmed when a forty-gun ship called the *Lynne* crashed into the ship on which Equiano was sailing. On the night of the accident, one of Equiano's fellow sailors, John Mondle, had been unable to sleep because he had a troubled conscience and had decided that he needed to change his life in order to avoid damnation. John Mondle vowed to give up drinking and gave away his liquor ration. In the accident, the prow of the *Lynne* smashed straight through John Mondle's bunk. However, as he was awake repenting of his sins, he survived unscathed. For Equiano, Mondle's survival showed the power of providence.

The end of the Seven Years War with France was, however, to give Equiano reason to question providence. When the war ended, Equiano, like the pressed sailors who had fought alongside him, believed that he would be free to go. While he had served his master in the Navy, little difference had existed between Equiano's life and that of other sailors. Perhaps the major difference was that he had not been entitled to a share of the money raised from ships seized as prizes. Equiano's slave status and lack of rights only became clear when he was seized by Pascal, forced into a boat and taken up the Thames until Pascal could find a ship prepared to take Equiano to the West Indies to be sold. Despite his years of loyal service, Equiano was not even allowed to collect his belongings and his much treasured copy of the Bible.

Pascal seems to have made the decision to sell Equiano on a whim. Pascal had found himself a new mistress, who wanted to rid the household of any reminders of her predecessors. This included getting rid of Equiano, who had been a favourite of Pascal's former mistress. Pascal had little difficulty showing where his loyalties lay and Equiano was soon on his way.

Although many of Equiano's shipmates promised to come to his aid, they were not able to prevent him being taken to the West Indies, where he was sold to a Quaker, Robert King. Equiano was fortunate to find a humane owner. It is ironic that Equiano was to have a Quaker owner while the Quakers were also to play a leading role in ending slavery. From this point on Equiano was determined to gain the freedom that he was denied by the end of the Seven Years War, but he was determined to do it by the legal route of saving sufficient money to buy his freedom rather than simply escaping.

King was, by the standards of the day, a reasonable slave owner. For King there was no need for harsh punishments. If slaves needed punishing then King simply sold them, but, because he was much nicer to his slaves than many other slave owners, most slaves worked hard in order to stay with him. King recognised the hard work that Equiano had put into his education and decided to give him a little more maths schooling and make him his clerk. He also recognised that Equiano had skills as a sailor, which could be useful in trading sugar between the West Indies and America.

Serving on his master's boat, Equiano made 15d per day, while slaves from other masters might get between 6d and 9d. The master made about 3 or 4 shillings in profit from each slave each day. As a clerk, King reckoned that Equiano was the best of his type. Free clerks were paid between £60 and £100 per year, while Equiano earned himself little more than a shilling per day. On the other hand, King earned thousands of pounds from Equiano's work. Equiano showed the money that could be made by slave owners and was appalled by the waste of life caused by harsh slave owners. As he saw it, there would be no need for the Middle Passage and importing slaves from Africa if owners were decent to their slaves.

In his work for King, Equiano travelled between the islands of the West Indies delivering slaves and transporting sugar and rum. It gave him the opportunity to observe and record all the horrors of the plantations. He noted the slave who had a leg amputated for running away and the owner's justification that it prevented other slaves doing the same. He was shocked to find a slave having his ears chopped off 'bit by bit' for going with a white prostitute, while African girls were regularly robbed of their virtue. Instruments of torture like the muzzle and the thumbscrews are also recorded. Equiano was unusual in that, despite being a slave for much of his life, his skin remained unmarked, a testament to his loyalty and the value he held for his masters.

While working for King, he divided his time between working as a clerk and serving under Captain Farmer on King's boats. Farmer and King used to compete for Equiano's service. In the end Captain Farmer won, and Equiano spent most of his time in the boats. This was to Equiano's advantage, as he was able to use these voyages to earn money to buy his freedom. He started with 3d and invested all of it in a glass tumbler, which he bought on St Eustasia (a Dutch island). When he returned to Montserrat, he sold it for 6d and bought two glass tumblers. Alan Sugar would have been proud of him. However, trade was not easy as slaves had no legal rights. At times he found his entire stock seized by whites on a whim and he had no legal redress. He could ask Captain Farmer to intervene on his behalf, but even then his lack of legal rights put him at a severe disadvantage.

Equiano was determined to buy his freedom and be free under the law. He had a strong sense of justice, and even though there were opportunities to take short cuts he resisted them. A French captain offered to pay all of Captain Farmer's crew high wages if they served en route to France. While many accepted and Equiano was tempted to go to France and then make his way back to England, he decided to remain loyal to King. Eventually King accepted £40 as a fair price for granting Equiano manumission. It is interesting to note that King was also, to some extent, concerned with a sense of justice. He accepted £40 from Equiano, having rejected offers of over £100 from other slave owners for the services of Equiano.

Once free, Equiano was determined to move to England. He was disgusted by the immorality of the West Indies and how slaves were treated. However, he was offered employment by King as a free man and he accepted the job. Life as a freedman was, at first, a disappointment to Equiano, as he rapidly found that even freed slaves had no legal rights and that racism was almost as much a block to improving his life as slavery had been.

Working for King, he made a series of voyages to Savannah. Here he found that whites took his goods without paying and wanted to flog him for trying to defend his rights. Equiano ended up in hiding in a friendly house and fearing for his life. Once again he relied on Captain Farmer to extricate him from an impossible situation. When Captain Farmer died during a voyage, it was left to Equiano to take charge and guide the ship safely home. The voyage showed that Equiano had indeed learnt the navigation lessons taught to him by Farmer and he must have enjoyed the title Captain Vassa, which was bestowed upon him on his return.

The death of Farmer marked another turning point for Equiano, and he finally cut his ties with King and signed on a ship bound for London. On his return he met Pascal and Miss Guerin once again, but was disappointed by their responses. Pascal refused to give him any prize money as he claimed he was a slave and had no right to a share in the prizes. Miss Guerin was unable to find employment for him. Undeterred, Equiano tried to make a living as a hairdresser, using the skills he had acquired in the Navy as a teenager. He also set about completing his education and learning to play the French horn. However, he soon ran out of money and returned to the sea. He signed up for a series of voyages to the Mediterranean, which took him to Portugal, where the ship was searched by the Spanish Inquisition, and to Turkey, where he was offered two wives as an inducement to accepting a job.

Returning to London, he was employed by a Dr Irving who was experimenting with methods of desalinating seawater. It was as an expert in desalination that Equiano signed up to the Arctic expedition of 1773 aboard the *White Horse* (a young Horatio Nelson was also on this mission). No route around the Northwest Passage was found, and the *White Horse* got stuck in the ice. He did, however, see plenty of walruses, or seahorses as he called them, and some polar bears. The mission nearly came to grief when Equiano set fire to the ship by knocking over the lamp he was using to help him write his diary. The crew extinguished the fire, the ship was pulled from the ice and both Equiano and Nelson returned safely.

While in England, Equiano fought strongly against slavery. In 1786 he joined the 'Sons of Africa', a small group of ex-slaves who campaigned to end slavery. He contacted Granville Sharp, the white abolitionist, to try to prevent the kidnapping of a black slave and he spoke at public meetings alongside Thomas Clarkson. He encouraged another slave, Ottobah Cugoano, to publish an account of his life in 1787, and in 1789 Equiano published his own autobiography. The book was a national bestseller, running to several editions. It was also a bestseller in the USA, Holland and Germany. In Ireland he sold almost 2,000 copies of the book. His book showed the white population the reality of slavery and made it impossible to justify slavery on the grounds that slaves were well dealt with and enjoyed their lives.

Equiano settled his conscience by becoming a Methodist. He claimed he never understood the Quakers because their services were silent. He was offered employment as a missionary in Africa, helping resettle slaves in Sierra Leone, but died before he could make this happen.

In 1792 he had married an English woman in Soham, Cambridgeshire, and they had two daughters. By the time of his death in 1797, his book had made sufficient money that he left a sizeable estate to his heirs. However, despite his campaigning and the success of his book, slavery and the slave trade were still legal in the British Empire when he died.

It was not until 1833, almost forty years after Equiano died, that slavery was finally abolished in the British Empire.

36

The American Invasion of Cumbria

The eighteenth century had been an intense time on the battlefield for Britain as it fought to exert its influence in Europe and extend its control to distant parts of the world in wars like the War of the Spanish Succession, the War of the Austrian Succession and the Seven Years War.

By the 1770s, Britain already had extensive foreign possessions and was already a global power, able to deploy force around the world thanks to the Royal Navy. For instance, where now we might send planes to bomb, then we could send ships to bombard and raid. But in the late eighteenth century, we were in for a shock. We were about to discover that founding colonies didn't necessarily guarantee their perpetual obedience. Not only that, but we were about find out that rebel colonists, with the help of a Brit who'd found a new allegiance, could even challenge us by means of the sea, even in British home waters and on the British mainland.

In 1778, the thirteen states of the United States had declared independence from British rule and were fighting to maintain that independence against George III. He, in turn, was determined that the colony should be recaptured. This war sparked an unexpected 'invasion', now commemorated by plaque in the Cumbrian town of Whitehaven describing the raid as the 'only unfriendly American invasion'.

The Continental Navy (the navy of the American rebels) was

formed by John Adams in 1775 and its main job was to disrupt supplies arriving in America from Britain. Understandably, being small and comparatively inexperienced, it had relatively little impact on the Revolutionary War as compared with the Royal Navy. (Though obviously we can't pat ourselves on the back too much, since we lost the war.) Through the work of one John Paul Jones, however, it did rather unexpectedly manage to make its mark around the shores of Britain – although, frankly, there were Americans who would have far preferred it to be more effective a bit closer to home.

John Paul Jones had a rather astonishing career. He was born in July 1747 in Kirkcudbright, Scotland. Nothing astonishing about that, obviously, except that he wasn't John Paul Jones when he was first given a name; he was just John Paul. He added the Jones to his name when he relocated to Virginia and this was one of several reinventions that were to characterise his career.

He began his life at sea as a thirteen-year-old apprentice, sailing on the *Friendship* under Captain Benson, based in the Cumbrian port of Whitehaven. He then got a sort of lucky break (lucky for him, very unlucky for some of the senior officers) in 1768 when, during a voyage, the captain and commanding officers died of yellow fever. The young John Paul took charge and was able to bring the ship home safely. The Scottish owners promptly gave him a well-deserved pay rise and made him master of the ship.

However, he did not always find the job of being master an easy one. Two years later he found himself imprisoned in Kirkcudbright because he had flogged one of his crew, who had later died from his beating, leaving John Paul accused of being 'unnecessarily cruel'. He then followed this up by stabbing and killing a mutineer named Blackton in a dispute over wages. John Paul was clearly not the kind of nice, cosy, 'my-door-is-always-open' boss with whom you could sit down and discuss your problems. This time John Paul was forced to flee to Virginia, where his brother was based. It was here, according to local legend, that he added the Jones to his name, inspired allegedly by one Willie Jones of Halifax, a statesman and eventually a delegate for North Carolina to the Continental Congress of 1780.

He had found a new land, a new name, and now a new allegiance as well. In 1775, John Paul Jones headed north to join the newly formed Continental Navy and he set sail for France in 1777. By this time France had entered the Revolutionary War on the side of the American rebels, and they were basically happy to host pretty much anyone who wanted to have a go at the British. Jones and his crew were perhaps not the ideal team. Perhaps not surprisingly, given his track record, his crew thought his discipline too harsh; even his officers thought he was too aloof and allegedly had little confidence in him. Nevertheless, these misfits were to succeed in landing in Britain and subsequently capturing two Royal Navy ships.

John Paul Jones decided that he would target the place he had sailed out of all those years ago, Whitehaven. The Whitehaven ship he had sailed on had been called *Friendship*, but you can't help feeling that this name probably didn't really describe his feelings towards his old home port. No doubt he hoped his insider knowledge of the port would help him attack it successfully, but you can't help wondering whether he also wanted revenge for some unpleasant experience there.

In the eighteenth century, Whitehaven was not a quiet town on the Cumbrian coast but a thriving port based on the coal industry. It was the third-largest coal port in the country after Newcastle and Sunderland on the east coast. Whitehaven even had a swanky new Georgian centre based on a square grid. The coal came from a local pit at Saltom, which had been the scene of one of the earliest Newcomen steam pumps in 1715.

Jones's plan of attack involved lowering two boats from the USS *Ranger*. He himself, along with his trusted Swedish second-in-command Lieutenant Meijer, would be in the first boat and his role would be to disable the guns in the two batteries that lay to the south of the harbour so that all those involved in the raid could escape without being fired upon by the batteries. The second boat, under the command of Lieutenant Wallingford of the US marines, was to enter the harbour and set fire to as many ships as possible before returning to the *Ranger* for a safe getaway.

The original plan, however, proved rather hard to execute. In fact, it was extremely hard. Rowing against the tide proved tough work for Jones and his boat. After a lot of exhausting endeavour they failed to land at Lunette battery, the outermost harbour defence, as the sea was too rough and the shore too rocky. Instead they rowed past the battery – fortunately for them unseen – and landed at dawn in the main harbour. As it was a cold night, the guards had retreated to the warmth of their guardhouse. John Paul Jones led the assault himself, and by climbing on the shoulders of his fellow sailors he was able to surmount the defences and surprise the guards, who were taken prisoner without bloodshed.

His next action was to stand on the battlements to let Lieutenant Meijer know that he had been successful. There were assorted factions in the ranks of the attackers and until they were sure that their leader had indeed actually taken the battery they weren't very keen on proceeding with the raid. In fact, Jones had invited Meijer to join him purely because he trusted him and he worried that without his loyal lieutenant there was a real possibility that the remainder of his crew would have rowed away, leaving him alone on land. Ah, the joys of having a loyal team behind you.

Having alerted Lieutenant Meijer, John Paul Jones then set about spiking the guns at the Half-Moon Battery. Spiking the guns was a fairly literal process in the sense that it meant he hammered iron spikes into the touch hole on the canons, which prevented them being fired.

Once Lieutenant Wallingford and his marines were sure that Jones had dealt with the battery they landed at the Old Quay. The plan was to set fire to the shipping lying in the harbour. Their first stop, however, was Nicholas Allison's public house. Well, it was a cold night. Their excuse, however, was that they needed to ensure that nobody raised the alarm and they needed to find a light to set fire to the ships. Anyway, the local newspaper recorded that they made 'very free with the liquor', which may, of course, be one reason why so few ships were to end up actually being destroyed.

When John Paul Jones caught up with Lieutenant Wallingford's party, he was, not surprisingly distinctly unimpressed to find out that as yet no ships had been set on fire because the marines had found it easier to find the booze than find a light.

Eventually the invasion started getting serious. The raiding party boarded the nearest boat, the *Thompson*, and took the boys who had been left in charge prisoner. They also captured the ship next door, the *Saltham*, and took the boys there, dressed only in their shirts, prisoner as well. The attackers then finally succeeded in setting light to the *Thompson* by setting fire to a barrel of tar by the main mast.

As time was pressing on and it was now daylight and they had managed to set one ship on fire, Jones and his men returned to their boats and set sail. Jones claims that he did not leave until he was confident that the fire on the *Thompson* was well alight, and he hoped that the fire would spread to the warehouses and other ships.

However, the raid had now gone on so long that, by the time Jones and his crew were rowing out of the harbour, the locals had managed to remove the spikes from the cannon in Half-Moon Battery and proceeded to open fire on the retreating sailors. In some ways, however, this turned out to be fortunate for Jones, since the shots demonstrated to the crew of the *Ranger* that at least some of the raiding party were still alive and the ship consequently moved closer in to collect the escaping raiders.

Meanwhile, back in Whitehaven, the locals were attempting to put out the fire and stop it spreading to neighbouring ships and warehouses. One of the attackers, Irishman David Freeman, seems to have been disgusted at the destruction that setting fire to the ships and harbour would cause to the innocent people of Whitehaven. He had broken ranks and warned the locals, who then had had time to react and call out the fire brigade. This is a rare example of a member of the attacking force trying to limit the damage rather than maximise it. Jones would not have been happy.

The danger of having numerous ships packed together in the harbour, where they were beached and unable to move at low tide, adjacent to warehouses storing huge amounts of coal, sugar and flammable goods, had not been lost on the locals, who had provided themselves with fire engines. The people of Whitehaven now turned out in force and successfully prevented the fire from spreading. In the end only the *Thompson* was damaged, and even here the damage was restricted to the cabin. This prompt action meant that the raid in fact caused relatively little damage – one ship damaged and a couple of young sailors seized as prisoners. However, it has not been forgotten either in Cumbria or the USA.

Jones's adventures were not at an end, though; not by a long way. Once on board the USS *Ranger* again, Jones headed north across the Solway Firth and decided to use his local knowledge of the area to try and seize Lord Selkirk, whose home was on St Mary's Isle close to Kirkcudbright.

For Jones, Lord Selkirk was in some ways a strange target since he had actually expressed views in favour of the American revolutionaries. For the crew of the *Ranger*, the motivation was probably simple greed. They were after rewards and prizes, which, apart from the liquid contents of Nicholas Allison's pub in Whitehaven, Jones had so far been unable to provide. As a consequence they were, yet again, starting to lose faith in their captain.

When the raiding party turned up at his home, however, Lord Selkirk was not there and his pregnant wife was instead left to face the armed sailors. She got no help from the local men, who had run away because they mistakenly assumed that Jones was leading a press gang and was intent on pressing them into the Royal Navy. So Lady Selkirk dispatched her servants upstairs and dealt with the sailors alone. She gave them a glass of wine, which they accepted, and demanded a receipt for any of the goods which the sailors insisted on taking. In the end the sailors took only one silver plate and, in fact, Jones would later buy the silver plate from his crew and return it to Lady Selkirk. Theft on a grand scale this was not.

Sailing back to France, where the *Ranger* was based, Jones did at last have some success. He was able to capture the Royal Navy ship HMS *Drake*. This was a rare victory for the Continental Navy, demonstrating that the Royal Navy was not always invincible, even when close to home waters. What's more, in 1779, a year after the Cumbrian invasion, Jones was back in action, now captain of the *Bon Homme Richard*, which had been given to the Americans by the French. This time he managed to capture HMS *Serapis* at the Battle of Flamborough Head off the Yorkshire coast.

Jones's leadership qualities seem to have been better on sea than on land, and he appears this time to have had his crew behind him. While in Whitehaven they had been after booze and ditching their captain, at Flamborough they responded to his flamboyant jibe to the British ('I have not even begun to fight yet!') by persevering and eventually winning.

Jones's exploits, despite their occasionally comic nature, had been something of a shock to the British, who responded by strengthening their naval defences, a move that was to stand us in good stead during the Napoleonic Wars and help prevent further invasions.

Captain Jones went on to be awarded a military medal by King Louis XVI of France and then, in a rather unexpected move, was appointed as vice-admiral in the Russian Navy by Catherine the Great, changing his name to Pavel de Zhoves. It's a rare thing to have taken charge of ships in both the Russian and US navies. However, his time in Russia was overshadowed by sexual accusations. Jones continued to regard himself as American, and after he died in Paris in 1792 his body was eventually, in 1905, returned with much ceremony to the independent USA for which he had fought.

Today, of course, the USA is one of our strongest allies. In this tradition, in 1999 the US Navy was granted the 'freedom of the water' by the people of Whitehaven and the declaration ended up on the desk of President Clinton. Equally, at the quay in Whitehaven there is now a statue of John Paul Jones spiking the cannons that were supposed to defend the harbour. There are few places that have put up statues to someone once regarded as a traitor, but then this is *Unexpected Britain*.

37

Britain Enters the Rocket Age
– to Fight Napoleon

The French had helped the American revolutionaries, but as radical ideas began to flourish in assorted countries (including here), the French were to see a revolution of their own. Edmund Burke (Irishman and Whig in the party politics of Parliament), who had defended the American Revolution, by contrast attacked the French Revolution in a 1790 publication called *Reflections on the Revolution in France*. Other radicals, however, including Mary Wollstonecraft, Thomas Paine and William Godwin, had more sympathy with the revolution. Thomas Paine wrote his famous *Rights of Man*, subtitled 'Answer to Mr. Burke's Attack on the French Revolution'. In Ireland, the example of the French Revolution would help lead to the rise of the United Irishmen and the rebellion of 1798. However, after the Revolution in France came The Terror and the guillotine and then Napoleon. Soon we would be fighting the French yet again.

A lot of people tend to think of rockets as a particularly hi-tech form of warfare. There's plenty of talk about the sophisticated technology behind the German V1 (though that was technically a jet, not a rocket) and the V2 in the Second World War, and how they helped usher in the Space Age and a world of ICBMs and guided missiles. What gets much less attention is the fact that the British Army and British Navy were among the pioneers of using rockets in warfare in the West. Not only that, but they were using them in quantity and with plenty of impact about a century and a half before the V1 and the V2 ever lifted off. The industrial and scientific revolution of the late eighteenth century wasn't just going on in laboratories and factories – it was taking place on the battlefield as well.

Sir William Congreve was born in 1772, the son of Sir William Congreve – the shared name must have been confusing at times because they both ended up in the same line of work. William Congreve the elder happened to be comptroller of the Royal Laboratory at Woolwich Arsenal (the same arsenal, incidentally, that gave rise to the football team before they moved north of the Thames). He was therefore very interested in artillery and how to make it better – or, in other words, scarier and deadlier.

Now, it happened that, in the late eighteenth century, the British Army had been having some rather nasty and unnerving experiences with rockets in India. Our men had had rockets fired against them in a number of wars against Mysore, and it hadn't been pleasant. The Mysore Army contained specific rocket units designed to fire masses of rockets at the tightly packed infantry formations which were a feature of the battlefields of the day. At the Battle of Pollilur in 1780, it is thought that a rocket may have ignited British ammunition stores. The effect was often terrifying and sometimes devastating. The rockets could pass right through a formation, killing, maiming and lacerating. On one occasion, heavy rocket and musket fire caused the then Colonel Wellesley, none other than the later Duke of Wellington, to abandon an attack. When Seringapatam fell to British forces in 1799, effectively ending the war, hundreds of rockets and launchers were captured. Some were brought to Britain and displayed as war trophies in the Royal Military Repository at Woolwich.

This is where Congreve the younger comes in again. Congreve had read Mathematics at Cambridge and was an inventive kind of chap. In 1804, he proposed building a weapons system that consisted of an oar-powered floating armoured battery. Perhaps not surprisingly, it was never built. He was to have more success with rockets.

Probably inspired in some sense by what he had read and seen of Indian rockets and perhaps by the efforts of other Western rocket pioneers, Congreve set about developing his own rockets for the British armed forces at Woolwich. He bought skyrockets from manufacturers in London and then, experimenting with different designs, managed to produce a rocket that could travel 2,000 yards, well over a mile. Eventually he had a design that he thought was ready for action. However, rather than executing a land-based initial attack, Congreve decided in 1805 to launch a sea-based rocket attack on the French port of Boulogne. Considering uncertainties about the new weapon and the uncertainties of wind and waves in the English Channel, this seems an unwise decision. The British ships, loaded with almost 600 rockets, anchored off Boulogne and launched the attack. The results were unimpressive. The rockets went in assorted directions, with few heading toward the target. Congreve returned to researching and refining the rockets, including some experimenting with bigger rockets and longer-range rockets. After another year he had rockets he thought were an improvement and another attempt was made to attack the French fleet at Boulogne, this time with thousands of rockets. This time, even though the attack wasn't devastating, some fires were lit and generally the operation was regarded as something of a success. That attack at Boulogne was to be the first of plenty.

In September 1807, for instance, during the war in Denmark, British forces had surrounded Copenhagen but the Danes had refused the terms, so British troops started to bombard the city. The bombardment went on for several days and included hundreds of Congreve rockets. Hundreds of buildings were destroyed, hundreds killed and in the end the Danes gave in.

Congreve rockets were once again present at the Battle of the Basque Roads in 1808 and at the Walcheren Expedition in 1809, where HMS *Galgo* was specially converted to fire them.

Soon Congreve rockets became a regular feature of land battles in the Napoleonic Wars, as well. They were present at the Battle of Leipzig in October 1813, when the 2nd Rocket Troop of the Royal Artillery was the only British unit present at the so-called Battle of the Nations and managed on its own to put to flight a French column – 2,500 French troops were so shocked by the rockets that they surrendered. The Tsar of Russia must have been mightily impressed, as he took the Order of St Anne off his own chest and pinned it on the troop commander. Congreve rockets were there in Spain at the crossing of the River Bidossa the same year, and in 1814 at Toulouse, as Wellington's troops pushed into southern France. Some rockets even featured in the Waterloo Campaign.

But it wasn't just in Europe that the British armed forces were using Congreve's terrifying weapons; they were also in action across the Atlantic. When the War of 1812 broke out with the United States, a number of Royal Marine rocket detachments went into action, seeing service, for instance, at Fort Oswego and Lundy's Lane, at the Battle of North Point, at the Second Battle of Lacolle Mills and at the Battle of Cook's Mills. In 1814, at Bladensburg in Maryland, the Royal Marine Artillery Rocket Brigade put to flight American militiamen and opened the road for British troops to attack and destroy much of Washington.

Congreve rockets continued to be used on occasion after the end of the War of 1812 and the Napoleonic Wars. They were used, for instance, in the wars in New Zealand and, according to an American Civil War memoir, the Confederates under Jeb Stuart even used Congreve rockets during that war on just one occasion. However, as the Confederates found out, the Congreve rocket was not very accurate, and later in the nineteenth century Hale's design of rocket went into use with the British Army instead. Conventional gun artillery was improving fast, though, and in the First World War it would be this that would terrify and slaughter infantry, not rockets. On the other hand, in the Second World War the Russian Katyusha rocket system achieved something of the effect that

Congreve had once dreamed of, and today's Multiple Launch Rocket Systems continue the tradition on the battlefield.

Congreve himself went on to design assorted other things before getting caught up in a fraud investigation, after which he moved to the south of France. He died there in 1828, being buried in Toulouse, the scene of one of the uses of his rockets over a decade earlier. Presumably, the local populace didn't hold it against him too much.

38

The Germans Who Served
the King

Ultimately, despite advances in science and technology, victory on the battlefields of the Napoleonic Wars was still largely created by the character and training of the fighting men involved. However, by no means were all of those who helped the British Army achieve its triumphs British themselves.

German troops served in the British Army. This may seem a strange idea to those brought up on regular doses of *Dad's Army*, but truth is often stranger than fiction and in the early nineteenth century there was an entire unit comprised of German soldiers.

Britain's Hanoverian royals of course had strong connections with Germany, and Germans had fought for Britain before, like the troops from Hesse and other places in Germany who fought for Britain during the American Revolution. However, the King's German Legion was something rather special.

In 1803, French forces under General Mortier invaded and occupied the Electorate of Hanover. The Elector of Hanover was, of course, Britain's King George III. The Hanoverian army, led by King George's seventh son Adolphus Frederick, Duke of Cambridge, was willing to fight the French, but the politicians of the Electorate decided that this was a lost cause and made an agreement with the French. Adolphus Frederick returned to England and appealed to officers and other ranks of the Hanoverian army to join him.

The duke's first appeal drew a limited response, attracting

officers like Baron Christian von Ompteda, but few other ranks. A second appeal was much more successful, and by the autumn of 1803 there was a steady flow of recruits passing through the port of Husum in Schleswig-Holstein, en route for Heligoland, where they were picked up by British naval transports.

The volunteer émigrés made up two regiments of cavalry, two light battalions, four line battalions, two batteries of horse artillery and three batteries of foot artillery, plus a unit of engineers. These troops were to be known as the King's German Legion under the command of the Duke of Cambridge.

Many troops were garrisoned at Bexhill. The village, with a population of about 2,000 living in around 100 houses, must have been swamped by the rapid arrival of between 5,000 and 6,000 Hanoverian soldiers. However, the Hanoverians generally seem to have made a good impression. Locals were impressed by the care that they took of their horses, which must have created work for the local blacksmiths. The landlord of the 'Queens Head' discovered a business opportunity by making boots of a specific design favoured by the Hanoverians. Church services were conducted in German and German hymns were sung. 'The New Inn' at Sidley acquired a bowling alley to occupy the new arrivals. And the Hanoverians brought an extra bit of excitement to the local social scene. The parish register records several marriages between local girls and the Hanoverian soldiers.

At Bexhill, the King's German Legion was part of a brigade led by Major-General Sir Arthur Wellesley (the future Duke of Wellington). It was as part of Wellesley's army in the Peninsular War that the King's German Legion made its first contributions to the British war effort against Napoleon.

Admiral Nelson's victory at Trafalgar in 1805 had ended Napoleon's plans to invade Britain. Hooray! But in Europe, until 1808, French forces were unchallenged. Boo! In April 1808, however, Napoleon placed his brother Joseph on the Spanish throne. Britain saw an opportunity in the situation, and in August 1808 an expeditionary force led by Wellesley landed in Portugal. Hooray!

The King's German Legion played little part in the early fighting and was not involved in Wellesley's first victory against the French at Vimeiro on 21 August 1808. Wellesley's victory, though, was sufficient to persuade the French to leave Portugal. However, the Convention of Sintra, which allowed the French to sail home safely in British ships, caused such a stir that Wellesley was called home to explain his actions. This left the remaining British troops under the command of Sir John Moore. The Hussars of the King's German Legion performed with distinction at Benavente during Sir John Moore's epic retreat to La Coruña in the autumn of 1808.

In 1809, the King's German Legion saw action in northern Europe as well as in Spain. Not, sadly, with much success, or indeed any success. The legion was part of an ill-fated expedition to the Low Countries. The idea was to destroy the French fleet while at anchor at Flushing and in so doing help the Austrians in their fight against the French. Some 39,000 troops, including some from the King's German Legion, landed at Walcheren in July. The expedition was a complete disaster. The French fleet had moved from Flushing and the Austrians had been defeated and were negotiating peace with Napoleon. Of the 39,000 troops landed, only 106 were lost in action. Walcheren fever, however, killed more than 4,000 and in February 1810 more than 11,000 of those who had been involved were still laid up on their sickbeds.

In Spain, however, troops of the legion were about to enjoy significant military success, although they would suffer major casualties in so doing. During April 1809, troops of the King's German Legion were among those that Wellesley commanded as he marched eastwards into Spain. He met the French, led by Napoleon's brother Joseph, in a bloody battle at Talavera. Wellesley had about 20,000 men under his command, of whom about 3,000 came from the King's German Legion. The remainder were either British or members of the Spanish army. King Joseph of Spain had about 45,000 soldiers. The battle lasted two days before King Joseph decided to retreat and leave Wellesley in control of the battlefield. Wellesley's forces suffered 5,363 casualties. The King's German Legion suffered 42 per cent either killed or wounded. The victory at Talavera established the credibility of the King's German Legion as a fighting force. They were accepted as being on a par with British soldiers by the press and the public in Britain. One publisher who did not share this admiration and produced an article defaming the legion earned himself imprisonment and a fine of £1,000. The authorities were prepared to defend the reputation of the legion. Sir Arthur Wellesley was rewarded for his victory by being made Duke of Wellington.

Despite his victory, Wellington was eventually forced to retreat and organise the defence of Lisbon. He finished the year constructing a huge defensive barrier known as the Lines of Torre Vedras. The villages in front of the Lines of Torre Vedras were burnt so that the attacking French would be left with the choice of either storming a prepared position or slowly starving. Not the most appealing of choices, really.

The following year, 1810, would see Wellington and the troops of the King's German Legion glad of the time they had spent preparing their defences. Napoleon's so-called luckiest general, Massena, tried once again to capture Portugal. His attack in September was beaten off at Bucaco. The French lost over 1,000 men but the legion lost only three officers and forty-seven men either killed or wounded.

Massena and his men spent the winter of 1810/11 camped looking at the walls of Torre Vedras and starving. In the spring of 1811, they had no option but to retreat.

The year 1811 marked a turning point in the Peninsular War as Wellington's army started to turn defence into attack. The King's German Legion continued to gain valuable battle experience. In March, the 2nd Hussars captured two French cannon in a cavalry charge at Barossa and were awarded three cannon as booty for their efforts – not as portable as medals or cash, but impressive nonetheless. In May, at Fuentes De Onoro, they lost eight officers and 145 men helping

Wellington push General Massena out of Portugal. At the Battle of Albuerra, also in May, they suffered heavy casualties, as did both the French and English armies. The legion lost eight officers and 105 men. The legion finished the year on a high point, with the 2nd Hussars capturing ten French officers and 200 men at the Battle of Arroyo dos Molinos. In the end, Napoleon lost patience with Massena, said a firm *au revoir* to him and replaced him with General Marmont.

As Napoleon shifted his attention to Russia in 1812, his forces in Spain suffered further defeats. At Salamanca, Wellington crushed the French army of General Marmont. The Hussars of the legion distinguished themselves by capturing four enemy cannon and two standards. However, it was in the follow-up to the battle that the legion really triumphed. At Garcia Hernandez, the two heavy dragoon regiments of the legion charged three French squares in the space of forty minutes. They captured 1,400 men for the loss of six officers and 121 men, of whom fifty-two were killed. The authorities recognised the courage and commitment of the legion and decided the troops should be entitled to the same conditions as soldiers in the British Army. The officers were even entitled to a pension. The position of the legion was recognised further when they were given the honour of leading the Anglo-Portuguese forces into Madrid. So we have Germans leading the English and Portuguese through Spain having beaten the French.

The decisive battle of 1813 was at Vittoria, and Wellington's victory sealed the fate of King Joseph and the French forces in Spain. The legion again played an important role. This time it was Captain Augustus Hartmann and the artillery who made the decisive contribution. By massing all his forty-five cannon in the centre of the line, Hartmann experimented with a tactic that Napoleon, himself an artillery expert, was to use two years later at Waterloo. Wellington's victory allowed his troops to press northwards into France. It also encouraged the Austrians to take up arms against the French and thus marked the beginning of the end for Napoleon.

The King's German Legion emerged from the Peninsular

War with major honour. It had established itself as a committed and professional force to be treated with respect by the British. However, Waterloo was still to come.

When Napoleon escaped from Elba in March 1815, he gathered an army and headed for Belgium. He planned to defeat the British army of the Duke of Wellington and the Prussian army of General Blucher and re-establish French control of Europe. The decisive battle was fought in June at Waterloo, just outside Brussels, and the King's German Legion played a major role in the bitter fighting.

In front of Wellington's forces lay the farmhouse of La Haye Sainte. It was here that he stationed Major Baring and six companies of the 2nd Light Battalion of the King's German Legion. In total there were about 376 men. The defences of the farmhouse were somewhat weakened as the troops had burnt part of the gateway to keep warm on the night before the battle.

The French made repeated attempts to capture the farmhouse and drove the Hanoverians out of the orchard. However, for much of the day Major Baring was able to resist the French pressure. The burnt gateway was barricaded with the bodies of dead French soldiers, who had been bayoneted trying to force their way through the Hanoverians. Major Baring reported that the dead bodies made an efficient obstruction. The riflemen were running out of ammunition by mid-afternoon. They sent messengers asking for supplies but none arrived. They raided the bodies of fallen comrades for spare ammunition until this, too, was exhausted. The French set the farm on fire but the Hanoverians were able to extinguish the fire using cooking kettles. However, in the end the lack of ammunition was too great a disadvantage and the remnants of the light battalion were forced to retreat. The courage of the battalion was shown by their commander, Major Baring, who had three horses killed beneath him during the battle but continued fighting until the end of the day.

The fortune of Colonel Ompteda at the battle showed something of the character of the King's German Legion.

Ompteda had been with the legion since it was formed and he commanded the 2nd King's German Legion Brigade. The young Prince of Orange ordered Ompteda to charge a French column to relieve the pressure on La Haye Sainte. Ompteda pointed out that this would be suicidal, as a unit of French cuirassiers were positioned where they would be able to take Ompteda's men in the flank. The young prince refused to listen, so Ompteda rode off to lead his men into what he knew would be a trap. He was determined to do his duty and follow orders, even if it was likely to kill him. He asked Lieutenant-Colonel von Linsingen to look out for his two fifteen-year-old nephews, who were also to take part in the attack. Ompteda led from the front and, while his men did disrupt the French attack on La Haye Sainte, more than 130 of his 200 men were wiped out by the French cuirassiers, just as Ompteda had predicted. Lieutenant-Colonel von Linsingen was unable to prevent the death of Colonel Ompteda, but he was able to save his two nephews. Crawling out from beneath his dead horse, von Linsingen was able to identify the teenagers and drag them away from the action.

The defence of La Haye Sainte by the King's German Legion had slowed down the French attack and had given more time for General Blucher (those Germans again) and the Prussian Army to arrive and save the day. Napoleon was defeated, and his dreams of Empire ended, for the last time.

In February 1816, the King's German Legion was disbanded. However, they were not the last German soldiers to serve in the British Army. In 1856, for instance, 10,000 Germans were recruited into the British German Legion to serve in the Crimean War. The unit never saw combat and was disbanded in 1857, when many of the personnel went off to a settlement in the Eastern Cape. Married men were preferred for the settlement. As a result, members of the British German Legion built the garrison church in Colchester and married local girls so that they were eligible for the mission. There were as many as sixty marriages per day in order to clear the backlog before the legion was disbanded and set off for the Eastern Cape.

39

A Canned History

Even the best soldiers need feeding, and as the advance of science set out to cater for the needs of the soldiers and sailors of the Napoleonic Wars, French flair and British entrepreneurial spirit laid the foundations for a product that still dominates so many shop shelves all over the world.

'An army marches on its stomach' is a quote attributed to Napoleon. As he marched his armies all over Europe, from Spain to Moscow, he must have had plenty of time to ponder the issue. In 1795, he offered a reward of 12,000 Francs to anyone who could solve the problem of how to preserve food for his army.

A Paris chef, Nicolas Appert, took up the challenge. Since wine could be preserved in glass bottles, he decided to explore methods of preserving food in glass jars. He experimented with a wide variety of meats, eggs and vegetables. His most ambitious experiment was to try to preserve a whole lamb. His method involved boiling food inside corked jars.

After fifteen years of experimenting, Appert was confident that he had solved the problem of preserving food for Napoleon's soldiers even though he was unable to explain how or why his methods worked. In January 1810, he presented his idea to the Emperor Napoleon and was awarded the 12,000 francs prize. Like a good French academic, he wrote up his work in a book – *The Art of Preserving Animal and Vegetable Substances* – and applied for a patent, which was duly granted. He set up the first food-bottling factory at La Maison Appert in the town of Massy, near Paris.

While Appert had discovered food could be preserved by boiling it, it was in England that the idea was used in conjunction with tin cans to start the whole tinned food industry. England and France may have been in the middle of the Napoleonic Wars, but news of what Appert had discovered spread fast.

A Frenchman called Philippe de Girard brought the idea to England. He claimed there was too much red tape in Napoleonic France and he came to London to experiment with preserving food in tin cans. He made contact with the Royal Society and invited them to taste his preserved milk and stews. However, it would have been unpatriotic for George III to grant a royal patent to a French man in the middle of the Napoleonic Wars. Girard therefore passed on his ideas to Peter Durand, a merchant of Hoxton Square, Middlesex, and by August 1810 Durand had the royal patent.

The method patented by Durand was broadly similar to that described by Appert. However, it makes specific mention of preserving food in tin cans as well as glass and pottery. Durand experimented with preserving various soups and stews. His interest was in preserving food on a much larger scale than Appert. In one tin he succeeded in preserving thirty pounds of meat. With an eye on exploiting his patent, Durand gave tinned meat to the Royal Navy, who tried it out on voyages of between four and six months. On returning, the remaining tins were examined by members of the Royal Society, who declared that the food was perfectly preserved. However, even the Royal Society would have been unable to explain how this had happened.

Durand, however, was not interested in setting up a canning business himself, and, having proved that his idea worked, he sold the patent to Bryan Donkin and John Hall for £1,000. Donkin was a London engineer who already had an impressive record. He had made his money by taking a French idea and adapting it to the English market. He had made a machine to mass produce paper in continuous rolls rather than having to make each individual sheet separately. The Fourdrinier machine ended up being named after the financiers who had invested their money in Donkin rather than the engineer himself. Nevertheless, by 1810 Donkin had built eighteen Fourdrinier machines in different mills. His business was making over £2,000 per year but he was looking for a new challenge.

So Donkin went into partnership with John Hall and John Gamble. Donkin built a new factory in Bermondsey, London, where his existing factory was already making the Fourdrinier machines. He spent three years perfecting the process of manufacturing the tins and preserving the food. In June he sent a sample to the Duke of Kent, who served it to Queen Charlotte and other members of the royal family. The duke sent a letter to Donkin expressing his delight at the tinned beef. Donkin, not unreasonably, reckoned that the letter would help him secure business in his target market, the sailors of the Royal Navy.

While Donkin took care of any engineering issues, John Gamble handled much of the day-to-day running of the business and he seems to have been very thorough. Bermondsey was well placed for supplying the docks on the River Thames, and Donkin and Gamble had agents at the docks advertising their product and touting for business. The tins themselves were made by hand from sheets of tinplate. They came in different sizes and, ranging from four to twenty pounds in weight, by modern standards were very heavy. A tin in the Science Museum measuring fourteen centimetres by eighteen centimetres and filled with veal weighs in at seven pounds. Wow. That would make for a heavy shopping basket. Production was tightly controlled and each can was numbered. It was also kept for a time at a specific temperature. The food was priced between 8*d* per pound for carrots to 30*d* for beef. Quality control was tight as a food scandal would have been suicidal for the new industry.

Tinned food revolutionised life in the armed forces. In the

Royal Navy it ended the days of a monotonous diet of salt beef and bully biscuits. In 1813, the Navy bought 156 pounds of Donkin food. It was served to the sick and those who had scurvy as it was wrongly believed that scurvy was caused by a lack of fresh meat. 'I think it is a most excellent thing for the ship's company, and particularly those in a convalescent state. Two men, who were very ill and weak, have considerably recovered from the use of it these last few days,' wrote Captain A. W. Schomberg of HMS *York* in 1814.

In the Army, the Duke of Wellington wrote enthusiastically of the benefits of Donkin and Gamble food in the Peninsular War. It was also a staple of explorers and those looking for a way through the Northwest Passage. Fearful that their ships would be trapped in ice, these expeditions took enough food to last three years. Parry took Donkin food on his 1825 expedition. One tin was found in 1829 by Captain Sir John Ross and it was opened by scientists in 1958. Sadly, some of the iron and tin had dissolved into the food and scientists described it as having a 'pronounced bitter taste'.

In Chile, a cove was named Caleta Donkin because Captain Fitzroy and his crew were so delighted with their canned food.

In 1821, Donkin dissolved his partnership with Hall and Gamble and ended his interest in canning. John Gamble remained in the canning business but moved to Cork, Ireland, to take advantage of the fresh Irish beef. Donkin pursued other engineering interests, working with Mark Brunel (father of Isambard Kingdom Brunel) on a tunnel under the Thames. In his obituary the Royal Society noted that 'his life was one uninterrupted course of usefulness and good purpose', which is more than can be said for most of us.

By 1850, the canning industry was ready to increase its target market by moving from explorers and the armed forces into the domestic market. As more people moved into the towns and urban farms were pushed out, there was a market for tinned food. However, it was almost destroyed by a food scandal. In January 1852, meat inspectors found that tins of meat bound for the Royal Navy in Portsmouth contained rotten meat. Not only that, but the 'meat' contained bits of heart, tongue and dog. The tins had been supplied by a Stephan Goldner, who had undercut other suppliers and sourced his tins from what is now Hungary. Does this sound familiar? More than 6,000 pounds of Goldner's meat, costing nearly £7,000, was disposed of. Confidence in the tinned food market was severely shaken.

It was condensed milk, which appeared in the 1850s and was a commercial success, that convinced the general public that tinned food was safe.

40

A Maverick Scottish Surgeon
at the Cutting Edge

It wasn't just in food that science in Britain was making great advances in the early nineteenth century. Advances were taking place in a wide range of areas, including medicine.

Thanks to a string of hospital soap operas, we're now very used to thinking of surgeons as the superstars of medicine. In this TV world, surgeons have the power of life and death and patients and other medics look at them in awe as, firm of jaw, they wield their scalpels. But it hasn't always been this way. In fact, in the long history of medicine, while doctors have been respected for thousands of years, for surgeons it's all been a little more recent. It took a medical revolution, particularly in Scotland, to set them on the path they're on today.

When Robert Liston became a surgeon at Edinburgh Royal Infirmary in 1818, surgeons had only just begun to be accepted as professionals. The Royal College of Surgeons was less than twenty years old. Until 1745 they had been joined together with barbers as part of the Company of Barber-Surgeons. Hence, of course, all those jolly, red-and-white-striped, blood-and-bandages barber signs that you still see today.

When surgeons were granted a royal charter to become the Royal College of Surgeons in London, the Royal College of Physicians was the first to insist that they must be qualified physicians or doctors before they could become surgeons. The surgeons responded to this snub by insisting that surgeons kept the title Mr rather than prefixing their names with Dr, as they still do today. It's delightfully ironic that the medics many non-medics would regard as the most doctorly of doctors don't even call themselves 'doctor'.

The repertoire of most surgeons in the late eighteenth century was limited to amputations and the removal of bladder stones. All operations were carried out without anaesthetics, antiseptics or any form of blood transfusion. Surgeons were justifiably feared and patients only visited them when they could no longer cope with the pain of a disease or when death seemed even more likely off the operating table than on it.

Robert Liston was born in 1794 and was the son of a Scottish clergyman, Henry Liston, who appears to have had a hobby inventing new musical instruments – a far more soothing and peaceable occupation than that chosen by his son.

It was a time of enormous change in Scotland. In many parts, particularly in the Highlands, the clearances were destroying societies that had existed for many centuries, driving people off the land into cities or abroad. In the cities, an industrial and scientific revolution was also changing lives.

Robert Liston was educated at Edinburgh University and qualified in 1818. He was a flamboyant and brash character who found it difficult to get on with his contemporaries in Edinburgh. He revelled in confrontations. His response to a patient who had locked himself into a cupboard because he had changed his mind about having a bladder stone removed was to break down the door, seize the patient and go ahead with the operation anyway. Similarly, in an altercation with a Dr Knox, Liston felt perfectly justified in flattening Dr Knox in front of his students. Dr Knox had obtained the body of an attractive woman, Mary Paterson, within four hours of her death. Liston, however, suspected Dr Knox had been complicit in her death. The thought of her body being preserved in whisky and then dissected by students who may have known her well understandably offended Liston's sense of decency. However, Liston had no qualms about flattening his fellow professional. Actually, to be fair, it's the sort of incident you can probably still find in some hospital soap operas today, though it's hopefully rather less common in real life.

Anyway, in the light of all this it is unsurprising that the medical profession in Edinburgh took delight in recording Robert Liston's mistakes.

With no anaesthetic available, speed in particular was the hallmark of a good surgeon at the time. Liston was able to amputate a leg in less than two and a half minutes and his fastest amputation lasted a mere thirty seconds. Liston's operations were often carried out in public and fellow surgeons, students and the general public came to watch the show. He would begin preceding with his catchphrase, 'Time me Gentlemen, please', and would save time by clasping his knife between his teeth while operating – something you hopefully won't see in hospital soap operas these days.

Liston's speed, however, was not without its problems. In one famous, or indeed infamous, operation he removed one of his patient's testicles as well as his leg. As one might have said in the days of the barber-surgeons, a little bit too much off the side. Another spectacular mishap occurred when a single one of Liston's amputations managed to cause three deaths. The patient, unfortunately but not that shockingly, died of septicaemia. However, in the frenzy of trying to amputate quickly, Liston also accidently managed to cut off the fingers of his assistant, who then also died of septicaemia. Not only that, but Liston managed to cut through the coat of a spectator, who had come closer to get a good view. The spectator thought he had been stabbed and is reported to have died of the shock. This is the only recorded operation with an impressive 300 per cent mortality rate.

Robert Liston was, however, more than an entertainer or crowd pleaser as a surgeon. He was prepared to operate on patients who had been rejected by others. He took four and a half minutes to remove a scrotal tumour weighing forty-five pounds, which the patient had been carrying around in a wheelbarrow.

Robert Liston's abrasive character and confrontational manner led to him being ostracised by his colleagues. In 1840 he moved to Clifford Street in London and became Professor of Surgery at University College Hospital. In London he left a legacy that included the 'bulldog' locking artery forceps and a leg splint used to stabilise dislocations and fractures of the femur. These specialist pieces of kit, which form the basis of modern equipment, show that Liston was genuinely a serious surgeon who was determined to make improvements in surgery. His legacy was recognised by University College, who instigated the Liston Medal in his honour. It was at University College that, in 1846, a year before his death, he became the first surgeon in Europe to carry out an amputation using a general anaesthetic and thus introduced pain-free surgery to this country.

Of course, while Liston deserves the credit for being the first surgeon to have the courage to use ether as an anaesthetic, some of the developmental work took place in the USA. The English chemist Humphrey Davy had been the first to discover an effective anaesthetic when he discovered that inhaling nitrous oxide (laughing gas) numbed the body to pain. Surgeons took little notice of Davy's work, but nitrous oxide became a recreational drug, used on both sides of the Atlantic as entertainment. Spectators would turn up at fairs to watch the effect that it had on people and to laugh at their intoxicated behaviour. These entertainments also featured the use of ether, and it was ether that was to provide the stronger and more effective anaesthetic. Medical student William Morton used the drug on a recreational basis and realised its potential for medical use. In September 1846 he carried out a tooth extraction at Massachusetts General Hospital using ether and this began a rush to use the drug. Within three weeks John Collins Warren had used ether to remove a tumour from a patient's neck, and by December 1846, less than three months since William Morton's initial experiment, Robert Liston was ready to usher in a new era in England.

However, rather unfairly for Liston, it is James Simpson

who has been given most of the credit for the development of anaesthetics in the UK. Simpson, like Liston, was trained at Edinburgh University. He was a child prodigy who started at university aged fourteen and took his finals aged eighteen. He then had to wait two years to qualify as a doctor as he was considered too young. He became Professor of Midwifery at Edinburgh University in 1839 and therefore would have been working in Edinburgh at the same time as Robert Liston. Simpson's search for an alternative to ether that could be used in childbirth, sniffing his way along the range of solvents he had acquired from the local chemist, is well known. The danger of this approach, which frequently left him unfit to lecture at Edinburgh University and which could have easily killed him rather than produce a breakthrough, is rather less appreciated. Simpson's fame comes from the fact that he helped persuade celebrity mothers like Queen Victoria and Catherine Dickens to use chloroform in childbirth. It is more surprising to learn that this doctor, who was entrusted with delivering the children of royalty, should have entertained himself by giving chloroform to his guests to liven up his dinner parties. Even the cook was said to have imbibed chloroform, which was mixed into some sort of cocktail.

While some of Liston's mistakes were spectacular, so were many of his successes. The advances he made helped prepare the path for surgery to become a respectable, and indeed essential, part of modern medical life. A host of actors and actresses have donned surgical scrubs, entered TV studios kitted out like operating theatres, and uttered immortal lines like 'Swab, please, nurse'. On his death, Liston was given a glowing send-off from his peers in *The Lancet* and 30,000 mourners gathered on the streets of Edinburgh. You'd have to be a pretty big soap star to get 30,000 mourners.

41

Pembroke's Ships, from Wales to the World

One of the key factors in the Industrial Revolution was Britain's flourishing global trade and the powerful navy that protected it. But the Royal Navy didn't just help create the Industrial Revolution; the Industrial Revolution helped create a new navy too, a navy of steam and metal.

Today, with a Royal Navy facing severe cuts, it's sometimes hard to imagine the full might of the Navy at the height of its power around the globe, when it was a key component – in some senses perhaps *the* key component – in maintaining and expanding the British Empire and generally expressing British imperial might around the world. Some places in Britain today linked to that history are very well known; places like Chatham and Portsmouth, for instance. Some are less widely known, but still have amazing histories. One example is Pembroke Dock.

By the early nineteenth century, the area already had a long association with the sea and shipping. The Vikings had spent time there, and kings of England had set off from the area with fleets to attack Ireland.

Iron and timber and manpower were cheap in the area, and in the eighteenth century the Royal Navy had paid a local private dockyard to build some ships. HMS *Milford*, for instance, was launched there in 1759. In 1776, it won a victory over the American privateer the *Yankee Hero* after the US ship's crew made an extremely unfortunate mistake. They chose to chase HMS *Milford*, thinking it was a merchant ship. When they realised their mistake, things suddenly swapped around and the Americans ended up being chased by the much larger *Milford*. After the *Milford* managed to put a broadside into the *Yankee Hero*, its captain, with a large section of his crew dead or wounded, was forced to surrender.

Eventually, with the Napoleonic Wars having placed a renewed focus on shipbuilding facilities, the Navy tried to develop its own dockyard on the site of Pembroke Dock and a purchase price of £4,455 was suggested. However, when a deal proved impossible the Navy decided to build its own dockyard in the area: Pembroke's Royal Naval Dockyard.

They didn't waste much time. The last ship built at Milford for the Royal Navy in the period was HMS *Rochfort*, launched in 1814. HMS *Lapwing* was used as temporary accommodation at Pembroke Dock and by 1816 they were launching ships from the new dockyard. The first two ships to be launched were the little frigates HMS *Valorous* and HMS *Ariadne*. Okay, they'd managed to miss the Napoleonic Wars, but still a century of spectacular shipbuilding activity lay ahead of Pembroke, and what a century it would be. A century of vast technological change and a century of global British naval activity. Pembroke would have a whole thirteen building slips and by the time the last ship was launched in 1922 something in the region of an amazing 250 ships had been built there.

A number of ships for the royal family were built at Pembroke. For instance, twin-paddle steamer HMY (that's Her Majesty's Yacht) *Victoria and Albert* was built for, yes, Victoria and Albert, being launched at Pembroke in 1843.

But it's the warships that were built there that are Pembroke Dockyard's main contribution to British history and which give it a unique place in the story of British sea power. HMS *Rodney*, for instance, launched at Pembroke in 1833 and carrying ninety guns, saw action in the Mediterranean and in the Crimean War, where her guns were used at Sebastopol and then became a flagship in Chinese seas. In 1843, HMS

Tartarus, Pembroke's first steam warship, was completed. And fifty-gun frigate HMS *Constance* launched at Pembroke in 1846, rounded Cape Horn and served on the Pacific Station. Courtenay on Vancouver Island is named after *Constance*'s then captain, who led an expedition against the locals while at Fort Victoria (now Victoria, the capital of British Columbia). In 1862 HMS *Prince Consort* was launched, becoming the first ironclad screw ship out of Pembroke. The huge, 14,900-ton HMS *Hannibal* was launched at Pembroke in 1896, becoming part of the Atlantic Fleet before serving as a troopship in the Dardanelles Campaign and ending up as depot ship in Alexandria, Egypt.

In the early twentieth century, Pembroke built three giant armoured cruisers: HMS *Duke of Edinburgh* in 1904, HMS *Warrior* in 1905 and HMS *Defence* in 1907. By the outbreak of the First World War, all three ships had already had interesting careers. *Defence*, for instance, escorted newly crowned George V when he set off on a visit to India and subsequently served on the China Station. *Duke of Edinburgh* had served with the Mediterranean Fleet and rushed to help those in danger after the SS *Delhi* sank off Morocco in 1911. *Warrior* had served with the Channel Fleet and then with the Mediterranean Fleet.

Then, in 1916, all three ships fought in the Battle of Jutland. HMS *Duke of Edinburgh* went on to serve elsewhere (on the North America and West Indies stations). For *Warrior* and *Defence*, however, Jutland was the end of it. *Defence*'s magazines exploded after it was hit by German shells, killing all aboard.

It wasn't just in the empire's wars that Pembroke ships played a key role. For instance, HMS *Erebus* was launched at Pembroke in 1826. In 1840, it set out from Tasmania under the command of James Clark Ross to explore Antarctica. The famous Antarctic volcano Mount Erebus is named after this Pembroke ship. The *Erebus* unfortunately then became part of the Franklin Expedition, sent along with HMS *Terror* to try to navigate the Northwest passage. The subsequent disappearance of the expedition is one of the great tragedies of British exploration history.

Things didn't always go smoothly with the shipbuilding and launching process. HMS *Cockchafer*, for instance, was launched successfully in February 1881 as the band played and crowds cheered. But even as it was taking to the waters, shipwright Samuel Ellis Ball lay dying on HMS *Nankin*, the dockyard hospital ship. Ball had fallen while working on the stern of the ship and had suffered terrible injuries. He finally died just a few hours after the ship that he had helped build was launched. It wasn't just the dockyard workers themselves who were vulnerable. In March 1856, Mrs Mathias, the wife of the high sheriff, stood on a platform to name HMS *Janus* and HMS *Drake*. As the ships moved off into the water, HMS *Janus* hit the platform on which Mrs Mathias was standing, destroying it and sending her and her children flying. They were all rather luckier than Samuel Ellis Ball, but the cheering for the ships was, predictably, rather cut short. A bit of a disaster also happened to new royal yacht *Victoria and Albert* in 1900 when an attempt to move it from the dry dock left the vessel keeled over on one side with a large dent in it.

Many fascinating characters served at Pembroke dockyard, including, for instance, Watkin Owen Pell, superintendent of the dockyard in the 1840s. He had lost a leg in a naval battle in 1800, and is said to have used a telescope to watch over his dockyard domain and the activities of it staff. He used to ride a donkey around the dockyard, sometimes even venturing with it onto the ships being built there.

The naval presence became a key part of the local landscape and economy and this wasn't down to just the shipyard itself. For instance, barracks were built for troops who would defend this key strategic naval base if it was ever attacked. Two massive Martello tower fortifications were built in order to defend it. The town, still called Pembroke Dock today, grew up around the dockyard.

But naval shipbuilding at Pembroke would not last forever. The last big warship built at Pembroke was armoured cruiser

HMS *Defence* in 1907. Shipbuilding did continue, along with some submarine building (another technological innovation). The First World War naturally saw a surge in demand for repair work, and in 1918 the future US President Franklin D. Roosevelt visited. However, shortly after the war, naval shipbuilding at Pembroke came to an end. The last Navy ship launched there was the Royal Fleet Auxiliary tanker *Oleander* in 1922. Work at the Navy dockyard ceased in 1926, causing devastation to the local economy.

It was not, however, entirely the end of a military presence at Pembroke Dock. Some naval activity was to remain, and the Second World War was to bring another major period of British military activity. Pembroke Dock became a major base for RAF flying boats during the desperate battle to keep the Atlantic supply lines safe from U-boats.

In 1956, the last Pembroke-built ship afloat, the in some senses rather strangely named HMS *Inconstant*, which been launched long ago in 1868, was broken up in Belgium. The following year, in 1957, the RAF announced big cuts to its activities at Pembroke Dock. The story of the Navy's Pembroke dockyard remains an amazing and somewhat unexpected part of Britain's history and heritage.

42

Educating Britain

During the nineteenth century, while Britain fought to build its predominance around the globe, at home another battle was starting: the battle for social justice. The nineteenth century saw, for instance, the Chartists fighting for greater political rights and the Great Reform Act of 1832. It saw the Tolpuddle Martyrs and the start of trade unions; it saw Elizabeth Fry and the fight for prison reform; it saw the beginnings of socialism; and it saw the beginning of the battle for women's rights. However, then as now, a vital component of social justice was a good education. The question, though, as always, was how to provide it. No, panics, confusion and controversies over education aren't a new thing. Not at all.

Britain's schools had fallen behind the standards of Britain's commercial rivals. Industries were concerned about workers who had not mastered the three Rs – reading, writing and arithmetic. Inspectors reported huge differences between the best and worst schools inspected. The churches worried about the moral standards of the young. Politicians were anxious to prove to taxpayers that money spent on education had not been wasted. Teachers worried about making the most impact while spending least. While many of these issues may be familiar today, they were also the issues faced by Victorian educational pioneers as they sought to give the country an education system that was fit for purpose.

Education choices and schooling depended entirely on social class and the wealth and aspirations of parents. For the aristocracy and upper middle class there were the nine traditional public schools: Eton, Winchester, Westminster, Charterhouse, St Paul's, Merchant Taylors', Harrow, Rugby and Shrewsbury. The curriculum consisted of classics, mathematics, a modern language, two natural sciences, history, geography, drawing, and music. The activities of these top nine schools were investigated in the Clarenden Report in 1864 and regulated by the 1868 Public Schools Act. While there had been criticism of these schools for being too focused on the classics, they had been reformed by heads such as Thomas Arnold and they represented the upper end of the educational establishment.

Beneath this elite group, the Taunton Report decided schools would be divided into three groups. First-grade schools were for upper- and upper-middle-class boys, who were bound for university and the older professions. These schools would teach boys up to the age of eighteen or nineteen and the subjects would be very similar to those in the top public schools. Beneath these were second-grade schools aimed at providing members of the newer professions, the Civil Service and the Army. They kept boys until they were sixteen or seventeen and taught two languages and Latin to their pupils. The third-grade schools were for lower-middle-class boys, small tradesmen and superior artisans. They left at fourteen or fifteen, by which time they were expected to have learnt some French and Latin. This was the system enshrined in the 1869 Endowed school Act. However, two-thirds of towns had no secondary schools at all, so provision of secondary schools would remain poor until the Balfour Act at the beginning of the twentieth century.

At the elementary stage there was a huge variety of organisations and individuals competing to provide a basic education. The two largest organisations were the Church of England and the Nonconformist churches. Their efforts were supplemented by private dame schools, which were run as nurseries to allow women to keep working. Some industries set up schools and charities provided education for the poorest in ragged schools.

The Anglican Church created the National Society for the Education of the Poor in Accordance with the Principles of the Established Church. It ran national schools in many villages, which were designed both to teach pupils a moral education and to provide some instruction in the three Rs. These schools did not receive any state funding and the Church of England was quite clear that their role was to educate a new generation of Anglicans. By 1832, there were more than 12,000 such schools in the country.

Many national schools were based on the Madras system, introduced by Andrew Bell to maximise the amount of knowledge which could be obtained from a small number of trained teachers. This was a system which Bell had developed from his time in India. He had observed children teaching each other to write by copying the letters written by one child in the sand. Bell showed how one eight-year-old who had been taught to write could then teach a group of twenty children how to do it. He called this method 'the steam engine of the industrial world' and he adapted it for use in national schools. The master taught the lesson to the best students, who in turn taught it to the younger pupils. It was a perfect system for rote learning. What the master wrote on his board was copied by the monitors, who wrote it on their slates and showed it to the younger pupils, who copied it on to their slates.

In competition with the national schools were those schools funded by the Nonconformist churches. These were funded by the British and Foreign Schools Society to ensure that Nonconformists did not lose out. By 1851 the census showed that there were nearly as many Nonconformists as Anglicans in England, and in the new industrial cities Nonconformists may even have outnumbered Anglicans. Nonconformist schools did not receive funding from the government either and were dependent on parents paying for their children. However, in Joseph Lancaster's school in Southwark no child was ever turned away for being unable to pay.

Like the national schools, the Nonconformist schools based their education on the three Rs and a good dose of moral education. The leading light of the Nonconformist schools was the Quaker Joseph Lancaster. He set up his school in Southwark and more than 7,000 children passed through its gates while he was in charge. He copied the teaching methods of Bell and adapted the monitorial system. In 1803 he published his *Improvements in Education*. He encouraged schools to organise their pupils into groups of similar ability rather than of a similar age, with a monitor for each ability group. He also laid out a system of rewards and badges for monitors to encourage them to carry out their responsibilities. As a Quaker, Lancaster was opposed to all forms of corporal punishment and preferred to encourage pupils to reflect on the morality of their actions. He set up about fifty schools around the country on these principles.

Andrew Bell and Joseph Lancaster were two of the best-known educationalists at the beginning of the nineteenth century and the teaching methods they advocated dominated elementary education. They met very different fates. Andrew Bell was very careful with his money, which ended up being used to establish Madras College in St Andrews, where he was born. Joseph Lancaster fell out with other Nonconformist reformers and left the country for New York. He established schools in New York, Canada and Venezuela, but they all failed to make any money.

Monitorial schools provided a basis of the three Rs and as a result were important in providing the economy with the huge number of clerks required to keep track of what was being made in the Industrial Revolution. However, they did little to provide the skilled engineers that were needed to drive it. The government thought this was the responsibility of industrial leaders. As a result, there was little technical education in Victorian times.

Girls received less education than boys. By 1851, only 55 per cent of girls could read and write compared to 70 per cent of boys. The wealthy could afford a governess. The quality of governesses was inconsistent. While some were studious, most provided an education which would fit girls for their role in society. They were taught to sew, to play music and to speak some foreign languages. Those who could not afford a governess might pay for a private school, but the curriculum would be dominated by the social role of making girls into good wives and mothers. After all, women were not allowed to attend university and therefore could not enter the professions. Victorians saw little point in educating girls for jobs which were closed to them. Even at elementary schools, girls and boys were taught separately. The schools had separate entrances for girls and boys, and they had separate teachers and separate classrooms.

By 1861, the government was forced into action. It was suffering as the industrialisation of Prussia was making Prussia an effective rival to Britain. Driving the Prussian economy was a national education system, which was much more geared to the demands of the economy and which did more than deliver the three Rs in a repetitive fashion.

The Newcastle Commission was established to investigate. It confirmed that there were huge differences between the best and the worst elementary schools in the country. It suggested that about 120,000 children from the poorest families did not go to school at all, either because there was no school available or because families preferred to send children to work rather than to school. Even though the government had passed laws forbidding child labour this was still an issue, particularly in rural areas where children were essential to bringing in the harvest. The commission was also critical of the education provided by the established elementary schools, finding that it was concentrated on older pupils at the expense of the younger and less able. They also found a lot of private schools that were little more than nurseries. The government responded to the Newcastle Commission with the Revised Code in 1862 and Forster's Education Act of 1870.

The Revised Code introduced a system of payment by results. The government had become alarmed at the amount of money being spent on education. In 1860, it had spent over £1 million for the first time. While the figure may have shocked MPs, it was insignificant compared to the £78 million they felt justified in spending on the Crimean War. The basis of the system was accountability. Schools would get 4s per year for every pupil who attended regularly and up to an extra 8s if pupils could prove to inspectors that they had made sufficient progress in the three Rs. Robert Lowe claimed in the House of Commons that 'if it is not cheap, it shall be efficient; if it is not efficient, it shall be cheap'. Either way, the taxpayer was a winner. Sort of.

There was no agreement that the Revised Code was the best way forward. To critics like Matthew Arnold it made the inspectors accountants, looking at attendance and the three Rs rather than the broader education of the children. Others pointed out it would narrow the curriculum almost exclusively to the three Rs, as these were the only subjects examined. Some critics pointed to problems with the fairness of the system. To its supporters, the Revised Code dealt with those schools identified as inadequate by the Newcastle Commission and it made schools accountable.

There is no agreement about whether it worked, but it lasted thirty years before the government decided that it was more important to promote a broader curriculum and that collaboration between schools and a greater role for local councils was a fairer approach. To its supporters it worked. Costs fell, inefficient teachers left and the standards in the three Rs in the poorest schools rose. Critics point out that overall standards in the three Rs did not rise, teachers' wages fell and there was a problem attracting good teachers into the system. The curriculum did narrow, and some pupils were forced into school for the inspector's visit even though they were in a state where they needed to be isolated or kept in bed because of infectious diseases. Frequently there were bitter disputes over the standard of inspections and whether inspectors were consistent.

Forster's Education Act established that voluntary schools that already existed, like the British and national schools run by the Nonconformists and the Anglican Church, would continue and be publicly funded. Where there were no voluntary schools, locally elected school boards would be established to set up and run board schools, which would be funded by the government. Women were allowed to both stand and vote in school board elections, and this was the first step into local politics for women like Elizabeth Garrett, the future suffragette. Board schools were allowed to charge fees if they thought it was necessary. For the first time, Britain had a national system of education for those aged five to ten. It was a start.

Girls' education in the later nineteenth century made great steps forward as middle-class women sought to open up suitable careers for single middle-class women and saw education as an important step forward. Dorothea Beale turned Cheltenham Ladies' College into a model of high-quality education for girls when she took over in 1858. Roedean and Frances Buss's North London Collegiate were founded in the 1870s. Both included Latin and the sciences in the curriculum.

At Cambridge, Emily Davies established Girton College in 1873. London University admitted women from 1878, and Oxford followed suit in 1879. Therefore, by the end of the century there were routes to enable middle-class girls to get an academic education and by gaining access to university they were able to start competing for entry into what had once been male-dominated professions like medicine.

For working-class girls, opportunities were more limited. They received a similar education to working-class boys after 1870, though classes were divided and taught in single-sex groups. The girls were also given some training in sewing, knitting, cooking and cleaning to help prepare them for life.

In the end, it was not until 1880 that the government made school attendance compulsory up until the age of ten and not until 1891 that it gave children a right to a free education. In 1899 it raised the school leaving age to twelve, but it was not until 1902 that Balfour's Education Act set out to tackle the problem of providing a proper secondary education for English children.

43

Percy Pilcher's Plane: How a Briton Almost Beat the Wright Brothers

By the late nineteenth century, the great industrial, scientific, social and commercial advances of the previous hundred years, in which Britain had played such a leading part, had created a world that was beginning to look, in some senses, a little like our own. In the final years of the nineteenth century and the first years of the twentieth century would come another revolution: the revolution of flight.

We're all so used to the idea that manned, powered, heavier-than-air flight started in America in 1903 with the Wright brothers taking a short hop in their biplane, but what if things had been different? What if, instead of Americans in the twentieth century, it had been a Briton in the last years of the nineteenth century who had first managed to master the ideas that would enable us to send a human being soaring aloft (or at least a few feet off the ground) on wings in powered flight? This is the story of one Percy Pilcher. Percy Pilcher, a great name. His full name, in fact, was actually Percy Sinclair Pilcher, but Percy Pilcher sounds more fun, and Percy Pilcher's plane even better.

Percy, of course, was not the first Briton to take a passionate interest in winged flight. The hundred years before Percy had already seen major work in the field from a number of Britons.

Sir George Cayley, for instance, played a major role in

establishing the basics of aeronautics with his work at the end of the eighteenth century and in the early nineteenth century on such fundamentals as aerofoils and designs for fixed-wing and multi-wing aircraft. Late in the nineteenth century, Francis Herbert Wenham worked on cambered aerofoils and even on a wind tunnel. Later still, Horatio Phillips did more work on aerofoils and multi-wing aircraft.

And now we come to Percy Pilcher. Percy was only young when his father died in 1874, and his mother died soon after, in 1877. In 1880 he was put into the Navy as a cadet, and he soon found that his passion in life was engineering. At first this was marine engineering. In 1887 he resigned from the Navy and became an apprentice at Randolph Elder and Co. shipbuilders on Clydeside, and this was to be followed by a period working at the Southampton Naval Works. But it was already becoming obvious that Percy had dreams of engineering that would not conquer the waves but conquer the sky instead. In 1890, he published *Gliding*.

In the early 1890s he returned to Glasgow and became an assistant to the John Elder Professor of Naval Architecture, John Harvard Biles. He lectured on the subject of marine engineering to the Naval Architecture students, but his passion for matters of the sky continued.

In 1895 he built a glider called the *Bat*, which he first took to the air at Cardross. Pilcher was now taking this all very seriously. That same year he travelled to Germany to meet the man who was then perhaps the world's leading expert on building hang-gliders, Otto Lilienthal. Lilienthal above all had understood that the curved shape of birds' wings is crucial in giving them lift and that this was the area the pioneers of winged human flight should be looking at.

Inspired by his discussions with Lilienthal and further developing his own ideas, Percy went ahead and built two more glider designs, the *Beetle* and the *Gull* (clearly a man inspired by nature as well). Then he went on to build a glider called the *Hawk*, which had the world's first sprung, wheeled undercarriage.

Percy, however, could be in no doubts about the dangers of what he was doing, particularly after the events of 8 August 1896. On that day, his great mentor Otto Lilienthal stalled and crashed. He was rushed by train to Berlin for surgery but died shortly afterwards. His last words allegedly were, 'Sacrifices must be made.'

Even the death of Lilienthal, however, would not stop Percy. In the *Hawk* he made flights of up to 750 feet. And it wasn't just him flying. Dorothy Pilcher, Percy's cousin, also flew the *Hawk*. This was, after all, the 1890s, not the 890s. Women could fly as well.

But Percy wasn't satisfied with just gliding, hugely daring though that was. He had his eyes set on an even bigger prize: not just winged flight, but *powered* winged flight.

Already in 1896 he had filed a patent for a design of a powered aeroplane, and he was determined to make one work. French-American aeronautical engineer Octave Chanute had been working on getting extra lift by using multiple wings, and Percy also explored this approach. In 1896 he left Glasgow University to work for the Maxim & Nordenfeld Company, where he worked with Sir Hiram Maxim (the man who designed the Maxim machine gun and who had himself already experimented with ideas for a steam-powered plane) on propeller designs. In 1898 he formed a business partnership, Wilson & Pilcher, with Walter Gordon Wilson, a distinguished engineer who would later become hugely important in the design of the first tank.

By 1899, Percy had a triplane and a lightweight engine to power it. The excitement and anticipation must have been intense. But days before what was supposed to be its first flight, the crankshaft broke. Pilcher desperately needed sponsorship, so instead of just cancelling the demonstration entirely he decided to fly the *Hawk* instead.

On 30 September 1899, Percy Pilcher took to the air at Stanford Hall near Market Harborough. Tragically, it was to be his last flight. Like Otto Lilienthal, Percy would not live to see the era of manned, powered, heavier-than-air flight.

The *Hawk* smashed into the ground with a crash that could be heard hundreds of yards distant, and Percy was terribly injured. He remained unconscious, dying two days later at Stanford Hall.

It is fascinating to contemplate how close this British aviation pioneer may have come to being the first human being to master manned, powered, heavier-than-air flight. He was buried in Brompton Cemetery, London. A memorial stone column marks the spot where he died at Stanford Hall just before the end of the nineteenth century. Just over four years later, in a new century, the Wright brothers' machine would take to the air, and just over a decade after that planes would be flying and fighting in the First World War; a war, of course, in which the works of Percy's colleagues Sir Hiram Maxim and Walter Gordon Wilson would also play a huge and lethal role. Sir Thomas Sopwith himself died as recently as 1989, at the grand old age of 101.

44

A British Attempt to Blast the Art World

Nineteenth-century British pioneers played a crucial role in the development of photography. In the second half of the century, photography's capacity to cheaply and quickly capture reality and an increasing interest in the art of distant countries that Europeans were now encountering were two major factors leading Western artists to explore forms of work less closely linked to traditions of portraying reality and idealised reality.

In recent decades, with the appearance of artists such as Damien Hirst and Tracy Emin, we've got more used to the idea of the UK as a home to adventurous modern visual art.

However, compared to the visual revolution happening across the water in mainland Europe, British art of the nineteenth and early twentieth centuries can sometimes be considered conservative and rather more in love with traditional genres such as landscape and portraiture. Yes, we had the rather jolly Pre-Raphaelites, but even they, despite the innovations they brought, deliberately sought inspiration from the past.

The second half of the nineteenth century in mainland Europe had already seen such visual experimentation as Impressionism, and the Vienna Secession. In the twentieth century, the pace of change was even faster. Already by 1905 France had the Fauves, and by 1907 Picasso was painting the angular lines and distorted faces of *Les Demoiselles d'Avignon*, and by 1911 Germany had the revolutionary art movement Der Blaue Reiter, featuring such artists as Kandinsky and Franz Marc. By 1915, Kazimir Malevich, artistic exponent of Suprematism, would be pushing abstraction to its very limits with his work *Black Square on White*.

Well, Britain is never quite going to take the place of France or Germany or Russia in the history of early twentieth-century modern art, but it was, in the period before the First World War at least, home to one genuine stab at a radical, revolutionary art movement with plenty of passion, debate, falling out and eventual disillusionment. It was called Vorticism.

Having said all that, even Vorticism had foreign roots and something of a Continental outlook. At the heart of the movement was a man born in 1882 and named by his parents Percy Wyndham Lewis, but now known generally as Wyndham Lewis because he apparently didn't like the name Percy. Lewis's father was Captain Charles Edward Lewis, who had fought in the American Civil War, but by 1897 Percy was being educated at the not hugely revolutionary Rugby School, followed by the rather more revolutionary Slade School of Art. He then followed all that up by living and travelling in mainland Europe and experiencing Continental art movements such as Cubism, Futurism and Post-Impressionism. Perhaps inevitably, on his return to Britain he fell in with fellow fans of cultural revolution the Bloomsbury Group and spent time at the famous Omega Workshop, which aimed to produce the Bloomsbury ethos in concrete, artistic reality. Again perhaps inevitably, a spat developed which led to Lewis walking out of the Omega Workshop, taking some other artists along with him, to found his own workshop, the ostentatiously revolutionary, or at least rebellious, Rebel Art Centre. If you're determined to be an art rebel, why hide it?

Like all the most famous art movements, it needed a catchy title. Lewis regarded the kind of adventurous, brash, colourful, angular art the movement was after as a sort of combination of Cubism and Futurism, a sort of Cubo-Futurism. Ezra Pound, however, came up with the name Vorticism. And what does a revolutionary new art movement need after a catchy name? Yep, a manifesto. Oh, and its own magazine as well, of course.

The first issue of a magazine named *BLAST* appeared in the summer of 1914, carrying the manifesto of Vorticism. Among the signatories of the manifesto were, of course, Lewis and Ezra Pound, but also artists such as Henri Gaudier-Brzeska and Helen Saunders. *BLAST* basically set out to blast the Victorian heritage in Britain and propel the country into the future. *BLAST* demonstrated its radical ambitions in the words used, in the works of art portrayed and in the dramatic typography and graphic design of the magazine itself.

Linked to the movement were also artists such as David Bomberg, Christopher Nevinson and Jacob Epstein. Epstein's *Rock Drill* is an extraordinary work of sculpture by any standards.

In the summer of 1914, the Vorticists were basically determined to make the country ready for a much more exciting, dynamic, explosive, intense future. Unfortunately for the Vorticists, and even more unfortunately for the vast numbers who were about to die and be maimed, the exciting, dynamic, explosive, intense future that Britain was about to face wasn't quite the thrilling new age of revolutionary development that Lewis had dreamt of during his artistic stay in Europe or when he set up the Rebel Art Centre. Instead it was, of course, the First World War.

Vorticism did not, however, immediately die as the first shots of the global conflagration were fired. Yes, even at the beginning of the war, plenty of people were nervous and anxious about where the war would lead, but also plenty of people were excited as well. The second issue of *BLAST* proudly announced itself as a WAR NUMBER when it appeared in 1915, and carried on its cover a work by Lewis with the title *Before Antwerp*, showing an angular rank of soldiers thrusting guns forward amid a dramatic, angular landscape. It even included an article by Henri Gaudier-Brzeska submitted from the trenches. In the same year that the guns were thundering in France and Belgium, the Vorticists held an exhibition at a gallery in London.

It is impossible now to know what would have happened to Vorticism if the First World War had never occurred. Would it have gone on to become a well-known and famous art movement, or would it have quickly degenerated into personal quarrels and disappeared?

But the war did happen, and an art movement that sought to portray the excitement and drama of an age made by machines suddenly had to face up to the hugely more intense experience of war made by machines. Some of the Vorticists experienced it first-hand. Henri Gaudier-Brzeska died in the trenches. Nevinson volunteered for the Friends' Ambulance Unit and was deeply affected by what he saw. His early work *La Mitrailleuse*, portraying a machine-gunner, still shows the angular intensity and fascination with machinery that linked him to Vorticism, but by 1917 he was painting *Paths of Glory*, a painting depicting dead British soldiers face down in mud, with a sea of barbed wire beyond, in a portrayal that has almost no artistic links to Vorticism.

Lewis himself served as an officer in the Royal Artillery. A photo of 1917 shows him in officer's uniform looking rather like the now much more famous (though fictional) Captain Edmund Blackadder. He spent much time as a forward observer and must have seen a lot of the horror of the war. Unlike the situation with Nevinson and *Paths of Glory*, however, Lewis even in 1919 could paint a recognisably Vorticist painting such as *A Battery Shelled*, though other non-Vorticist elements were also beginning to enter his repertoire.

But by the end of the war Vorticism as an art movement was finished. Its members – those still alive – scattered, and the future in 1920 looked very different to how the future had looked in 1910. Epstein went on to become the best-known visual artist who had been linked with Vorticism. Two of the other well-known Vorticists, Wyndham Lewis and Ezra Pound, however, would eventually become known for extreme right-wing views, something which discouraged a lot of people from taking an interest in their Vorticist work.

However, in at least one area, the influence of Vorticism and *BLAST* lives on. Its use of big, bold, brash typography and dramatic angular graphic design was influential in the graphic design revolution of the 1920s and 1930s which remains so important to graphic designers even now.

45

Terror from the Sea in the First World War

In 1914, the British Empire seemed in some senses at its height. The late nineteenth century had seen a wave of expansion, particularly in Africa. The empire had faced major difficulties fighting both Zulus and Boers but in the end had triumphed in both instances. The Royal Navy was a unique force. Queen Victoria had died in 1901, and her son Edward VII in 1910, but Britain had George V.

But the four years of bitter warfare that started in August 1914 were to shake many of the British imperial certainties of the nineteenth century, and the world that Britain would be part of after the war was finished would be a very different world indeed.

Most people are very well aware of the First World War and a lot of its key events, and that awareness is only going to increase with all the First World War centenaries coming up over the next few years. Many are even aware of the Zeppelin and Gotha air raids against Britain. But one of the lesser-known events of the First World War is another one that brought the war to the home front in a way that almost seems strange to us now, accustomed as we are to the idea of the Royal Navy 'ruling the waves' for long periods of the last few centuries.

During the First World War, far away from the trenches of the Western Front, the German Navy repeatedly attacked towns on England's coast – so frequently, in fact, that we can't really include every incident here.

Britain declared war on Germany on 4 August 1914. The Germans were wary of facing the full might of the Royal Navy, so they devised a raiding strategy in the hopes that it would enable them to do a bit of damage to Britain and perhaps sink a few British ships without having to run into a big, scary chunk of our Grand Fleet. Less than three months after our declaration of war, in the early morning of 3 November, just two days after our worst naval defeat in a very long time (HMS *Monmouth* and HMS *Good Hope* were sunk off the Chilean coast in the Battle of Coronel with a total loss of 1,570 men) and with the First Battle of Ypres still raging on the Western Front, a German cruiser squadron that had slipped across the North Sea was closing in on the unsuspecting east coast town of Great Yarmouth. It was a Tuesday.

The German squadron, commanded by Admiral Franz von Hipper, had three battle cruisers, an armoured cruiser and four light cruisers. The British forces that would tackle this mighty array consisted of a minesweeper, a few destroyers and a few submarines. Considering the imbalance in forces, we didn't do that badly. The minesweeper HMS *Halcyon* spotted and challenged the incoming German squadron and things got lively for it and for HMS *Lively* as it tried to make smoke to hide the ships and the Germans tried to sink them. The Germans then laid mines off the coast and attempted to shell Great Yarmouth, but they only managed to devastate the beach on this occasion. One British submarine was sunk by a mine while trying to pursue the German squadron, and by the time our big ships eventually turned up the Germans were long gone across the North Sea, though one of their ships also hit a mine in the end as well.

It hadn't exactly been a stunning success for the German Navy, but it hadn't been a huge success for Britain either, considering how a powerful German squadron had managed to cross the North Sea, shell Britain and return without being caught. The following month they tried again, and things were about to get a lot more serious.

As people in Britain were preparing for Christmas, and as it was becoming increasingly obvious that the troops were not going to be 'home by Christmas', on Wednesday 16 December Admiral Hipper arrived once again off the east coast, this time with an even more powerful squadron.

The big difference this time was that he also had a big chunk of the German High Seas Fleet in reserve further out in the North Sea, hoping to ambush any of our ships lured out. This was quite a coincidence as, since our codebreakers had managed to work out that a German squadron was leaving harbour, our Navy also had a lot of ships out trying to ambush the Germans. In the days before radar, and before much in the way of aerial reconnaissance was possible, trying to work out who exactly was where and doing exactly what in a big ocean was inevitably quite a challenge. On this occasion both sides failed to ambush anybody and failed miserably to do much damage to each other at sea.

On land, though, it was a very different situation. Hipper had split his cruisers into two groups and at around eight in the morning both detachments started shelling coastal towns. *Derfflinger* and *Von der Tann* shelled Scarborough, hitting assorted buildings like Scarborough Castle, a number of churches and even the Grand Hotel. The bombardment went on for about half an hour and killed or fatally wounded a number of people, including fourteen-month-old John Shields Ryalls. The ships that had shelled Scarborough then moved further on to bombard Whitby, killing more people there as well and hitting other buildings, including a coastguard station and Whitby Abbey.

Meanwhile, the other part of Hipper's squadron was shelling Hartlepool. Here shore batteries opened fire with some success and managed to disable two of *Blücher*'s guns and force it to retreat further out to sea. Nevertheless, the German ships did huge damage to the town. They fired hundreds of shells at it, hitting hundreds of houses, steelworks, gasworks, churches and railways. Large numbers of people were killed and injured. Light cruiser HMS *Patrol* tried to exit from

Hartlepool harbour but was hit by German shells and had to be run aground. Eventually Hipper's squadron escaped to Germany largely unscathed. By the end of the day, well over 100 civilians were dead or fatally wounded. There was general outrage in Britain about the killing of civilians and people also weren't hugely happy about the Royal Navy's failure to stop or intercept the raiders.

And it wasn't over. Not by a long way.

As well as big raids, like the attack on Scarborough, Whitby and Great Yarmouth, the war was also to see a significant number of much smaller raids. For instance, on 16 August a German submarine arrived off Whitehaven in Cumbria and fired a few shells. It was apparently targeting a chemicals plant, but missed. All it managed to do was start a few fires, and the only casualty was a dog.

In spring 1916, the big German ships returned in another attempt to lure some of our Navy into a trap. Early in the morning of Tuesday 25 April, around 4.10 a.m., with most people in bed, the German battle cruisers opened fire on Lowestoft. They fired for about ten minutes and damaged hundreds of houses and two gun batteries, killing three people. They then moved along the coast to Great Yarmouth and again opened fire there. But fog was a problem for the attackers, and when reports arrived of a clash between German and British ships further out to sea, the German ships abandoned their bombardment and departed. Once again a kind of cat-and-mouse game was played out between British and German ships, and once again the German raiders eventually returned to Germany without huge damage being done to either side, although the German ship *Seydlitz* had hit a mine during the operation and HMS *Conquest* and HMS *Laertes* had both been badly damaged by German shellfire.

In some ways it's easy all these years later to dismiss these incidents as minor compared to the carnage and slaughter that was going on at the same time on the Western Front, but when you look at actual photos of the damage done to familiar-looking British homes in familiar-looking British seaside towns by huge naval shells, it is still something of a shock. If it's still something of a shock to us now, it must have been much, much more so at the time.

The small raids continued. For example, on 11 July 1916 another German submarine had a go. *U-39* appeared off Seaham Harbour and at about 10.30 p.m. fired thirty-nine shells. Deciding how many shells you fire depending on your U-boat number has a certain bizarre, almost comic element to it. But there's nothing funny about the fact that Mary Slaughter, who was visiting from Hebburn on Tyne, was tragically killed by one of the shells.

In 1917, surface ships had another go. On 25 January 1917, German destroyers fired sixty-eight shells in half an hour at Southwold. Fortunately there were no casualties this time. This was a bad year for the Kent coast as well, particularly in the Margate, Ramsgate and Broadstairs area, which got attacked on a number of occasions. On 4 September 1917, Scarborough came under fire again. This time it was from a U-boat in Cayton Bay. The bombardment seems to have lasted about ten to fifteen minutes and about thirty shots were fired, some perhaps at minesweepers in the bay, but, deliberately or not, many fell in the town as well and three people were killed and a number wounded. On 14 January 1918, Great Yarmouth got hit yet again. On this occasion fifty shells were fired in a very short space of time and four people were killed. In February 1918, a child was killed and several people wounded by shells in Dover (quite a few people know that the port suffered bombardment in the Second World War, not so many that it was extensively bombed and shelled in the First World War as well).

46

Airships *versus* U-Boats

But even while the German raids of the First World War on the British coastline were going on, a perhaps even more vital battle was being fought further out to sea.

A lot of Britons are familiar with the Battle of the Atlantic in the Second World War, and the hugely significant role of Allied air power in defeating the attempt by Germany's U-boats to throttle Britain's shipping lifelines. What far fewer people are aware of, however, is a rather similar battle that took place decades earlier and saw British airships battling the submarine menace in order to keep supplies flowing to Britain.

In early January 1917, as troops on both sides on the Western front struggled against the bitter weather and British troops prepared to launch operations again in the Ancre sector, a very different battle was about to start out at sea. On 9 January, Kaiser Wilhelm II announced that unrestricted submarine warfare would commence in February. It was a dramatic move that would help bring the United States into the war on the Allied side, a development that would in turn become one of several factors that made Germany's defeat inevitable. However, it would take over a year from America's declaration of war on 6 April 1917 before American manpower began to have a significant impact on the fighting on the Western Front, and in the meantime German U-boats would play havoc with the vital shipping lanes that fed the Allied war effort and played a huge part in feeding, in an even more literal sense, the people of Britain.

Britain, with its vast empire and vast merchant fleet, had become reliant on imports to live. It was reckoned that if the U-boats could sink 600,000 gross registered tons of shipping each month, then Britain would eventually collapse. In April 1917, U-boats sank over 840,000 gross registered tons. It rapidly became obvious that, even with Allied forces advancing (slowly and at enormous cost, admittedly) on the Western Front, Britain could still face defeat. The U-boats did not manage to reach their target the next month, but in June of the same year, they did sink almost 670,000 gross registered tons of shipping. It was a major crisis.

Though submarines had been used in war before (for instance, in the American Civil War), submarine warfare was essentially still a new skill in the First World War and so was anti-submarine warfare. Extensive use was made of anti-submarine minefields, particularly in the Channel. More sophisticated methods of detecting submarines by sound were developed and more powerful depth charges were developed to use against them once they were found. In an attempt to lure U-boats into a trap, small, innocuous-looking merchant vessels were armed with hidden weapons. Assorted operations were carried out against ports from which U-boats operated, including bombardment and, of course, the famous raids on Zeebrugge and Ostend. One of the most crucial factors, however, that would save Britain's merchant lifeline in the First World War (and obviously in the Second World War) was the development of a sophisticated convoy system. Intelligence on German U-boat operations and the skilled use of surface vessels were vital in the success of the convoy system, but so was the use of air power. Of all the numerous convoys that had air support, only six actually suffered U-boat attack, and they only had five ships sunk.

The Germans made great use of rigid airships, where a covered metal framework contained gasbags. We didn't make much use of rigid airships against U-boats, except for in the use of the mighty *R-29*, which took part in three attacks against U-boats, one of which, with help from surface vessels, ended in success.

Almost all the airships Britain used against submarines in the First World War were of the non-rigid type instead. Our non-rigid airships came in a variety of shapes and sizes, but perhaps the most significant in the area of anti-submarine warfare was the SS Zero (SSZ) type.

Compared to many aircraft of the time, some types of airship were well-suited to anti-submarine work because of the length of time that they could stay in the air. British airships had already started some anti-submarine patrols as early as the summer of 1915. While early patrols had usually been around three hours long, by early in 1916 patrols of six or seven hours were becoming common. Airships operated out of a number of airship stations both in Britain (including Mullion, Anglesey Airship Station, Pembroke Airship Station and Howden Airship Station) and in Ireland. Once the convoy system really got going, airships played a valuable role in escorting them as well. Airships flew 2,000 escort missions in 1918. Not all the convoys escorted were the classic ones focused on the Atlantic. For instance, airships based in Scotland did escort duty with convoys heading to Norway. It wasn't just convoys that airships helped protect.

Often the value of aircraft against the U-boats seems to have been as a deterrent and in the ability of the aircraft to direct surface units to the locations of U-boats. However, the airships were perfectly prepared to have a go at U-boats when the opportunity arose. For instance, on 7 December 1917, airship *SSZ.16* set off in the morning from the Pembroke Airship Base and headed out over the Irish Sea on patrol. The airship was returning home later in the afternoon when the crew spotted a submarine on the surface. While they were trying to work out whether the submarine was friend of foe, the submarine helped them decide the matter fairly abruptly when its deck gun took a shot at them. The commander of the airship, Flight Lieutenant John E. Barrs, immediately ordered his wireless operator to open fire on the submarine's deck with a Lewis gun. This prompted the gun crew to abandon their gun and race for cover inside the submarine. As soon as they did, the submarine dived. The airship promptly manoeuvred itself over the area and dropped two bombs. One exploded about 25 feet distant and the other was closer but didn't explode. The airship then marked the area where the U-boat had submerged with flares and, after stopping to brief two destroyers making for the flares, headed for land.

Gradually, the combination of measures adopted began to turn the tide against the U-boats. The tonnage of ships they sank gradually began to decline and the number of U-boats sunk began to increase. By the last five months of 1918, the average monthly sinkings amounted to well under 200,000 gross registered tons. By contrast, in 1917, sixty-one U-boats were lost, already over a quarter of the total available, and in 1918 eighty-two were. The airships had helped to save Britain and prepare the path to victory.

The Allies would win the war at sea. Instead of German U-boats starving Britain, the Allied naval blockade of Germany would prove a major factor in the war, by blocking Germany's access to the natural resources that it needed in order to fight the war and by leaving much of the German civilian population with much restricted access to food.

47

The 1920 Bloody Sunday

By the end of 1918, the First World War, with all that bravery and sacrifice, with Ypres, the Dardanelles, the Somme, Passchendaele and all the rest, was finished. But another war that had been simmering during the global conflict, one even closer to home, was about to break out fully.

For a country to suffer one 'Bloody Sunday' is tragedy enough, but for a country to suffer three events which have been given this moniker within 100 years shows the scale and bitterness of the conflict within Ireland in the last century.

Ireland's first Bloody Sunday was in November 1920, when British forces attacked a Gaelic football match at Croke Park during the Irish War of Independence. Another Bloody Sunday then occurred the following year in Belfast when Unionists turned on Catholics, causing huge amounts of death and destruction as the War of Independence drew to a close. Yet a third 'Bloody Sunday' was, of course, 30 January 1972. Most readers will be familiar with many of the events of this third Bloody Sunday, but far fewer will know quite so much about the first.

By 1914, Irish Nationalists had persuaded the British government to grant them Home Rule. However, in so doing they had infuriated Protestants in the north of Ireland, who denounced any attempt to impose on them rule from Dublin. The Unionists began to arm themselves to resist Home Rule. Ireland looked to be on the verge of civil war. But when the gunfire started in earnest, it wasn't to be in Ireland. Not just yet.

The outbreak of the First World War initially seemed to offer the British government unexpected relief from a problem with no easy answers. Suddenly Germany was the enemy, as both the Irish Volunteers and Unionists offered to fight for Britain rather than fighting each other. The British government promptly breathed a sigh of relief and promised to focus again on Home Rule after the war was over.

The sighs of relief, however, were comparatively short-lived. The Easter Rising of 1916 put the problem centre stage again, and the ruthlessness of Britain's suppression of the rebels raised Irish sympathy for them. The Irish Republic that Patrick Pearse had declared on the steps of the Post Office in Dublin in 1916 may not have lasted very long, but the idea of an Irish republic independent of Great Britain would prove harder to eliminate. A threat to impose conscription on Ireland didn't exactly win the British government many friends in Ireland either.

The Armistice with Germany came into effect on 11 November in 1918. In the elections of December 1918, Sinn Féin won 73 of the 105 seats, while the more moderate Home Rule Party won only 6 and the Unionist Party a mere 26. It was clear that the majority of Ireland wanted independence from Britain and that they thought Sinn Féin most likely to provide this independence. Sinn Féin's solution was to refuse to take up their seats in London and instead to set up their own parliament, the Dáil Éireann, in Dublin and declare Ireland to be independent of Great Britain. The British government, having just defeated Germany, was in no mood simply to let Ireland walk out of the empire, and thus the Irish War of Independence began.

On the one side was Michael Collins and the IRA, fighting to remove Ireland from British rule and defend the new republic. On the other side was the British Army and the RIC, the Royal Irish Constabulary.

However, fearing they would need more firepower, the British government recruited additional groups to assist the RIC. The Black and Tans were a group of ex-soldiers whose uniforms were a mixture of army khaki and the dark green of the police. They soon acquired a reputation for ruthlessness which was even more colourful than their uniforms. In addition, other ex-soldiers formed the Auxiliary Division.

Michael Collins was waging a guerrilla war against the RIC, targeting police stations and police officers. As well as firepower, therefore, the British also needed information. A special intelligence unit was therefore formed to try to identify and track down the IRA leaders. This became known as the Cairo Gang, either because they met at the Cairo Café in Dublin or because many had served in the Middle East during the First World War.

Collins, afraid of the impact of British counter-insurgency measures, decided that if the IRA in Dublin was to survive they needed to wipe out the network of British spies and he drew up a list of fifty British intelligence officers that he planned to kill. That list was reduced to thirty-five by Cathal Brugha, the Irish Minister of Defence, who felt there was insufficient evidence against some names to prove that they were working for the British. Collins recruited a small assassination squad known as the Twelve Apostles, and on the morning of Sunday 21 November they set out to kill their thirty-five targets. It was a bloody morning in Dublin. Thirteen people were killed and six wounded. The dead included eleven British military intelligence officials and two auxiliaries. One IRA man, Frank Teeling, had been wounded and captured. Collins and his squad had assassinated only a third of the men they had targeted, but the killings had all taken place in a small area of Dublin and tensions were running high.

The GAA, the Gaelic Athletic Association, had scheduled a game of Irish football to be held at Croke Park that afternoon. The GAA had been set up in the late nineteenth century as part of an attempt to revive Gaelic identity. The GAA had strong links with the IRA and many members of the GAA were also members of the IRA and vice versa. The GAA had organised the game between Dublin and Tipperary as a way of cheering up the people of Dublin in the middle of the war and to raise funds for Republicans. Michael Collins was aware that the British might target the game for reprisals, but by the time this was realised it was too late to cancel the game. However, some Republicans did encourage their wives to stay at home rather than attend the game.

As the crowd of about 5,000 gathered inside Croke Park, outside the ground Major Mills was coordinating the British response. The British sources say the plan was to surround the ground and at the end of the game an announcer with a megaphone was to tell the women and children to leave, while all men would be searched for weapons. The stated aim was to arrest those who were armed and who were suspected to have taken cover inside Croke Park after the morning's shootings. If that was the intention, rather than to execute a more straightforward reprisal as claimed by Republican sources, it did not go to plan.

The game started at 3.15 p.m. and ten minutes later auxiliaries, RIC and Black and Tans forced their way through the turnstiles at the canal end of the ground, firing revolvers. Machine-gun fire erupted from an armoured car stationed outside the ground. (The film *Michael Collins* shows the armoured car inside the ground, but it remained on the outside.) Panic spread through the crowd and across the pitch as people dived for cover. After ninety seconds indiscriminate firing, Major Mills regained control. British forces had fired 120 rounds of rifle ammunition, fifty rounds of machine-gun ammunition and an unknown number of revolver rounds. They had killed seven people and five more died later from their wounds. About sixty people were injured. There were also two who died in the crush to escape.

One footballer, Michael Hogan, was killed and another, Jim Egan, was wounded but survived. The dead included Jeannie Boyle, who had gone to the match with her fiancée and was due to be married five days later, and two boys aged only ten and eleven. While some were able to escape, like John Symnottm, who swam across the canal to get away, the vast majority stayed and were searched. No weapons were found.

Exactly what happened in Croke Park and who fired first has remained a matter of controversy. The accounts from spectators tend to suggest that it was Black and Tans and auxiliaries who opened fire as they stormed the turnstiles. These accounts make no mention of the possibility that spectators were either armed or opened fire. RIC accounts are adamant that they were fired at from inside Croke Park as they approached and that they only returned fire. They blame IRA men for the casualties because they used the crowd as cover to escape arrest. However, sources at the *Manchester Guardian* suggest that the RIC confused ticket sellers who were stationed outside Croke Park with IRA sentries when they started firing. It is likely that some of the crowd were armed. One revolver was found on the ground outside Croke Park, where it had been abandoned by someone escaping the scene. Some sources lay the blame on RIC cadets, who were the least experienced people involved and were alleged to be trigger happy. The consensus seems to be that on this occasion the Black and Tans were not the worst offenders and have been blamed largely because of what they did elsewhere.

The violence of Bloody Sunday did not end at Croke Park, however, and continued into the evening. Two high-ranking IRA men being held in Dublin Castle, Dick McKee and Peadar Clancy, were shot dead while, it is said, attempting to escape.

Reactions to Bloody Sunday have been very varied. The international press expressed shock at the scale of the violence, but in London the attention was directed to the British officers who had been the victims of Michael Collins's Twelve Apostles. They were given a parade through London and burials at Westminster Abbey and Westminster Cathedral. Major Mills was embarrassed by the ill discipline and indiscriminate firing. He resigned. The British military concluded that the Crown's forces had acted indiscriminately, but the enquiry was held in secret. Witnesses were not allowed lawyers and the results were kept secret for eighty years. For the GAA it was a simpler affair, as Hogan became a martyr, a memorial was built for him and a stand named after him.

The events in Croke Park have helped shape both British and Irish history. It gave many of the people of Dublin additional reasons to support the Dáil in the War of Independence. The elimination of the Cairo Gang was also a serious blow to the British government's counter-insurgency efforts. In 1921 a peace deal was signed and in 1922 the Irish Free State came into being.

In 2007, when the Irish Rugby Union was looking for a stadium to host internationals while its own stadium at Lansdowne Road was being redeveloped, the GAA offered it the use of Croke Park. When the English rugby team turned up there were many Republicans who felt that singing 'God save the queen' and 'long to reign over us' at Croke Park, a place of martyrdom for the Irish, was a step too far. They may have felt it was justice when Ireland hammered England 43-13. In May 2011, the queen herself visited Croke Park as part of her tour of the Republic of Ireland and in so doing tried to draw a line under that period of British history.

48

Women on the Ball

Much as sport plays a role in the story of the battle for Irish independence, it also plays a role in the story of the battle for women's rights in this country.

By the 1920s, much of the modern sporting year was already present. Sports fans could divide their time in the winter between football and rugby. The Football League had two divisions, with a third added during the decade, and the FA Cup final was contested at Wembley Stadium. Rugby had already divided between a professional Rugby League and an amateur version, Rugby Union. International rugby existed in the form of the Four Nations. In the summer there was a cricket league and international matches. For tennis, fans could visit the centre court at Wimbledon. The Grand National was at Aintree for those with an eye on a bet on the horses.

However, one of the surprising sporting stories of the early twentieth century was a sudden explosion of women's football and an even more sudden halt to the expansion of the game. On Boxing Day 1920, 53,000 spectators gathered at Goodison Park not to watch Everton but to watch Dick, Kerr Ladies take on the ladies' team of the Arundle Coulthard Foundry in a charity match. So many spectators gathered that day that many thousands were unable to get into Goodison and remained stranded in the streets outside. A year later, on 5 December 1921, the Football Association met in London and banned women's football.

Football can trace its roots to medieval times. There were many examples of villages competing with each other or sections within villages competing to carry, kick or by some other means get a ball to some loosely defined goal. There were no rules about numbers in a team or even a definition of what constituted a goal. It was an excuse for mayhem and general rowdiness. Unsurprisingly it was condemned both by the Church and a series of kings from Edward II onwards, who preferred their subjects to be practising the longbow and preparing for war rather than fighting each other.

The tradition of football was kept alive in the nineteenth century by the public schools. However, each school had its own rules, its unique scoring system and even its own shape of ball. While it might be fine for William Webb-Ellis to pick the ball up and run with it at Rugby School, this was not the situation everywhere. The confusion was resolved in the 1860s when Ebenezer Morley founded the Football Association and attempted to define a set of rules. Public schools were outraged that the FA tried to outlaw the practice of 'hacking', which, as the name suggests, was the tactic of kicking the shins of the opposing team until they gave up.

By the 1880's football had spread from the amateurs of the public schools to the northern cotton towns. It had also become a professional game. The practice of paying players began with recompensing them for injuries and time off work. It then spread to offering good players non-existent jobs in local factories. James Lang, a Glasgow shipbuilder, was prompted to move south to Sheffield by the offer of a job in a Sheffield steelworks and playing for Sheffield Wednesday. At the forefront of the drive for professionalism was Preston North End, led by chairman William Sudell, who was determined to create a successful professional club. The showdown came in 1884 when Preston drew Upton Park in the FA Cup. It was a competition between the overtly amateur public school and Oxbridge graduates of Upton Park and the covertly professional cotton workers of Preston. The match ended in 1-1 draw but the following day the FA accused

Preston of playing a professional team. The FA had to decide whether the future lay with the professionals of Preston or the amateurs of Upton Park. Reluctantly, Charles Adcock persuaded the FA that paying players was the honest thing to do and the professional game was born. (It wasn't the end of Upton Park F.C. though; their players went on to represent Britain in football at the 1900 Paris Olympics and win! At the time football was only a demonstration sport, but a gold medal was later awarded for the achievement.)

It was at this point, with public school amateurs and working-class northerners arguing over the soul of the game, that there is the first mention of women playing football. In May 1881, a Scottish suffragist named Helen Matthews organised an international between an England and a Scotland team. The ladies met at Easter Road, Edinburgh, in front of a crowd of more than 1,000. The Scottish ladies won 3-0 and Helen Matthews played in goal. The Scots played a 2-2-6 formation, favouring an attacking phalanx to force a way past their opponents. Both teams are said to have played in 'high-heeled boots'.

A return fixture a week later in Glasgow, however, was a bit of a disaster. The match came to a dramatic end in the second half when there was a pitch invasion and the women had to retreat to their horse-drawn omnibus. Stakes were thrown at the omnibus and, according to some accounts, a baton charge by the police constables was needed to extricate the women. The remaining fixture of the three-match series in Kilmarnock was abandoned and the women fled south of the border to try their luck in northern England.

Two further games were arranged. One in Blackburn attracted a crowd of 4,000 and was won 2-1 by the English. A second at Cheetham Football Club, Manchester, once again ended in a riot. The entry fee of between 1s and 2s was considerably more than was paid to watch the men. Few paid for entrance, most instead gathering outside the ground trying to get a glimpse of the ladies in action. The crowds evaded the constables charged with keeping them out, the stadium was taken over and once again the women were forced to take to their high heels and escape in the waiting wagonette.

There were no further games in 1881, and for more than a decade there were to be no more ladies' football matches. It had been a novelty and attracted some attention, but the majority still regarded football as a rough man's game and unsuitable for women.

On 1 January 1895, however, Lady Florence Dixie made an attempt to revive football for women by founding the British Ladies' Football Club with her secretary, who had the impressive (if perhaps fictitious) name Nettie Honeyball.

There had been some progress since Mrs Matthews attempted to start ladies' football. Players no longer had to wear high-heeled boots. Instead they had men's boots but made in smaller sizes. However, they did still wear bonnets and the game had to be stopped if any woman headed the ball and it dislodged either bonnet or hairpins, which had to be replaced before the game could resume. Lady Dixie firmly believed that football was excellent for women's physiques and predicted a day when it would be as popular with girls as with boys.

The British Ladies' Football Club divided into a north and south team. On 23 March 1895, 10,000 spectators gathered at Crouch End in London to watch the north team beat the south team 7-1. The press hated the spectacle. Nonetheless, the British Ladies' Football Club went on tour around the country and in the following six months they played thirty-four games. However, the strains of playing so often and being amateurs took their toll. By September 1896, the ladies could field only a few players. They were also broke and ended up in Exeter with insufficient funds either to leave or to pay their hotel bill. They appealed to the Mayor of Exeter, who refused to pay, and in the end the ladies had to be rescued by friends. The activities of the British Ladies' Football Club came to a sorry end.

However, the ladies left behind a mystery about the identity of one of their star players. She was listed on the team sheets as the fourteen-year-old Miss Daisy Allen, but many in the crowds suspected foul play and thought Daisy Allen was a boy. Miss Allen thus acquired the nickname 'Tommy'. The Victorian press were unable to solve the mystery. The team photographs show women, but a reporter quoted one of the team as saying that 'Tommy' was the son of one of the married women.

Women's football was eventually rescued from obscurity by the unintended consequences of the First World War. With the men away fighting, the FA were forced to abandon professional football for the duration of the war. By 1916, Lloyd George had realised that the key to victory in the war was going to be increasing the number of soldiers in the Army and producing more shells and ammunition. The introduction of conscription solved the manpower issue, and taking the suffragettes up on the suggestion that women could work in the munitions factories helped resolve the munitions crisis. Employers were happy to employ women as their wages were much lower than those of men and the government was driving down the price it was prepared to pay for ordnance, so cost savings were essential.

The women worked twelve-hour shifts alongside the men, and in their short dinner breaks they also played football alongside the men. These informal contests rapidly grew into munitions factories forming their own teams and providing public entertainment.

The first recorded match was on Christmas Day 1916 in the Cumbrian town of Ulverston. A team of women from the local munitions factory took on and beat women recruited from the local town. Funds raised went into supporting war charities. The next year saw an explosion of such games around the country raising money for war charities and providing much-needed entertainment. A game at Motherwell in June 1917 attracted a crowd of 10,000. Blythe Spartans Munitions Ladies' Football Club on the Tyne took on a team from visiting Royal Navy Ships. One of the largest of these fundraising games was one organised by the Dick, Kerr Ladies at Preston on Christmas Day 1917. Thousands of spectators gathered to watch the game and raised £600 for the local hospital at a time when that was a lot of money.

By the end of the war, women's football was thriving and was a popular attraction. In the north-east the munitions factories had organised the Munitionettes' Cup, and there were also plenty of teams in Lancashire and Cumbria. However, the leading team was Dick, Kerr Ladies of Dick, Kerr Munitions, with their manager Albert Frankland, who watched visiting teams and offered their best players a deal. Lily Parr was the star of the team. She was strong and fast, standing six feet tall, and she once managed to break a male goalkeeper's arm with the power of her shot. She was also the first woman to be sent off for fighting and in her first year scored forty-three goals for Dick, Kerr Ladies.

To generate more publicity and to provide sterner opposition, Frankland arranged for the ladies to play a series of international matches against the French. In 1920, a French team visited to play four games. The press were distracted by the French teams' shorts, which they considered far too short and tight. They were also shocked when the two captains, Alice Kell and Madeline Bracquemond, kissed each other at the final whistle of the final match. The Dick, Kerr Ladies won the first two matches at Preston and Stockport and drew the third. In the final match, at Stamford Bridge, the English finished with only ten players after Jennie Harris was knocked out. The French won 2-1. In the autumn of 1920 the England Ladies travelled to France, where they played in front of crowds of more than 20,000.

Dick, Kerr Ladies were sporting superstars of their day. They were the first team to play a match under floodlights when they borrowed search lights from the Army and used them for an evening kick-off. They had begun life as ordinary working-class girls, doing tough manual jobs in munitions factories. Through football they appeared on Pathé newsreels, the company filming many of their games. They had travelled abroad and their names were known in the press.

However, all that suddenly came to an end in December 1921, when ladies' football was banned by the FA. The FA alleged that football was too dangerous for women, that there were too many financial irregularities in the charity fixtures and that women were being paid excessive expenses for playing the game. As a result, it forbade any of its members using their grounds to host fixtures.

Without venues, and in the face of opposition from the FA, the ladies' football game dwindled.

But this early explosion of women's football was a sign of things to come, both in terms of women's sport and generally in terms of women's freedoms and place in society. In February 1918, women over the age of thirty had been given the vote. From November 1918 they could be elected to Parliament. In 1928, all women over the age of twenty-one could vote.

49

Dylan Thomas and the Coffee Shop

The 1920s and the 1930s were a time of great change and experimentation in Britain, including the arrival of jazz, the Flappers, the General Strike and the effects of the Wall Street Crash. It was a time of ideologies, as significant numbers of Britons turned either to communism or to fascism. Pressure for freedom grew in parts of the empire. Britain was hit by the great Edward VIII abdication crisis of 1936, the same year that, further to the south, would see the outbreak of the Spanish Civil War. It was a period of intense literary experimentation.

In the annals of great world art and literature there are many iconic locations, and the grandest of locations aren't always the most important in peoples' lives. In Castle Street in Swansea in the 1930s lay the Kardomah Café. Swansea wasn't the only place in the world to have a Kardomah Café in the 1930s, not by any means. In fact, a lot of 1930s towns and cities had Kardomah Cafés. But the Kardomah Café in Castle Street in the 1930s was special because it became a meeting place for Dylan Thomas and a bunch of young talents who would become known as the Kardomah Gang, or the Kardomah Set, or the Kardomah Boys – well, you get the concept. One of those groups of mates that became such a feature of British cultural life in the middle of the twentieth century. It wasn't a formal gang, with everybody necessarily all there at the same time, but just a focus; some fascinating people with a shared love of ideas and conversation and laughter.

Dylan Marlais Thomas had been born shortly after the start of the First World War, on 27 October 1914, in a semi-detached house at 5 Cwmdonkin Drive, Swansea. He was his parents' second child and only son. Dylan was not at the time a popular first name; in fact, by calling their son Dylan (after a minor character in the Welsh folktale collection *Mabinogion*), his parents helped ensure that it would eventually become far more popular. Dylan grew up in Swansea but often had summer holidays at his aunt's farm in Carmarthenshire. His father taught at Swansea Grammar School and in 1925, just before he was eleven, Dylan went to school there. His father, handily enough, ran the school magazine, and soon after Dylan got to the school he had his first poem published. He would later become editor of the school magazine as well.

He did not have a stellar school career but he was good at English, which also happened to be what his father taught. So in 1931, aged just sixteen, Dylan left school and got a job as a trainee reporter at the *South Wales Evening Post*. He didn't have a stellar career as a reporter either, and eventually was invited to leave, but what he did do in the early 1930s in Swansea was join a drama group, spend quite a lot of time in pubs and write some amazing poems. Between 1930 and 1934 he would fill four notebooks with a total of over 200 poems, including perhaps half of the poems for which he is now so famous. And, of course, he hung out with the Kardomah Gang.

One of the key members of the gang (apart from Dylan obviously) was Charles Fisher. Like Thomas, Fisher had been born in 1914. Dylan had met Charles at Swansea Grammar School, and when they left school Charles also got a job at the *South Wales Evening Post*, where Charles' father happened to be head printer. Handily, located just across the road from the newspaper offices was, yep, the Kardomah. Dylan and Charles had already frequented the Kardomah while still at school and now began to spend quite a lot of time there in between their assorted reporting journeys. Charles Fisher would go on to become a writer and journalist in Canada and only died in 2006.

Daniel Jones, an aspiring composer who dreamt of composing a symphony, was another member of the Kardomah Gang. He did indeed go on to compose twelve symphonies and a huge amount of other work, as well as taking time out to be a codebreaker at Bletchley Park during the war. Artist and writer on art Mervyn Levy was another member of the gang.

Distinguished painter Alfred Janes would become a member of the set as well. He had been born in Castle Square, Swansea, and then gone to Swansea Grammar School and on to Swansea School of Art. He would share a flat with Dylan and Mervyn Levy in London and paint their portraits and the portraits of other members of the gang, including Daniel Jones and Vernon Waktins. Vernon Watkins was, like Dylan, a poet, and the two became very close friends. Allegedly Vernon was one of the very few people to whose advice Dylan would listen. They remained friends even after Dylan failed to turn up to fulfil his duties as Vernon's best man at his wedding in 1944.

Other names from the set include the politically left-wing Bert Trick, and the talented John Pritchard and Tom Warner. It was an impressive collection of individuals talented in a range of areas.

The Kardomah Gang would not, however, last forever and nor would the Kardomah Café as they knew it in the 1930s in Castle Street.

As the 1930s advanced, Dylan's fame began to spread and he began to spend time in other places as well as Swansea. Then, in February 1941, the Luftwaffe got involved. The Swansea blitz went on for three nights. By the end of it, hundreds were dead and injured and the Kardomah Café was hit badly. Fortunately, it wasn't the end of the Swansea Kardomah Café. Instead it was relocated to a new address in Portland Street, not far away from the original site.

50

The Second World War's Battle of Graveney Marsh

Tens of millions of people were killed in the Second World War, a vast ideological conflict that still helps shape how we see the world today. It was a period that included appalling and enormous atrocities like the Holocaust, but also one that included a myriad of small events, some of which even included an element of humour, even when the lead was flying.

The last battle fought on the British mainland is often said to have been the Battle of Culloden in 1746, but in September 1940 the 'Battle of Graveney Marsh' raged (if briefly and perhaps with rather more confusion than actual rage) on British soil.

The Battle of Britain had begun in mid-July 1940. Having conquered Denmark, Norway, Belgium, Holland and France in 1940, Adolf Hitler ordered Herman Goering and the Luftwaffe to prepare the path for the invasion of Britain. In the first wave of attacks Goering targeted shipping in the Channel and coastal defences. Next Goering switched attacks to focus on RAF airbases and radar installation, hoping to destroy the RAF either in the air or on the ground. On 7 September, however, the Luftwatffe changed tactics again and started large-scale bombing raids on London. One of the most decisive days of the battle was 15 September, now remembered as Battle of Britain Day. The Luftwaffe suffered heavy casualties and on 17 September Hitler called off Operation Sea Lion, the invasion of Britain, to prepare his forces for the invasion of the USSR. However, the Luftwaffe continued to mount daylight attacks on London before switching to attacking by night and the Blitz.

Just over a week after Hitler had postponed the invasion, Junkers 88 bomber 8099 of Kampfgeschwader 77, nicknamed *Eule*, the Owl, set off on a mission to bomb London. The plane was piloted by Unteroffizier Fritz Ruhlandt, a veteran of the campaigns in Poland and France. His radio operator was Unteroffizier Erwin Richter, whose bravery had already earned him an Iron Cross. The rear-facing 7.92 mm machine guns were operated by Gefreiter Reiner. They were flying one of the Luftwaffe's newest and finest light bombers. It was an updated version of the original with improved navigational equipment and bombsights. The plane was only two weeks old. The crew are likely to have been very well aware of the risks they faced, particularly after nine Ju 88s were lost by Kampfgeschwader 77 over Gravesend the previous week.

As *Eule* flew over the Medway with fifty-four other bombers from Kampfgeschwader 77, it was struck by anti-aircraft fire and lost power in one engine. Ruhlandt had no choice but to break formation and head for home while the remaining German aircraft pressed on. Ruhlandt was passed by the remainder of the German aircraft as they returned to their bases after their mission. As he limped over Whitstable he was spotted by two Spitfires, who gave chase. *Eule* dived for cover but was unable to shake off the two Spitfires, their pilots disabling the remaining engine. By now *Eule* was too low for the crew to use their parachutes and Ruhlandt had no choice but to try to make a wheels-up landing on Graveney Marsh. He made a good job of the landing and brought the plane to rest on the marshes at Seasalter, close to the Sportsman pub. All the crew survived uninjured, but so did the Ju 88, complete with all its hi-tech equipment.

The London Irish Rifles territorial unit had been billeted in the Sportsman pub for the duration of the Battle of Britain. They were part of the country's first line of defence. They had been busy during the Battle of Britain organising barbed-wire defences on the beaches to deter invasion and rounding up any Luftwaffe crew who bailed out. A Dornier Do 17 bomber had come down on the mudflats at Seasalter on 13 August 1940. A second had landed by the Neptune pub at Whitstable on 16 August. A certain amount of rivalry had developed between the various units stationed in the area to see who could round up the most airmen and collect the best souvenirs. On the afternoon of 25 September, neither the commanding officer of the London Irish Rifles, Lt Colonel Jack MacNamara, nor the officer in charge of A Company, Captain John Cantopher, were actually on duty outside the Sportsman. However, their men could see the downed aircraft and were anxious to seize their prize.

In the time that it took the London Irish Rifles to get organised, the Luftwaffe crew set about destroying their aircraft. They were under strict instructions from the Führer not to let valuable German hardware fall into enemy hands. Explosive devices were placed under the wing of the aircraft and in the fuselage, while Gefreiter Reiner removed his two machine guns from their rear mounts. It is not entirely clear whether Reiner was aiming at the approaching London Irish Rifles or was merely attempting to destroy important secret equipment on board the Ju 88 when he opened fire.

The London Irish Rifles had no doubt that the weapon was being aimed at them and their training kicked in. They hit the deck and returned fire with their 1914 vintage Lee Enfield .303 rifles. No clear order to fire was given and it was just an automatic reaction from the soldiers involved. The London Irish Rifles split into two groups, one giving covering fire while the other used the cover offered by a dyke to get closer to the aircraft. Much firing followed.

The Luftwaffe crew, however, could see that they were outnumbered and surrounded, even if they did have the advantage of two machine guns. When the London Irish Rifles got to within fifty yards of the plane, the Germans finally indicated that they were prepared to surrender. The firefight meant that there was uncertainty on both sides about what was happening, and more firing ensued before the surrender was finally accepted. No British casualties had been suffered. On the German side, despite being shot down and the ensuing firefight, only Erwin Richter had been injured.

The London Irish Rifles troops searched the plane, located one of the explosive devices and disarmed it. At this point their commanding officer, Captain Cantopher, arrived on a motorbike. He must have been in the vicinity and would have been disappointed at missing out on the action. Captain Cantopher appears to have been the only British soldier present who could understand German. He overheard the German crew reassuring each other that the second explosive device had not been discovered and that their plane would soon explode. Cantopher risked his own life to search the Ju 88 and disable the second explosive device before it could explode. He was awarded the George Medal for his courage.

Both the soldiers of London Irish Rifles and the Luftwaffe crew then retired to the Sportsman Inn. The British were elated after the excitement of their twenty-minute firefight. They had captured an enemy plane, which they could now identify as a new variant of the Ju 88 and one which they had been specifically briefed to try and capture. The Luftwaffe crew were no doubt relieved to be in one piece. Captain Cantopher, who seems to have been an officer of many talents, bandaged the injured ankle of Erwin Richter. The Luftwaffe crew swapped their insignia and souvenirs in return for cigarettes and pints of English ale. It is not known whether specific orders existed to stop captured Luftwaffe personnel exchanging their Nazi insignia for enemy beer. Piper George Willis, who had not even participated in the 'battle' but who was billeted at the Sportsman, recorded that he was very satisfied with his booty from the 'battle': 'We gave the Germans pints of beer in exchange for a few souvenirs. I got a set of enamel Luftwaffe wings.'

When the drinking was over, the prisoners left for a war spent in POW camps and the London Irish Rifles returned to fight on. Captain Cantopher went on to serve in Sicily and

Italy, being wounded three times and being promoted to major. The London Irish Rifles came out of this encounter unscathed but suffered their first casualty when Lance Corporal Cronin was killed by a bomb at Lyminge.

Members of the London Irish Rifles gathered in Whitstable in 2010 to commemorate the Battle of Graveney Marsh. Many pints, but no Germans present to exchange souvenirs.

51

Blue Streak and Putting Europe into Space

Germany surrendered in May 1945, and a few months later Japan did also. After terrible suffering, after Dunkirk and the Blitz and the Fall of Singapore, after triumphs like El Alamein and D-Day, the Allies had won. But the world of 1945 was very different to that of 1939. The world had been shocked by the Holocaust. Europe had been devastated. Britain was exhausted and massively in debt. The empire would soon start to split up. In 1948, British India came to an end. Soon the world would be split by a new ideological war, the Cold War.

The two powers that had come out of the war strongest were the United States and the Soviet Union, the two superpowers that would come to dominate the Cold War era. But Britain was not finished, and was still determined to play a major role on the world scene. It was planned that part of that role would be Blue Streak.

Yes, Blue Streak. It may sound like a man running naked across a rugby pitch on a particularly chilly January day, but in the end it became a major British contribution to human attempts to investigate space.

In the mid-1950s, the Cold War was at its height and the threat of nuclear war was very real. If the unimaginable should happen, the British government wanted to know that the British military could deliver nuclear devices to their intended targets. Originally it had been envisaged that jet bombers, our V-Force bombers, would deliver their deadly loads in the event of war. But even as the V-Force bombers were being developed it was becoming increasingly clear that, with advances in fighter technology and particularly in anti-aircraft missile technology, many V-Force bomber crews were going to find it extremely difficult, perhaps impossible, to complete their missions. So the search was on for a different method of delivering nuclear warheads.

The unexpected and distinctly unpleasant arrival of V2s in southern Britain during the latter days of the Second World War had brought home, rather too literally, the advantages (or disadvantages, in this case) of ballistic missiles. Fighters and anti-aircraft artillery could attempt to stop the winged V1s, and sometimes they managed to do so. Nothing much at that stage could be done about the V2s, which is why, as soon as they could, both the USA and USSR started work on rocket programmes based on the V2 design. Both nations were working on ambitious rocketry programmes in the 1950s that would eventually lead in the USSR to the 1957 launch of the R-7 (and its use to launch *Sputnik* later that year) and in the USA to the launch of the Atlas missile. Britain had also been researching rockets, and in 1955, the year before the Suez Crisis, it was decided that we, too, needed at least some form of medium- or long-range ballistic missile. Thus was launched the programme that would create Blue Streak.

The missile was going to be liquid fuelled and with a range of something like 1,500 nautical miles, which would mean, for instance, that we could hit Moscow. By 1958, work was pressing ahead on such matters as incorporating something like twenty to thirty decoys into the missile to counter any anti-ballistic missile measure the enemy might deploy. Rolls-Royce were building the RZ-2 rocket engine and De Havilland were building the airframe. North of Gisland, Cumbria, the Spadeadam Rocket Establishment was being constructed with a range of advanced facilities. Meanwhile, another British rocket, Black Knight, was being built on the Isle of Wight by Saunders-Roe and this was enabling research into development of a re-entry vehicle for the Blue Streak programme.

But fears were also rising about how vulnerable the weapons would be to attack while they were being prepared for launch, and also, above all, about cost. Yes, fears about the size of public spending are hardly a recent invention. Finally, in 1960, after already huge expenditure, the project was cancelled. A bit embarrassing. Well, actually, very embarrassing, so the government looked around for something else it could do with a partly complete medium-range ballistic missile programme. Obviously the options were fairly limited, but they did come up with something.

Britain already had a successful programme of launching rockets for scientific research. The first Skylark had launched from Woomera, Australia, in 1957. Hundreds of Skylark launches were to follow over the ensuing decades.

However, the USSR and USA had both already demonstrated that military ballistic missile technology could also be extremely useful for space research and launching satellites (and people) skywards. So it was decided that Blue Streak should become a space rocket. Actually, it was decided that both Black Knight and Blue Streak should become space rockets.

Black Knight led to the Black Arrow programme in 1964, constructing a three-stage rocket, built on the Isle of Wight and launched from Woomera; a British-built launch system that finally, in 1971, put a British satellite into orbit. Before the programme was cancelled, that is.

Blue Streak had a rather more European destiny. In the early 1960s, we weren't the only ones in western Europe interested in sending things into space. In 1957, the EEC, the European Economic Community, the forerunner of today's EU, was created. The decades after the Second World War saw the rise of the idea of European cooperation and integration, of a Europe that would construct and trade, not fight and kill.

In late October and early November 1961, a meeting at Lancaster House in London established the main plan of the European Launcher Development Organisation, ELDO. The idea was that we would supply the first stage, Blue Streak, of course. France would supply the second stage, called Coralie, and Germany the third, also known by a girl's name, Astrid. Italy would work on satellites, Belgium on guidance and the Netherlands on telemetry. The launch site wasn't going to be quite so European; it was going to be Woomera in Australia once again. On the other hand. the name of the rocket was going to be very European; in fact, it couldn't have been much more European. It was called Europa.

It took time to get things going fully, as tends to happen on projects like this, but in 1964, after extensive work on Blue Streak at Sapdeadam, launches started at Woomera. Initially these consisted of the Blue Streak launcher with dummy upper stages, and basically everything went fine. Blue Streak was largely performing well. Some problems became apparent with some of the other elements, but ultimately it was the British government that once again decided to terminate our involvement in another space project.

However, terminating our involvement did not terminate the project itself. The launch operation was moved to Kourou in French Guiana, and in 1974 ELDO became a key component in creating the new European Space Agency, an organisation that has achieved and continues to achieve so much in space.

Obviously the UK has made many other contributions to the exploration of space, particularly on the satellite front, and even more obviously we've gotten far more involved in Europe, after the UK, under Edward Heath, joined the EEC in 1973.

52

From Manhattan Project to Nobel Peace Prize

Blue Streak is an example of one approach to the Cold War, but others at the same time were taking a somewhat different approach.

How many UK winners of the Nobel Peace Prize can you name? Actually, more UK people have won than you might perhaps think when you consider that we're a country with a long and very active military history.

In 1903 we had Randal Cremer, proponent of international arbitration as a means of solving international disputes. In 1925, Sir Austen Chamberlain, as Foreign Secretary, got it for negotiating the Locarno Pact of that year, which was supposed to guarantee peace in Europe. Which it clearly didn't in the end. In 1933, Sir Norman Angell got it for things like being an executive committee member of the League of Nations. To be fair to him he did go on, in the 1930s, to actively oppose German, Italian and Japanese policies. In 1934, Labour politician Arthur Henderson got it for chairing the Geneva Disarmament Conference, shortly before Europe massively rearmed. In 1937 it was Robert Cecil, a big League of Nations guy, who won. The Friends Service Council (now known Quaker Peace & Social Witness) won in 1947, along with the US version, the American Friends Service Committee. In 1959 it was the turn of Philip Noel-Baker, a Labour politician who had helped start the League of Nations. He was also keen on multilateral nuclear disarmament (though not unilateral).

Philip had also won a silver medal at the 1920 Olympics. Betty Williams and Mairead Corrigan won in 1976 for their work crossing divides in Northern Ireland. And similarly, in 1998, David Trimble and John Hume got it after the Good Friday Agreement. In 1977, Amnesty International (which had originally been founded in the UK) won. And in 1995, it was Sir Joseph Rotblat's turn.

Sir Joseph Rotblat had a fascinating, and at times controversial, career that raises loads of key questions about the interaction of science, morality and politics in some of the most dramatic decades and events of the twentieth century.

Joseph Rotblat was born in Warsaw on 4 November 1908 at a time when Warsaw was under the control of the Russian Empire. As he grew up he became a distinguished physicist. He got an MA at the Free University of Poland in Warsaw in 1932 and a PhD from the University of Warsaw in 1938. But the world he had grown up in was about to change forever, and Joseph's life would change with it.

Rotblat had already been working as an atomic scientist in 1939, and as the war clouds gathered he won a Fellowship at the University of Liverpool and came to Britain, where he was to work alongside Professor James Chadwick, himself a winner of the Nobel Prize for Physics and the man who had demonstrated the existence of neutrons. Robtlat was from a Jewish family and the move to Britain probably saved his life. His wife, Tola Gryn, was tragically not so lucky. She was too ill to leave Poland before the war, and after the Germans invaded Poland she disappeared and Rotblat never saw her again. He never remarried.

By 1944, Rotblat, by now one of the world's leading nuclear physicists, was invited to join the team working to produce the world's first nuclear bomb. Being only too aware of the horrors of Nazism and fearing that the Germans would succeed in making their own nuclear bomb first, Rotblat agreed, thinking that if the Allies had a nuclear weapon then it might deter the Germans from using one and that then nobody would need to use the weapon. He joined the project.

However, when it became clear to him that the Germans would not be able to make a nuclear weapon before they were defeated, he made the decision that he could no longer justify working on a weapon of such staggeringly destructive powers. He therefore requested permission to leave the project and this was granted.

Ultimately, two nuclear devices were dropped on a Japan that did not have nuclear weapons. It shortened the war and saved the lives of huge numbers of Allied soldiers, but it also killed large numbers of Japanese civilians and it inaugurated a world of nuclear threat. Plenty of people today would argue that the threat of the use of nuclear weapons prevented the Cold War turning into a massively destructive non-nuclear war, while others would disagree and say that the proliferation of nuclear weapons is still a threat that could lead to their use.

Rotblat returned to Liverpool University, and when the war was finished he decided to stay in Britain and in 1946 became a British citizen. In 1949 he moved to St Bartholomew's Hospital Medical College (London University) to become Professor of Physics. He remained there until 1976, then becoming Emeritus Professor.

However, while his work there was valuable, including his work on radiation and cancer, it was his work elsewhere that would eventually lead to the Nobel Peace Prize.

By 1955 both sides in the Cold War had nuclear weapons, and in the bitter international atmosphere following the Korean War the threat of a nuclear war seemed very real indeed. That year, Rotblat became one of eleven signatories to a manifesto calling upon scientists to meet and cooperate on a programme to try to prevent nuclear war. Bertrand Russell was another signatory, and so was perhaps the most famous scientist of modern times, Einstein himself.

In 1957, in pursuit of this goal, he helped launch and became Secretary-General of the Pugwash Conference on Science and World Affairs. This was named after the village in Nova Scotia where the first conference was held, not after a rather jolly pirate cartoon character. Conferences took place regularly and included scientists from both sides of the Cold War divide. At a time of such deep divisions, not everybody appreciated his efforts. But many did, and Mikhail Gorbachev said that the Pugwash conferences and papers had played a crucial role in leading to the end of the Cold War.

In 1965 Rotblat was awarded a CBE, and in 1998 he accepted a knighthood, as Knight Commander, 'for services to international understanding'. In 1995 he got his Nobel Peace Prize, which, appropriately enough, was shared with the Pugwash movement. In his Nobel Lecture he stated that Pugwash wanted a war-free world and that to want that was not Utopian. He pointed out that, for instance, war within the EU was already unthinkable and that it was just as necessary to extend that situation to the major powers outside the EU.

In his fascinating career he had lived through a time of huge changes and huge events for Britain. That time saw, among other things, the Second World War, the Cold War, the coronation of Elizabeth II, the building of the welfare state, the Suez Crisis, the withdrawal from empire, British entry into the EEC, the three-day week and trade union militancy, the rise of feminism, the Troubles in Northern Ireland, Thatcherism, the Falklands War, the end of the Cold War and the collapse of communism in eastern Europe, the Afghanistan War, the Iraq War and huge social and cultural changes. Sir Joseph Rotblat finally died in 2005.

And that brings us from our journey, which started in pre-Roman Britain, thousands of years ago, almost up to date, and brings us to the end of this particular wander through Unexpected Britain.

This island is an amazing land with an amazing history and many amazing people. There is plenty more of Unexpected Britain out there that can be explored, and more history is happening every day. So we hope you've enjoyed this selection, and if we get to write more in this series we hope you'll enjoy those too.